Where There's a Will

Michael Heseltine was born in 1933, and was educated at Shrewsbury School and Pembroke College, Oxford. President of the Oxford Union in 1954, he was first elected to Parliament for Tavistock in 1966. Following a redistribution of parliamentary boundaries, he has represented Henley since 1974.

His political offices include Opposition spokesman on Transport, Parliamentary Secretary to the Ministry of Transport, Parliamentary Under-Secretary of State at the Department of the Environment, Minister of Aerospace and Shipping, Opposition spokesman for Trade and Industry and then for the Environment. In 1979 he joined the Cabinet as Secretary of State for the Environment and in 1983 became Secretary of State for Defence until his resignation in 1986.

He is married, with one son and two daughters, and now lives in Northamptonshire.

WHERE THERE'S A WILL

Michael Heseltine

HUTCHINSON

London   Melbourne   Auckland   Johannesburg

© Michael Heseltine 1987

All rights reserved

This edition first published in 1987 by Hutchinson, an
imprint of Century Hutchinson Ltd, Brookmount House, 62–65
Chandos Place, London WC2N 4NW

Century Hutchinson Australia Pty Ltd PO Box 496, 16–22
Church Street, Hawthorn, Victoria 3122, Australia

Century Hutchinson New Zealand Limited PO Box 40–086,
Glenfield, Auckland 10, New Zealand

Century Hutchinson South Africa (Pty) Ltd PO Box 337,
Bergvlei, 2012 South Africa

British Library in Publication Data
Heseltine, Michael
  Where there's a will.
  1. Great Britain – Politics and
government – 1979–
  I. Title
  320'.092'4   JN237
ISBN 0 09 172712 X (paper)

Phototypeset in Linotron Sabon, 11 on 12 point by Input
Typesetting Ltd., London SW19 8DR

Printed in Great Britain by Mackays, Chatham, Kent

Contents

To Anne

Acknowledgements

I am grateful to the following for permission to reproduce photographs and cartoons:

Gerry Crowther, *Daily Mirror*; *Daily Mail*; Greater London Records Office; NATO; *Daily Express*; Army Information Services; Nick Garland, *Daily Telegraph*; Trog; Jak, *London Evening Standard*, 19 December 1980; Nick Austin.

To all those who have helped, who for their sakes as much as mine must remain anonymous, my profound thanks.

Introduction

For anyone willing to serve his country, nothing can compare with membership of a British Cabinet. There is constant stimulus and excitement, a strong sense of opportunity and sometimes, if one is lucky, a sense of achievement. I have no doubt about my resignation a year ago, but anyone who claims to have left office with no regret must expect a sceptical audience.

Until I resigned from the Government, it never occurred to me that I would write a book. I have done so because ministerial office implants a habit which is not easily cured: the habit of thinking about government. Ideas come constantly to mind, with recollections of opportunities either taken in office or missed; and a new habit is formed, of exploring in discussion what can no longer be explored in action.

This book is the result. It is an account of some of the ideas which attract me and some of the ways in which I believe that political action could better the living conditions and raise the spirits and ambitions of very many British people. It also contains reflections on Britain's position in an ever-shrinking world. It is not a volume of memoirs: that comes with retirement. It is not a history of recent events: I remember Sir Walter Raleigh's warning that 'whosoever in writing a modern history shall follow truth too near the heels, it may haply strike out his teeth.'

I have not tried to cover the whole field of politics but kept to those parts of it where I have had a particular interest. In six and a half years as Secretary of State, first for the Environment and then for Defence, I learned a great deal. I make no claim to any special insights but offer some judgements to be examined by anyone who may be interested – and either used or discarded. Because necessarily I draw on my experiences, the reader who picks up, or even buys, this book must expect to find the author at the centre of many of its pages. It seems only fair to begin with that warning.

A British Secretary of State can easily believe that he is at the centre of the world. In a large department an ever-flowing stream brings problems to his desk, or to anywhere else where he may be working or relaxing. Holidays offer only limited protection. I was once lying on a lilo in the Atlantic, off the coast of Portugal. 'Ah, there you are,' said this head as it emerged from the waves, 'I've been looking for you everywhere, I've got a problem with this planning issue. . . .' Or again, there was the picture which the Press missed, of the minister on a Caribbean beach kitted out in flippers and mask, reading flash cables from a red box held by an immaculate member of the High Commission staff.

If you resign and leave all this behind, the stream of decisions which it seemed that you alone could make continues to flow as merrily as before with someone else's help. I found, as others have found, that when one chapter closes another opens. No longer was there anything to do in government, but neither were there the constraints of a parliamentary career which had been spent almost entirely on the front bench. So, within an unswerving conviction that this country should again elect a Tory government, it seemed to me that I might contribute a personal view to that kaleidoscope of opinion upon which the most successful political party in the democratic world depends.

Some of my perceptions are bound to be distorted. A departmental minister in Britain is not well placed to see every complex political problem in the round. He and his colleagues will all bring partial views to Cabinet where with luck and wisdom they will be reconciled in balanced and sensible decisions. But there are times when a minister faces an important decision which is his responsibility alone; where he must weigh all the evidence, make his judgement and defend it to his colleagues and to Parliament. These are the times when the most valuable lessons are learned. Government is an occupation like no other except in this: that you learn it only by doing it. So if I return more than once to particular episodes from my periods of office, it will be because they opened my eyes or enlarged my experience.

Although I have a certain fluency and familiarity with the spoken word, I find it less easy to absorb from or communicate through the written. In commerce that matters very little; in opposition politics some would say it is almost an advantage; but in government it is a massive burden.

So as a minister I invented systems to make arguments speak for themselves. It began in the Ministry of Transport, when I had to determine the outcome of public inquiries. Files piled high were an almost total deterrent. I asked for a map comparing all the routes for new roads, with pins to show where all the objectors were. Objectors were numbered and their arguments summarised in chronological order. The local issues stood out and the contentious areas were highlighted, and although it was often necessary to go back to the closely-reasoned submissions I did so from a background of familiarity with the problems which I had been able to absorb more easily in this way.

The paperwork never stops, although it is not uncontrolled. It is as if a department has a mind of its own. It knows just how much work to offer to a minister to keep him busy, but not so busy that he breaks under the strain and takes no decision. I was worth an in-tray about a foot high. It was always a foot high. If I was away for a weekend, a week or a fortnight, then a foot of paper would be waiting, threatening, and often hiding a political grenade which would explode if left too long.

You develop a nose, a second sense of where the danger lies – that is, if you are to survive. No one can survive unscathed. The pitfalls are too many, and if one is fortunate enough to have survived in a British Cabinet the overriding sense is one of gratitude.

One experience, which was more than an episode, was my involvement in the problems of Merseyside. As Secretary of State for the Environment, I was already chairman of the Liverpool Inner City Partnership when, after the Toxteth riots of 1981, the city and its troubles became a focus of national interest and concern.

I shall recount my Merseyside experience in some detail because it helps to illustrate the extent of urban reconstruction which is yet to be done. Part of the significance of Merseyside is that in its decline it represents most acutely a crisis that is to be seen to varying degrees in many provincial towns and cities. The further one explores the older industrial heartlands, the more examples one finds.

I felt a moment of pride a year ago at a headline in *The Times* which read: 'A land being born again.' It appeared on 21 March, 1986, above a report which told of wholesale renewal of cities and towns in the North-west of England, and of the flowering of experiments which had taken root, invariably with the active help of the Conservative Government, at the start of the decade. That day the Queen was to open the Greater Manchester Exhibition and Events Centre, housed under the majestic iron arches of the Central Station. The great building had been a disturbingly prominent token of emptiness and waste at the heart of the city since the last train had pulled out in 1969; it had now become a symbol of renewal.

The report also told the tales of Liverpool's Albert Dock which the Merseyside Urban Development Corporation had turned from a rotting wasteland into a humming waterside community; and of the tens of millions being invested in new commercial and residential building on the sites of the Salford and Preston docks. The newspaper's main advertising feature that day was itself a sign that the physical renewal brought about by government, local authority and business in essential partnership had laid the foundation, as we had intended, for economic regeneration.

My years in Government proved to me that British people, from the urban poor to the most élite units of our Armed Forces, from voluntary workers to the captains of industry, do indeed possess those exceptional qualities of character which are so often claimed for them, with tolerance, inventiveness and courage near the top of the list. From Cabinet level I had the advantage of an extensive view of our national capabilities and of our busy and gifted people, which left me puzzled that, with all our qualities and opportunities, our society was not as harmonious or prosperous as it could easily be. We suffer, as indeed we should, from spasms of self-doubt whenever we are shown the recurrent evidence of our economic insufficiency; but we do not then stir ourselves.

Too easily we see the need for change, as change in someone else. Alibis are easily substituted for action.

The evidence that things have been amiss is hard to dispute. Most measurements of national performance show Britain doing less well than our competitors in Europe, America or Japan over decades, in share of world trade, in manufacturing productivity, in increase of the average citizen's income. But our history does not indicate that failure is the natural condition of Britain, and there have recently been signs that a general recognition of the truth of our national condition is turning at last into a resolve to face change. I left office as convinced as when I entered it that our relative decline can be stopped, and with an anxiety to see the task continued.

The prime immediate need is for the Conservatives to formulate a national strategy for industry which will enable the workers, the managers and the owners of wealth to travel the same road to national recovery, with shared objectives and with the widest possible understanding and respect by each partner for the others' roles. This fundamental prerequisite for industrial success is present in the shared values and assumptions of our major industrial competitors, but it is not yet second nature within British society. It has been absent for generations.

I hope in this book to dispel the false belief which has misled too many in my party, that there is a heresy called 'intervention' to which unsound Conservatives have in the recent past been prone but which sound Conservative administrations eschew. The *laissez faire* idealists may hold that all government action, to the extent that it inhibits the free exercise of the citizen's will, must threaten his liberty and weaken his spirit. This is too romantic and impractical a guide for men and women who hold public office, and it has nothing to do with the Tory Party.

Conservative ministers and their officials, as in all previous governments, today intervene habitually and on an immense scale to limit the citizen's freedom of action and constrain the working of markets, and ordered government would be impossible if they did not. The need, surely, is not to wrestle with making respectable the idea of intervention but to make the reality of it more responsive and effective, so that a whole range of government activities which at present seem haphazard and sometimes shamefaced are in future co-ordinated and pursued with conviction.

Conservatives must feel confident in the proper uses, as well as the proper limitations, of government. Our history shows, and the elector knows, that we can be trusted not to overreach. We enjoy, too, the advantage that we carry no burden of dogma to limit our scope for practical action. We have proved that our philosophy of balance and partnership can work.

Tories are bold in bringing the resources of the State to the rescue of the needy; and this Tory Government has been uniquely bold in making the State disgorge and distribute wealth to fructify, as Churchill said, in the pockets of the people. We have given the right of ownership to a generation of council tenants: we will spread further this distinctively Conservative freedom and remove other barriers which deny so many families decent homes.

A new urgency must be shown and a new assault made on urban misery and squalor. If we fail, our failure will have cruel consequences for people who live in unacceptable conditions – the poor, lonely, elderly and unemployed. And behind their plight grows the ethnic minority: an urban programme must aim to lift the burden of discrimination, not least in jobs and housing, from the many city-dwellers who belong to ethnic minority groups.

We have turned back the Soviet-style State capitalism reflected in nationalisation and in its place we have given ordinary people the chance to become part-owners of great enterprises which previously could only pretend to be publicly owned. The managements of these enterprises have also been set free. We shall go on pursuing wider share-ownership, and planting everywhere this new popular capitalism and the responsibility which it brings.

Tories, who understand the liberating power of capitalism, understand also that this power must be harnessed. Tory capitalism is a caring capitalism, energetic but never rapacious, and ensures that the citizen who uses his economic freedom to enrich himself will also enrich society at large. We do not forget that the privileges which a free society bestows carry obligations as well. Our party's claim to office rests on our ability to demonstrate that the capitalist system, under Conservative management, can best generate wealth, create jobs and protect the people's savings, and that it will never fail to succour the needy. A democratic society will allow nothing less.

The opposition parties in Britain do not deserve election. Mediocrity and confusion are sown through many of their policies. Labour and the Alliance are both divided. Cardinal questions of nuclear weapons policy are fudged and have been exposed to the critical judgement of the people. Labour in particular seems resolved to weaken British defences and destroy the NATO alliance. While defence is the area of most visible deficiency, the confusion of the opposition parties extends as deeply into other areas such as economic policy and industrial relations. The opposition parties share the mantle, if not the intention, of advocating policies designed to undo the progress – especially the economic and industrial progress – which has been so hard won over the past eight years.

But it is not enough for Conservatives to be given office again merely because their rivals forfeit the electors' trust. The purpose of this book is to help persuade Conservatives and potential Conservatives of the immense scope and need for a practical Tory philosophy of partnership across the whole fabric of national life. The Tory Party's long experience, its national spirit, its refusal to ally itself with sectional interests, its dependence for office on the constant renewal of bonds with the industrial working class, give it not only strength but a unique aptitude for service.

The British predicament requires the devoted exercise of that special talent. There is a long and pressing agenda, and not much time.

1

Whitehall: An Encounter With The Private Sector

The present government was elected with the belief that Britain could be better governed. It was not just that we expected, as all new governments do, to make wiser decisions: we believed that the quality of administration could be improved.

Gone is the day when one could hold to the constitutional belief that ministers should concern themselves with policy and leave the execution of it to civil servants. That was all very well when you could get ministers and a row of quill-toting clerks into one office. Everyone then knew what was going on. But today the scale is huge and a different approach is required. Ministers cannot escape a responsibility to ensure that the management arrangements and functions within their departments can deliver the value for money to which the Government is committed. They will only partially succeed but the attempt is an important part of the pressure for efficiency.

To preach efficiency to the world at large, as governments do, we must ensure that government itself is efficient. It is not easy. All ministers come first to office as amateurs, most of them from the overwhelmingly amateur House of Commons.

The voters who choose an MP, the party activists who select a nominee for a safe seat, may not fully realise the responsibility which they carry: there is usually an even chance of any eligible MP becoming a minister at some time if his party takes power. In a governing party with, say, 350 MPs, many will not be candidates for office; some who have been ministers will be too old; others will have found that lack of time or talent or availability has ruled them out; the new entry will be unknown and untried. A Prime Minister may therefore have only two hundred people to fill one hundred government posts. It follows that relevant skills and experience will be at a premium in any team of ministers from any party. This in turn puts a responsibility on those at the top of the civil service who are in a position to provide the professionalism in administration and management which ministers can seldom offer.

The untrained minister can remain untrained. Men and women in middle life, on whom the favour of the voters and of the party leader has fallen for a season of uncertain length, have neither the time nor the inclination to take induction courses. Provided that civil servants are appropriately educated, experienced, trained and, when necessary, retrained this may not matter; but the longer I spent in office the more I was persuaded that members of the higher civil service are neither chosen nor trained to meet the exceptional demands of their jobs, although their intelligence and application carries the best of them a long way. Most civil servants do the job of policy-advising for which they are selected extremely well. But the talent to advise is very different from the talent to manage. Thinker–doers are in short supply. Thinker–advisers are the normal product of the system.

I was lucky in my initiation. To climb the greasy pole of politics most rapidly, it helps to enter the House of Commons when your party has suffered a serious electoral setback and faces perhaps four years in opposition. In 1966 only eleven new boys emerged as orphans of the storm.

My second piece of luck was to come early under the eye of Peter Walker, then Opposition spokesman on Transport. There is no more professional eye.

I spoke from the Conservative front bench for the first time some two years after entering Parliament and did not speak again from the back benches until eighteen years later. In office the amateur – the new junior minister – encounters the professional civil servant, and in theory the amateur takes charge. In practice, although much depends on the experience of ministers and the competence of officials, control of government departments is only nominally with ministers. Once they have established political control at the top – and

not every minister achieves even that – they find themselves
working through senior officials who are themselves remote
from the day to day workings of the department and who
can easily regard management as a secondary activity.

The present Conservative Government has begun the task
of creating for the first time the essential means of running
departments as they should be run. Notable progress has
been made, but there is a long road to be travelled before the
public sector can begin to set the private sector an example of
the proper management of resources. To be fair the private
sector has relatively simple numerate disciplines. The public
sector operates within a more complex and less easily defined
set of disciplines. But even this distinction should be
modified. This Government has shown that much policy
implementation can be given a numerate discipline. It was
one thing to promise to speed up the planning process. It
was another and more valid step to make every local authority publish detailed performance statistics to show how
long each application took to determine and to publish the
government's statistics for the handling of appeals as well.

The junior minister, unless he is lucky, has to fight to
survive before he can expect to assert himself and make
decisions. If the new man has a smattering of management
experience, which few have, it will prove priceless. His arrival
at his Whitehall desk is a moment of decisive importance,
for it is then that his officials will make their judgement of
him.

I once said, only half jokingly, to a junior minister: 'Whatever you do on your first day, do something. Better still, do
something big and, whether it is right or wrong, for good-
ness' sake stick to it. First, they will notice you are there.
Second, they will know that they cannot push you around.'
Many departments will respect ministers with minds of their
own, but there are officials who like nothing more than a
minister who asks to be briefed on his first day, asks for
advice about what he should say, goes off to a committee,
wins the battle there for his department, presents its arguments fluently in Parliament and causes the least disturbance
in its daily life by having ideas of his own.

It is perfectly possible for a minister to appear adequate,
perhaps excellent, provided he is adept at handling the flow

of files; but he will not be doing his duty. It is no criticism of civil servants to point out that they are ready enough to run a department if they are landed with ministers who are not disposed to run it themselves.

Someone must direct policy: the department will invariably have its own existing policy which, if ministers have no ideas of their own, will naturally continue to prevent a vacuum. Decisions have to be taken: if a minister cannot make up his mind, his officials may in despair try to help the process even to the point, if need be, of making it up for him. I would never belittle this process. It carries many a department through periods of indifferent political direction. Of course, such direction could hardly happen under a colleague of my own party, but there are always others!

I freely admit to the moments where the pure gold of the perceptive permanent secretary shone through. I have as many faults as the next man but I can, by and large, take decisions. Sometimes, however, your powers fail. You are tired. It is late. The issue is of secondary importance, only half understood, and you know in your heart that you have lost control of that meeting of civil servants waiting for the firm hand of government. You ramble, hesitate and suddenly the voice at your elbow takes over: 'I think that's most helpful Secretary of State. We'll proceed as you have outlined which, if I follow your argument correctly, I would summarise as follows. . . .' And the permanent secretary pours out a string of elegant phrases and concise instructions as tears of gratitude well up within you. And private secretaries – the permanent secretaries of tomorrow – make no mean fist of the same process.

A hazard for the junior minister is the private office, the small private fiefdom which, I was earnestly assured when I arrived green at the Ministry of Transport in 1970, was there to serve me. In the world outside I had run my own business and was naturally surrounded by the best and most senior people in the company.

At the Ministry I quickly found, to my considerable resentment, that while I was cutting my teeth as a parliamentary secretary my private office was staffed by young civil servants cutting their teeth on me. It was a training ground where the totally inexperienced were sent to find out what the world was all about.

Private secretaries came and went with a bewildering rush, and as soon as they began to know their job and became familiar, perhaps even friendly, with the minister they were promoted. From the minister's point of view this is a near-disaster, because he is totally reliant on his private secretary as his eyes and ears within the department.

Happily I again had Peter Walker as my apprentice-master when I moved to the Department of the Environment after four months. As Secretary of State he used his great administrative skill to run an enormous department in what I believe was the only way possible, by the widest delegation to his middle-ranking and junior ministers. He not only delegated but backed his subordinates' decisions and so strengthened each minister's authority.

Peter Walker's approach, now widely adopted, was a departure from the Conservative norm. Other Cabinet ministers even then were used to keeping power in their own hands. Junior ministers were to be seen and not heard. Their seniors kept them at a distance and so, of course, did the civil servants.

Today it is recognised that the complexity of government and the scale of most Whitehall departments would make the secretary of state's job impossible if he did not share the burden with his departmental colleagues.

I quickly saw also that Peter's methods were essential for proper political control. In an ill-organised department, whose ministers are not in regular touch with one another, the civil servants can secure the decision which they favour by sending a submission to the minister most likely to agree. They know each minister's instincts.

One essential innovation of Peter's was therefore the 9.15 meeting. It was not mandatory, but if he was in the office, as he usually was, at that time on a week-day morning, there was an informal meeting of all the department's ministers, without officials. The opportunity to keep in touch, to share each other's preoccupations, to take urgent decisions and to discuss events in the House the night before was invaluable.

When after two years I moved to the Department of Trade and Industry to be Minister for Aerospace and Shipping,

Peter took over the Department shortly after and brought with him his management techniques.

I found, though, that the Ministry of Aerospace had something of a life of its own within the DTI, and I decided to try to implant there the Walker-style of management which had so impressed me.

Cranley Onslow, the parliamentary under-secretary, Cecil Parkinson, my PPS (his first political post), and I held our own management meetingsm but three seemed too few, so we included one or two very senior civil servants and my press officer. We met as a team, and, I believe, enjoyed the same feeling of close and efficient control and of a common purpose. One of those civil servants, James Hamilton, was later to establish a significant precedent as the first engineer to reach the top of the civil service as permanent secretary at the Department of Education and Science.

When, in 1979, I found myself responsible for a large department, Environment, I again applied Peter Walker's method, adapting it for my own needs and, I believe, improving it. I encouraged the attendance of the ministers' PPSs, and also of the departmental Whips. Later, at the Defence department, I did the same.

The effectiveness of these meetings converted me from an earlier belief in the French *cabinet* system, which provides ministers with groups of political advisers. At the Department of the Environment I had Tom King and John Stanley as Ministers of State and four experienced parliamentary under-secretaries in Hector Monro, Geoffrey Finsberg, Marcus Fox, and Irwin Bellow. We also had our three PPSs, Tim Sainsbury, Keith Hampson and Anthony Nelson. I never felt the need for other political advice. My colleagues were articulate and supportive, and I can never remember an occasion where I felt that the inner anguishes of the department, and sometimes of the Secretary of State, were revealed in any sense that was disloyal to the general interests which we were serving. I therefore had the political input and the political confidence-building, together with eyes and ears open to my political surroundings, which I recognise to be a strength of the *cabinet* system and which is the justification for political advisers. I think that the 9.15 method is a better way. It gave me all I needed.

In opposition, from 1976 to 1979, I was an impatient shadow Secretary of State for the Environment. My interests and training were concerned with doing things. Like others I was frustrated by the usually fruitless carping process which characterises so much of opposition life. But at least when I was invited to be Secretary of State for the Environment, I had some knowledge of the responsibilities with which I was entrusted and was particularly fortunate in my ministerial colleagues.

I was lucky as well in that my first permanent under-secretary was Sir John Garlick, a dedicated civil servant whom I had known and with whom I had worked in the Ministry of Transport nine years before.

I invited him out to lunch, and there we renewed our relationship on the right footing, meeting outside the department, not on neutral ground but on my ground.

Sir John came, as I knew he would, unarmed. There was not a file in sight although, to the best of my recollection, there were references to the briefing that awaited me in the office. I was not quite unarmed: I came with the outline of my programme on the back of an envelope. I gave it to him and forgot it, but when I left the department after four of the happiest years of my life I had a kindly note from Sir John, who had by then retired. He wished me well and said that perhaps now I might like to have back the envelope, which he enclosed. My handwriting, as is well known, is appalling, and I have only with difficulty persuaded my publishers to reproduce it here.

I confess to some satisfaction that, as I took over one of the most exciting government departments, I was able to set out so clearly what I wanted to do and that so much of it was done.

The essential first lesson for a newly-appointed secretary of state, as I had learnt, was to know what one wanted and how to get it. The other lesson well learnt was of the constantly moving private secretaries, so the first requirement on my envelope was that I would interview the brightest candidates in the appropriate grade and that once I had chosen a private secretary he would stay with me to the day I left the department.

Again I was lucky. David Edmonds, who remained with

The crucial envelope

me as long as I remained in the Department of the Environment and then left to run the Housing Corporation, was an outstanding official and one of those with whom I worked closely who bred in me a profound admiration for the talent and loyalty of the best civil servants and a contempt for those who belittle them. In the Ministry of Defence I inherited from John Nott another quite exceptional civil servant, Richard

Mottram, who survived me in the private office but moved on promotion after a few months to take charge of the budgeting controls he had helped me to understand.

Of the words I had written on the envelope for Sir John Garlick, perhaps the most challenging were: 'Staff. Reduce level. Freeze on recruitment.' They were part of a revolution in Whitehall which has by no means run its course.

The Government had come to power pledged and determined to reduce the number of civil servants, which had reached its highest level since the war. I was fortunate in having as a Minister of State Irwin Bellow, now Lord Bellwin, who had been an outstanding civic leader in Leeds. He told me that he had managed to reduce the numbers of municipal employees there only by taking over responsibility for recruitment himself. This was an affront to the orthodoxy that ministers determine but civil servants execute. It turned out also to be a priceless piece of advice.

The Government was embarked on an exercise in staff reductions. It was agreed by the Cabinet that each of us would go back to his department and examine options for securing reductions over a period of years of 2.5 per cent, 5 per cent and 7.5 per cent.

In each department the immediate assumption when this news was received was that any shedding of staff must mean shedding of responsibilities. Nobody was prepared to concede that just by squeezing numbers it would be possible to make economies and still do the same tasks. After all, there were staff inspection schemes to ensure that there was no over-manning.

This immediate and universal assumption was in time revealed to be wholly unwarranted; but it was the point of departure for the briefing of ministers on the reduction of numbers which then ensued.

The preparation of option papers gave civil servants a field day. They took the parts of prosecuting and defending counsel, of judge and of jury. I cannot now recall the exact words in which I was told the facts of life, but I will never forget the general tone and sense.

There is, I admit, an element of parody in what follows, but there is also a broad vein of historical truth.

'Minister, we have been looking forward to playing our

part as this country adjusts to the recession,' I was assured, 'and of making a total commitment to the execution of the mandate which the electors have given this Government. We have carefully considered the options of 2.5, 5 and 7.5 per cent reductions in manpower which your colleagues in Cabinet have decided to explore, and we have broad recommendations for you.

'It has not been easy. The work that is done in this department – as you will be the first to recognise, Secretary of State, since you will now be responsible for it and your reputation associated with it – is of prime national importance. But we have not flinched from the challenge. Our advice is that, if your colleagues insist and if each of them is prepared to carry an equal share of the burden, it would just be possible for us to achieve a 2.5 per cent reduction. It would be unfair not to warn you that there will be pain, but acceptable and legitimate pain in the grave crisis which our nation faces.

'If you are prepared to reduce somewhat the standard of maintenance of the Government's estate, with the condition of your colleagues' offices making a contribution, we can make some economies in the Property Services Agency. If you are prepared to forgo some of the statistical returns upon which our judgement of safety in the construction industry is based, we will be able to make a small reduction in that directorate. If we no longer collect returns about the quality of housing provision, which we must in fairness point out means that standards will deteriorate without our knowledge, further economies can be made.

'In these ways and a number of others, with which we need not detain you, we believe we will be able to meet your colleagues' objectives.'

I later learnt that Labour had asked for similar manpower reductions a year or two before. No doubt the former option papers (known in Whitehall as 'horror comics') had been dusted off for me. No doubt the eloquent speech had been rehearsed with my predecessor.

The political menace behind the advice would not have been lost on the most naïve of Secretaries of State, but I was fresh from the hustings and my heart was bold. 'Go on,' I said. 'Let us consider the 5 per cent options.'

'Secretary of State, may I first say to you' – it was one of the senior civil servants speaking – 'that we consider ourselves extremely fortunate to have you, obviously one of the more determined, ambitious and talented members of this Government, in our department. Our responsibility is to protect you, Secretary of State, to ensure that all that you want for yourself is advanced, together with the interests of this department.

'Of course, if you insist upon urging us to recommend to you the 5 per cent staff reductions, we are not saying there are no options that could be considered. For example, we have considered the methods we use for monitoring pollution of waterways. If you are prepared to see increased levels of untreated sewage pumped into the rivers, then further economies could be found.' A harrowing catalogue was recited. At the end, not daunted, I asked for the 7.5 per cent options.

'Secretary of State', my principal adviser said, 'can I be quite honest with you? We have had conversations with some of our colleagues in other government departments. We know how much you care about the commitment of this Government and how determined you are to carry it out. We have been making some inquiries about the resolve of your colleagues. Secretary of State, none of your colleagues is going to consider the 7.5 per cent option. Do you think it wise, so soon in your political career and at such an early stage in this Government's fortunes, when the future is uncertain and your colleagues' resolve untested, to be out there alone, taking risks, sacrificing standards, abandoning the fruits of decades of social improvement?'

In twenty offices in Whitehall similar conversations were being held. I remembered Irwin Bellow's advice and put one last question: 'How many people are allowed to recruit to this department?' Notice was understandably required, but soon the reply came back: fifty-seven. There was only one decision to make, and I made it. I gave instructions that only one person would in future recruit to the department. That burden would be mine.

Four years later the DOE was 29 per cent smaller, employed 15,000 fewer people and remained in my view one of the most impressive and creative departments in Whitehall. I heard no more about the impossibility of a 7.5 per cent reduction in manpower.

After my crude but necessary decision officials from the personnel department paid me occasional visits to report on vacancies as they arose, and I approved or disapproved of their being filled. It was not scientific and my priorities must often have been wrong, but it was the only way to make the inroads into numbers which I intended. It was also the only way for me to find out the realities of our manpower requirements as against the superficialities which stared at me from the official briefing papers.

The threatened reduction of standards soon turned out to be one messenger lost here, one secretary there, one merging of two offices where work had previously been duplicated. It soon became plain that people were leaving the department at a rate of about 10 per cent a year. Some retired, some were fed up, but the rate of natural wastage was consistent. In the normal cause of events that happens in most organisations. It also seemed clear, after a month or two, that on average only four out of every ten of the resultant vacancies needed to be filled. Gaps could be closed by moving the existing staff. After six months, with the department already 3 per cent smaller, I handed the work on to two very capable civil servants with instructions to keep up the pressure and to refer to me only when they were worried about safety or security.

Looking back, it seems incredible that a department which was supposed to be efficiently managed could lose a quarter of its manpower and still in other respects be the same department. The only possible explanation was deeply disturbing: that the system of management was nowhere near equal to the task; and that the system of scrutinising Whitehall, the painstaking work done by the Comptroller and Auditor-General and his staff and by the Commons Public Accounts Committee, was defective.

I now decided that I must find out what was happening in my department and who was responsible for making it happen; who had set the targets, what the targets were and whether they were being monitored. Nobody could answer these questions for me. Nobody could recall them being asked before. Nobody had even the means of gathering the information. Frequently, the information did not exist.

My simple decision was to identify every person who would be able to answer my questions because he was familiar with the office or depot or laboratory where things were being done. Each such person, in private sector language, was a profit centre; and each was asked to analyse his responsibility, his activities, his authority, his manpower and his costs.

We did it in a matter of months and, I believe for the first time, public sector managers then had a clear set of objectives and costs. Anyone taking over a post would have an equally clear guide to his new responsibilities.

In creating the MINIS (Management Information System for Ministers) system we looked, first of all, for the man in charge of a definable and recognisable unit of activity. Each of those terms had to be defined but the task proved much easier to do than to describe. The excellence of the Civil Service once brought to bear, reluctantly at first but with increasing enthusiasm, soon found answers to the technical questions of what units of accountability there should be and in what form the answers should be returned. The head of each of the DOE's 57 directorates became the responsible officer. Usually each was close enough to the front line, the centre of activity, to know the names of his subordinates and the nature of their work. He was told the costs of the people working under his direct authority, and he analysed the time and cost devoted to each task. The result was a book which set out his management structure, his objectives and the costs of the work in hand, and set targets for six months ahead.

It was a chore, like all accounting, and no doubt largely for that reason had not been done in the public sector before. In the private sector the more numerate disciplines of the balance sheet impose it.

MINIS yielded a wealth of information and incidentally revealed how little authority and therefore accountability even senior civil servants had. Too few were answerable. Before its introduction too many responsibilities were undefined. Technical experts advised administrators. Progress slipped between the two. Numbers were set by staff inspection. Pay was negotiated separately. People, especially the fast-streamers, changed posts in the private office manner.

In the public sector there is not the same simplicity of purpose that the disciplines of the rate of return and of the balance sheet impose in the private sector; but it does not mean that there can be no assessment of the value of public sector work. A civil servant may tell you that he is responsible for policies about the permissible levels of pollution in the waterways of Britain. That is a worthy activity, but it does not tell you much about what he is doing. I wanted to know what standards had been set; whether higher standards were to be brought in, and when; what this would cost, and how the benefits were to be measured.

When the literacies of the Civil Service and the generalities of their intentions are turned into targets which can be monitored and costed, when information is conveyed in columns instead of screeds, then objectives become clear and progress towards them becomes measurable and far more likely.

An important benefit was the effect on senior managers of having to prepare the MINIS documents. They had to make sure that they knew in detail what was happening in their empires. I helped this process along by myself carrying out many interviews of those in charge, and although my questions were often superficial the prospect of a dialogue with the Secretary of State usually helped concentrate minds.

It was gratifying to find how many people felt that the exercise was beneficial, and the system was seen increasingly by civil servants as a useful management tool. One immediate gain from MINIS was that it brought rationality into the staff reductions: for the first time we could see what people were doing and what could be done with smaller numbers or cut out altogether.

The story of MINIS shows how slack the disciplines of the public sector had grown in comparison with those of the private sector. It would be unjust to blame civil servants entirely for this. The best of institutions and the most highly motivated people are bound to allow standards to fall if there is no known way of measuring those standards, no incentive to raise them and no interest in whether they are raised or not. The state of affairs that was discovered first in the DOE and then, inevitably, in every other department which came under examination, exposed the same slackness in the use of public sector manpower as the recession had exposed in the private sector.

A new age of more efficient management is now slowly coming into being, but movement is sluggish even though it is sometimes thought or claimed to be rapid; and unless Parliament and the public, who stand to gain much, are vigilant there is no certainty that the revolution will be completed. The power of the machine to resist this patently overdue change, in spite of steady pressure from the top, has been awesome to observe.

On one memorable occasion, I was asked by the Prime Minister to give my colleagues an account of how MINIS was helping the DOE to put its house in order. My fellow Cabinet ministers sat in rows while I explained my brain-child, each with his sceptical permanent secretary behind him muttering objections, or so I suspected. Any politician knows when he is losing his audience's attention, and I knew well enough. When I had done, there were few takers and absolutely no enthusiasts.

In the early days, permanent secretaries popped up all over Whitehall to explain why the MINIS system was unnecessary or inappropriate or both in their own departments. The Commons Treasury and Civil Service Committee, which described MINIS as 'a most important development', observed in March 1982, after three years of development of the system by the DOE, that nothing like it had yet been adopted in other departments. They were not impressed with the excuses which the permanent secretaries had given, and they noted that one permanent secretary had rejected MINIS without properly examining it. I do not know whether he was criticised, or rewarded in the next Honours List. I would be astonished to be told that he was retired early or posted somewhere less demanding. It seems unlikely in the extreme that anything occurred to encourage in him some degree of commitment to improvement.

The committee were also concerned that there was no clear orientation towards the achievement of efficiency and effectiveness at the higher levels of the civil service or in government generally.

At the same time academics in learned journals began to recall the failure of several past attempts to plant modern management techniques in the apparently alien soil of Whitehall. There was a strong school of thought that, once Heseltine had passed on, this attempt also would soon wither and die. There are several interpretations to be placed on the evidence of a former head of the Civil Service who said to the Treasury committee: 'There are not all that many Mr Heseltines around.'

I never expected that all ministers would prove enthusiastic managers, for the reasons I have given; but I was a little surprised that so many senior officials, whose duty to their ministers, it seemed to me, was to see that their departments were well managed, should have shown little interest in a device which was designed to make their task easier. It was encouraging, on the other hand, to see that many younger officials, less bound by past practice than their seniors and eager to see the performance of their service raised, became active reformers. I wish I could be confident that their devotion will be rewarded.

In 1982 the Government launched its financial management initiative (FMI) to secure the adoption in each department of systems which would enable managers to measure performance and secure greater value for money. The spur was the fact that the administrative costs of central government, the annual bill for running the machine, was approaching £14,000m. This was a level of expenditure well worth devising a system to control.

By 1984 most departments had, at last, adopted management information systems with some or most of the features of MINIS, and were using them to improve financial control. To quieten any suggestion of vulgar imitation, and to maintain understandable *amour-propre*, departments found different names and different acronyms: thus the Department of Trade and Industry introduced ARM (for activity and resource management); Agriculture sprouted both MINIM and the rustic-sounding MAIS; in the Home Office there is APR, and in the Health Department DMA. By 1985, the Lord Chancellor's Department had devised something which sounds a little more lordly: it is called LOCIS, for the Lord Chancellor's information system. There is no case for all these variants. I do not claim that MINIS is the last word. It is at least a bold attempt at a proper management accounting system. It was flexible enough to cope with all the vagaries of two of Whitehall's larger and more varied departments.

While MINIS was taking root at the DOE it was widely accepted that one department at least neither needed nor could accommodate such a system: the Ministry of Defence. If I remember my first conversation about MINIS with the new permanent under-secretary, Sir Clive Whitmore, it was relatively brief: 'I wonder if by chance you've heard of the MINIS system?' 'Yes, you may remember that I was in No 10 when you did that presentation.' 'Ah yes, I'd like to introduce it here.' 'I thought you might.' We never looked back.

We asked Mavis McDonald, who was in charge of MINIS at the DOE, to come and explain it to MOD officials. The MOD was vastly bigger – it had about three times as many non-industrial civil servants as the DOE – but that was of no consequence. The system was designed to be applied to any government department, local authority or any public sector body, large or small. All that was needed at the MOD was the will to apply the rigour of detailed management accounting to the public sector in a way that no one would hesitate to apply it to the private sector.

It would take at most a month to produce a model system that could apply across Whitehall. That is what is now needed to ensure that the best information is available, regularly updated, the tightest disciplines applied and comparability between departments achieved. The information should be published.

The virtue of MINIS or its equivalent is that it charts a whole department. Ministers and senior civil servants see not only the in-tray, the media coverage, the Parliamentary Question or the manifesto commitment. They also see the rest of the little-observed work of the department.

Being little observed does not mean that it is insignificant; but because it is out of the spotlight it can too easily be ignored. Most departmental work comes into this latter category. So MINIS is not just about measurement of output, or tighter control of staff costs; it is an attempt to open every door, to manage comprehensively as opposed to reactively or sporadically. It is to apply a common discipline most closely comparable with the private sector. Nor is MINIS necessarily about staff reductions. It is about costs, priorities and accountability. If, in the process of discussing the MINIS returns, it becomes apparent that some activity is not being adequately performed and needs higher quality staff, or just more staff, then a priority switch can take place. MINIS will have opened another door which could so easily have remained closed through lack of interest.

The difficulties must be recognised. Policy advice cannot be subjected to output measurements, and value-for-money criteria are likely to be highly subjective. Those departments or sections of departments more involved in executive work offer more straightforward measurements. But, whatever the problem, it remains right to know the cost of the policy advice that year after year is constantly prepared and updated. Requirements change and there needs to be regular monitoring to establish continued need.

Whitehall, properly managed within MINIS disciplines, would find a culture contrast between itself and many of the outside public organisations with which it has to do business. They have no such systems and, like Whitehall itself, will resist their adoption; but a strong lead and a gentle tug at the purse strings should prove persuasive.

There are two final problems. The more value-for-money criteria are applied, the slower the programme momentum may become. If civil servants are issued with general instruction to support, for example, home improvement, the money flows. If they are expected in each case to stand up against questions about the enhanced life of the property or the judgement of whether to rebuild or repair, a slower programme emerges. It would be the same in targeting regional expenditure to genuine new job-creating industrial support rather than to blanket capital support programmes; but one has only to set out the problem to realise that it is precisely this discipline of value for money that should prevail.

More difficult for politicians is the publication of such detailed information. As I have said, it opens every door in a too-closed society. That is a desirable objective within legitimate national security and commercial constraints. It will make Parliament, the media and the pressure groups better informed and reveal more clearly what is being done with taxpayers' resources. If the answers to inconvenient questions become clear, that may increase the inconvenience; but it does not make it wrong.

Ministers should take heart from the experience of the select committees. As their scope and scale has widened, they have not brought the workings of Whitehall to a halt, and public comment has reflected a proper appreciation of the strengths and weaknesses of such a system. Ministers are not destroyed by revelations of waste within their departments, when it is seen that ministers could not reasonably have known and have acted reasonably on what they did know.

A further sign that people understand the realities of ministerial life in a complicated and large department is a growing parliamentary willingness to accept the need for a Secretary of State to delegate to subordinate colleagues.

By 1984 there were a few civil servants at senior levels who were clearly committed to root and branch reform of ancient attitudes and practices; but report after report confirmed the degree of inertia which they would have to overcome. In 1985 a scrutiny of scrutinies was prepared by the Prime Minister's efficiency unit. Margaret Thatcher had noticed that it was taking in most cases at least two years, and often as long as five, to implement savings in Whitehall departments identified by detailed scrutinies of the kind begun by Derek (now Lord) Rayner. Available savings of £600m a year had been turned up in 260 such scrutinies, and the Prime Minister was naturally concerned to know what was causing the delay.

The short answer proved to be the one which was fully apparent before inquiries started: examination revealed that the sense of urgency which characterised the scrutineers did not characterise the officials who were called on to take corrective action. The report observed that the attitudes of both ministers and permanent secretaries were crucial and that, in three out of the eight cases which were studied, the permanent secretary's direct involvement had 'signalled the importance he attached to change'. The junior officials who wrote the report were too delicate – and who can blame them? – to do more than imply that, by leaving the matter there, five of these eight top civil servants did not appear to attach great importance to securing the savings. It might have led to different results if those who prescribed the economies had had a hand in securing them instead of moving on to new and different fields.

A few months later, in October 1986, the National Audit Office looked at the progress of the Financial Management Initiative in a dozen departments. The Comptroller and Auditor-General, Sir Gordon Downey, who is not given to overstatement, said that the 'timeliness' of the FMI was emphasised by the fact that every one of the departments he examined had found it necessary to enhance its existing management system or to introduce a new one in order to comply with what was asked of it.

Sir Gordon's overall verdict was favourable; his 'broad conclusions', noted in the Press, were that real progress was being made in the development of management systems, and that there were no serious shortcomings in the departments which his staff had examined; but his report was full of implied criticism, always in the mildest language, of slowness in one department, lack of commitment in another, inadequacy of the system introduced in a third. This was the position six years after the establishment of MINIS in the DOE had shown how great was the scope for improvement and how urgent the need.

The picture that emerges from between the lines of most of these reports reveals just how difficult it is to bring about a culture change, whether in the public service or anywhere else. It also raises another related issue. The Government had, as its principle task, to win the battle against inflation. It could not escape any more than its predecessors from a public linking of its determination in this field with its attitude to the pay of its own employees, and the conventional wisdom about pay is that of centralisation, standardisation and rigidity. Every exception is a precedent for the watchful union negotiator.

So civil servants were both harangued about the need for enhanced efficiency and rewarded with exemplary low levels of pay settlement, which created a climate which did not improve motivation. Both sides had a seemingly unanswerable case; but the civil service saw little of the benefits gained from the savings which they helped to achieve.

The combination which ideally we need, but which at the time I certainly never saw how to achieve, was one in which civil servants, in responding to the government's exhortations, would share in the rewards of enhanced efficiency. Later I shall argue for a way forward. To attract people of the highest quality and then motivate them is of the first importance.

One further point must be made. Public servants live in a climate of public accountability. They know, and ministers know, that when things go wrong, as they inevitably will, Parliament will expect to find a thoroughness of preparation and a detail of record quite unthinkable in the private sector. The effective implementation of policy will not always correspond to what Parliament regards as efficient. Ministers who seek effectiveness must be prepared to defend their decisions when the spotlight is turned on them.

By the time I moved to the Ministry of Defence in 1983, as is the way with political initiatives, the climate had changed. Unemployment had risen and the pressure for efficient use of manpower in the public service had correspondingly fallen. The Government's target for manpower economies in the 1983 Parliament was modest.

I was asked with great force: Why us alone? I was not persuaded. I had entered Government resolved to bring the discipline of tight management to the public sector, and my conviction was not a matter of mood or of fashion. To the day I left, the MOD reduced its civilian manpower as consistently as had the DOE. I made a concession to the changed climate: our manpower fell not by 6 per cent but by 4 per cent a year, but by that time the overall rate of reduction of the central government workforce was hardly falling at all except through privatisation.

Between 1983 and 1986 at the Ministry of Defence staff numbers were reduced by about 20,000, in addition to the reductions arising from the transfer of the Royal Ordnance factories out of the civil service. The reductions were achieved by improved efficiency, giving up tasks and by contractorisation. With the transfer of the Royal Dockyards to commercial management some 20,000 more people will

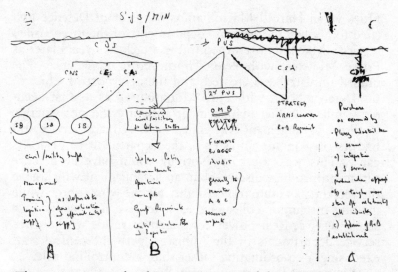

The new structure for the reorganisation of the MOD was drawn in an RAF VC10 on the way home from a ministerial visit to Kuwait

have moved out of the public service. Civil Service numbers in the Ministry will have fallen from around 250,000 in 1979 to under 150,000.

The very size of the MOD and its loose federal organisation, with central co-ordinating staff placed alongside single service structures, was a recipe for the wastage of effort; and the military and civilian staffs tended to report upward through separate chains, blurring responsibilities.

I decided I would have to have a wall-sized management chart produced so that everybody knew who was answerable to whom. It was a huge undertaking, but it was done; and it proved of immense value to me in the judgements I had to make about the department's future structure. There is no better way to learn about the department for which you are responsible, than to ask somebody to draw lines of accountability on a sheet of paper and put names into boxes.

The most important change to which the newly-assembled evidence pointed and which it helped to make possible was the completion of the reorganisation of the Ministry which had been contemplated for about thirty years.

There is no need to recount the blood-letting in the mid-

fifties when Harold Macmillan as Minister of Defence first
tried to abolish the separate departments of the three armed
services. Macmillan returned to the attack five years later as
Prime Minister, with Peter Thorneycroft at Defence. The
unified ministry was created, and the new post of Chief of
the Defence Staff, with Lord Mountbatten as its first occu-
pant; but a unified management structure did not emerge.
Until the arrangement was ended in 1981, each service still
had its own junior minister in the department to plead its
cause. This was anarchic. Nothing could have been more
certain to produce discord than an arrangement which gave
the Secretary of State responsibility for the whole show while
inviting his junior colleagues each to give his loyalty to a
single service. Real power continued to reside in the three
service departments of the Ministry, with the central staff
exercising a co-ordinating rather than a controlling role.

Abolition of the separate service ministers allowed for the
first time a community of interest in the political direction
of the department; but immediately below the Secretary of
State the potential for conflict remained embedded in the
structure of the department.

Although his position had been strengthened by my predecessor, John Nott, the senior serving officer, the Chief of the
Defence Staff, still had only a small planning staff. One rank
below him each of the three autonomous service chiefs had
his own much larger and competing planning staff. I
discovered to my astonishment that the three service chiefs
were not directly answerable to the CDS. Business was
conducted through the Chiefs of Staff committee and rested
on consensus.

The fiercely protected prerogatives of the Royal Navy, the
Army, and the Royal Air Force, had produced and sustained
for twenty years something which was indefensible not only
by modern standards of management in the world beyond
the services but by every rule of command taught to the
humblest uniformed recruit.

The potential for confusion or worse, and the actual triplication of activity, should have been dealt with years before,
and in his heart of hearts every senior officer and official in
the department must have known it. The MINIS exercise at
once showed me and everyone else where the weaknesses

were. As the evidence came in, I held long and detailed discussions with the chiefs of staff and a wide range of senior officers about the need for rationalisation but, knowing all too well the defeats which their predecessors had inflicted on mine, it seemed wiser to design a blueprint for change, and to do it in some detail, without their assistance. In the end I drew the skeleton of the proposed reorganisation in an RAF VC10 on the way back from a visit to Kuwait. To stand so apart from Field Marshal Sir Edwin Bramall and his colleagues, for whom I had the highest admiration, was without doubt the least comfortable position I adopted in government.

It was clear that my target must be the independent powers of the three single-service planning and equipment requirement staffs. I decided to bring them together in central planning and systems staffs with a new post of Vice Chief of the Defence Staff to take charge. He would also have under him the key policy and operations staffs. To put the realignment of power beyond doubt the Vice Chief was to be of four-star rank – the same seniority as the service chiefs – and all of them became answerable to the CDS. On the civilian side, the fragmentation of responsibility for finance and budget issues was also ended. The aim was a new machinery for reaching the key resource allocation decisions on a defence-wide basis, rather than by a process of fair shares for three competing service interests.

By the time the blueprint was ready to be put before the chiefs in a consultative document I felt I knew what had to be done. There was some scope for change but not much. The chiefs, steeped as they were in loyalty to their own services, disliked my proposals as I knew they would and on my suggestion exercised their right to take their objections directly to the Prime Minister. She put her authority behind me, and the chiefs, as I had also known they would, accepted the new command structure with a loyalty that was most impressive.

I hope the three services will appreciate, as time goes by, that this unification is in their own long-term interests. Allowing for the limitation of its size, we have today one of the most professional armed forces in the world. But as Mountbatten so clearly set out, and as the Falklands has recently proved, the conduct of war requires an integrated command. The earlier the most senior commanders think together and plan in concert with their equivalents in the other services, the wider and more valuable their experience will be.

The reorganisation of the Ministry brought to a conclusion a process begun 30 years earlier. Inevitably it provoked fierce and determined opposition from the interests concerned; this could be overcome only by the exercise of political will. The pressure now and over the next few years will be for 'modifications' to the new structure to assist the single service areas in the discharging of their responsibilities. The danger, as after 1964, is that there will be a slow drift away from the central determination of priorities towards a more federal structure. Ultimately these pressures can be resisted only by the Secretary of State himself. I am sure that my successors will see, like me, that with the increasing interdependence of the services, the key resource allocation decisions must be taken on a defence-wide basis on the advice of staff with tri-service responsibilities. In years to come people will perhaps marvel that things were ever done differently.

2

Whitehall: Up With The Leaders

Within a few days of starting my first government job in 1970, I discovered two things about the public sector: how different was the attitude to money, by comparison with the private sector; and how easy it was to adopt it.

I began my career as parliamentary secretary to John Peyton, the Minister of Transport, a veteran political officer, meticulous as to detail, with an intuitive judgement of Tory purpose. Like all new boys I was resolved to run the public sector, to the limit of my very limited power as a junior minister, on the same lines as the private. So when I was invited to approve £6m of investment by British Rail in electrification I asked to see the managers who wanted so much money. 'We would not advise that, Minister,' my officials said. 'If you start interviewing everyone who puts a request to you, and questioning their judgements, you will never cope with the work and we will never get any decisions.' My resolution extended to seeing the managers, but no further. They got their cash, and I had effortlessly crossed the divide which separates those who deal in their own money from those who deal in the taxpayer's.

That crossing was too easy. It roused all my latent anxieties about the adequacy of the financial disciplines in the public sector. I knew all about private sector disciplines, and I knew that they worked. In the 1960s, before I joined the Government, the publishing company I had helped create, Haymarket Press, had gone through a rough patch and, as chief executive, I had for a while authorised personally every petty cash voucher for 50 pence or more. There were not that many 50 pence pieces to go round. Today, thanks to

Lindsay Masters, Simon Tindall and their colleagues, it all looks very different.

From 50 pence to £6m was giddy progress. A rather slower rate of ascent took me in the next thirteen years to an annual budget at the Ministry of Defence of £18b. By then I had learned that it was wise to question many of the assumptions on which proposals to spend taxpayers' money were based. Everywhere I had found evidence that the public sector was not managed as it should be.

The thousands of jobs, or non-jobs, eliminated in those years at the Department of the Environment and the Ministry of Defence, with a consequent annual saving of over £100m, had all been scrutinized by each department's staff inspection system, and adjudged essential. Yet we did not so much cut them as smooth them away, almost all through natural wastage, without blood or pain or public attention. What we did should not have been possible.

The same hidden waste and potential savings lurked in every other government department and every local authority and public body. Indeed they lurked in much of the private sector as well. In spite of the great gains in efficiency made under Conservative government since 1979 I have no doubt that much costly fat remains on the body of the public sector. The question which my experience raised was whether the disciplines or the motivation of life in the public service should be changed; and if so whether the cure required manipulation or surgery. I have come to believe that quite severe surgery is still needed.

The working lives of all of us have been spent against a background of steady expansion in the public sector. Some governments have welcomed the process, others have set out to reverse it, but the growth has continued. As we squeezed the public body here, it expanded there, the two changes often directly related as some cuts in public spending led to higher costs in supporting the casualties of those same cuts.

The public expenditure indexation programmes, to which we have all put our names, left little opportunity for government to shift the thrust of national endeavour towards investing in the future instead of consuming today. Even the present Government, rightly cutting some expenditure to the very limits of political acceptability, has had to cut investment programmes time and again to pay the bills of our over-consuming society.

Of course there are pressures from those who pay the bills of the public sector to curb the role of the State. In the private sector growth is controlled by profitability. Inefficiency will show up. Management accountability can be traced back from the market place to that bottom line. I would be the last person to dismiss the comparative simplicity of that discipline, which teaches the person who runs a business that the bank manager is not just the friendly smiling fellow in the television advertisements. I remember a moment in my business life when every Friday the company finance director used to bring in the list of outstanding creditors. There were three columns headed: solicitors' letters, writs received and writs whose time limits for reply were about to expire. The bills in the last column we paid. In government service there is no equivalent discipline and no comparable measurement of success or failure. One dangerous consequence is that it encourages the debate to concentrate on the input and not the output, and it is meat and drink to the armies of special pleaders which now support every public sector programme.

The argument is simple but false: the input is cash; more cash buys more people and more people provide better services. It was easy but wrong to assume that Britain in 1979, with a record number of civil servants and of health service and local government employees, was enjoying public service of unprecedented quality. To proclaim it there were spending departments, trade unions, organised lobbies and specialist media correspondents. They were all infinitely sensitive to any whisper of a threat to the relentless assumptions of yet more expenditure, more consumption, more prestige and power in each department's hands at the expense (literally) of those who were producing the means to meet their ends.

We knew that Britain's private sector was over-manned, under-profitable and losing its markets with depressing regularity. The market place weighed the outputs and measured the decline. But the measurement of output in the public sector was low on the list of priorities; the customers were no match for the producers.

It is depressing how much of the vocabulary of the public

service enables those employed in it or speaking on its behalf to present any attempts to increase output or efficiency as cuts eagerly sought by a hard-faced government. The misuse of scarce resources cannot glibly be defended on the grounds of concern or care.

To challenge the vested interests of the public sector required a determination and an attention to detail not characteristic of most administrations. I doubt if any member of the present Government would claim that we made no mistakes, but I would be the first to claim that the Government exposed the public sector to something of the harshness of the experience which has been commonplace in the private sector during the 1980s. It did so with courage, and it was right. If there is to be a tomorrow for a civilised and caring Britain, it will have to be based on prosperity achieved through efficiency and effectiveness in public and private sector alike. No one who has served in government during the 1980s can have any doubt that the attainment of adequate standards, in the public as in the private sector, will be as hard as it is necessary.

I arrived in the Department of the Environment in 1979 with an obligation to contain the expenditure not only of central government but also of local government in England and Wales for which the department had supervisory responsibility.

I first entered that department as parliamentary under-secretary nine years earlier, when I detected in local government the same mistaken conviction that then possessed Whitehall, that there was no scope for pruning the size or the cost of administration, except possibly at the margin or by giving up what were always presented as essential tasks. I came to think that this widely proclaimed and generally accepted belief should be tested.

My suspicion fell on the worthy staff of the District Audit Service who, since the 1840s, had been watching local authorities to see that no unlawful use was made of public funds. I had never doubted that they discharged their duties conscientiously, but it struck me as possible that the relationship between council officer and auditor might have become too comfortable after years of friendly familiarity, and that the occasional scrutiny by an auditor from the private sector with a fresh eye would do no harm.

I therefore proposed that the Bill which was to bring about the 1974 reform of local government should allow private accountancy firms to undertake municipal audits, not supplanting but supplementing the District Audit. My modest idea roused surprising resistance, but after some argument it prevailed. The legislation was framed to allow this but I did not stay long enough to supervise its implementation.

It was not until 1979, when Margaret Thatcher invited me to join her Cabinet and take charge of that department, that I found how little had happened. The relevant clause of the Act appeared watertight: competition there would be. But I left the department. A new set of ministers took over. The continuity was broken. Administrative rules emerged and the private sector never had a chance. I hoped that the officials who had so deftly frustrated the minister's intentions felt some chagrin at finding me back at the department in 1979 and, worse, in charge of it.

I did not intend to fail a second time. I had plans for a more potent remedy, an Audit Commission which would bring some of the rigours of private sector accountability into local government. I thought it wrong in principle, as the 1976 Layfield Report had said, that councils should be able to appoint their own auditors. Awkward auditors do not get reappointed. I wanted a Commission, independent of both central and local government, which would appoint auditors as it chose from either the District Audit or private firms. This said, it is right to point out that the District Audit has provided a formidable bulwark against impropriety and irregularity by the Left, insofar as the law permits. The abuses of extreme councils are manifest. They would have been more widespread without the District Audit who have responded, in the quite different environment of the Audit Commission, in a way that again indicates that it is not the quality of the public servant that is deficient but the way in which he is expected to work.

It was important that the Commission should do more than simply see that auditors checked the books. It was important for the auditors to be required to express opinions

"That chain will have to go!"

Some of us felt that councils had more in reserve than they were willing to reveal when asked for cuts

on the way accounts were presented, and to actively promote efficiency and value for money. This the Commission is now doing with impressive success.

The Treasury raised objections and delayed for two years the establishment of the Audit Commission. At the root of their arguments was their instinctive hostility to anything which they cannot control or at least interfere in.

I was denied provision for the Audit Commission in the Local Government Planning and Land Bill in the first parliamentary session, which became the Act of 1980. After a renewed campaign it found a place in the Local Government Finance Act of 1982. The upshot was that it was April 1983 before the Audit Commission could start its vital work. We were fortunate to secure as the first chief executive John Banham, now Director-General of the CBI. He was later to report that the Commission in its first three years had discovered scope for improving management within local government which had a potential value worth billions of pounds a year – something, he noted accurately, which few people had accepted three years earlier.

If those improvements are achieved, and, slowly, they will be, two years will have been lost, to the great cost of both taxpayers and ratepayers. The Treasury's dialogue with the Public Accounts Committee revealed a preoccupation with the short term and a lack of imagination which blinded them to the importance of something that was in the mainstream of the Government's economic policy.

Tom King, without whose wise counsel and untiring effort my time at the Department would have been the poorer, bore the brunt of steering the local government legislation through Parliament and presided over its subsequent implementation.

In that first bill we were at least able to make a start by taking powers to require local authorities to publish the information essential for the performance of councils to be compared. That idea had been scribbled on the back of my envelope for Sir John Garlick, as the second of ten policy matters for early attention. The concept of comparability statistics is commonplace in the private sector. We wanted more of it in the public. If every local authority was compelled to make available details of its use of manpower and of the cost of providing each service, wide disparities between comparable councils would be revealed. Once rate-payers saw that they were paying twice as much for street-cleaning as the neighbouring borough, while having dirtier streets, we hoped they would want to know why.

I believed naïvely that the conscientious council of average competence would examine its weaknesses and learn from its betters; and that the occasional prodigal and obstinate council would be forced to improve its performance. The value for money debate is now entering into the local authority psyche. It has taken too long. The first reaction to improved comparative statistics was not to seek to emulate the leaders but to explain why the experiences of the leaders did not apply to the laggard authorities.

If local government has taken too long in accepting this principle, it is certainly right to have moved in this direction. The next stage is to apply the same lessons to central government. The National Audit Office could make use of outside consultants in value-for-money studies and in much more critical reporting on the efficiency of central government departments. Lord Rayner and the studies that carry his name have set a precedent, but *ad hoc* initiatives conducted on a one-off basis are no substitute for regular comprehensive scrutinies conducted at arm's length, published and later checked for implementation. If we are seeking a cultural change there has to be a permanence about the new atmosphere of accountability and it must extend throughout the public sector. Government imposed it on local government. What is sauce for the goose . . . !

In 1979 the pattern of local government had two peculiarities of special interest to me. More councils were under Tory control than ever before; and more people than ever before were employed by local government.

Local authority manpower had risen steadily for decades, except for a hiccup in 1976 when the International Monetary Fund took a hand in the Labour Government's economic management. The cost of wages and salaries had risen even faster and was now taking two-thirds of all current expenditure. We knew what the work of the Audit Commission was to prove a few years later, that the same services could be delivered in many cases at much lower cost and that the first step for most local authorities must be to reduce manpower.

The Government had been returned on a promise to cut out waste in local government and elsewhere. The Department of the Environment had to play its part and secure a decided fall in the numbers employed by local government. By 1983, after a battle which inevitably was fought trench by trench, numbers had fallen back to the level that prevailed at the time of local government reorganisation in 1974; but to bring this about we had to try to apply by remote control the same sort of pressure that we were applying in the department itself.

There was no wish to interfere in the priority of expenditure decisions of particular councils, and no attempt at first was made; but as time passed we were forced to involve ourselves more and more. In my first year I made a mistake. The local authorities, both Tory and Labour controlled, all assured me that local government had always complied with the overall expenditure guidelines set by central government. 'You won't need controls,' they said. 'We always stick to the guidelines.' They were telling me the truth, and I do not think that most of them realised any more than I how comparatively easy it had been for them to contain expenditure within government guidelines which had risen every year.

Now the guidelines were to be lowered, and the change in 1979/80 from Labour's proposed increase of 1.6 per cent to a decrease of 1.4 per cent – a reduction of 3 per cent after the financial year had begun – broke the habit of a lifetime for local government. The electoral timing meant we were late in asking for a revision of plans based on numbers already employed; but authorities with strong Conservative leadership invariably responded and achieved what we asked. We were seeking more ambitious targets in our own department.

Many councillors came with their officials to plead the impossibility of our requests. It was important to be armed with the facts. In almost every case the petitioners were not so equipped. Time and again visiting councillors, especially if they were Tories, would say: 'Yes, we agree that there is waste in local government, there is certainly fat to be shed, but you won't find it in our authority. Secretary of State, we assure you that we in Blankshire have cut services and staff to the bone.' Hardening my heart I would point out that I happened to have the figures for Blankshire; that its council was employing a larger workforce than ever before, not only in areas where its commitments had increased but in every department; and I was often able to add that I had comparative figures for similar authorities which were employing smaller numbers. Could the councillors explain? They seldom could, and their silence was the cue for the chief officers to move in. They had briefed their councillors for only superficial dialogue, and only when their front line collapsed did the officers try to ensure that at least the retreat was orderly. The best of the Tory authorities just got on; indeed, in London, under Horace Cutler, they were ahead of the game.

The experience showed me two similarities between local and central government: first, that there is little chance at either level of improved efficiency unless the elected minister or councillor insists on being told the facts; and that at both levels there is frequent reluctance on the part of officials even to consider the possibility that the regime they run may be slack.

The councillors at least had some excuse for being insufficiently briefed. Any system for calculating support grant becomes extraordinarily intricate, and there is no way of making it less so unless the methods adopted are so crude that they are difficult to defend. The needs of relatively poor populations in the urban centres are as different from the prosperous surburban communities as are their resources. Officers were able to tell most councillors whatever they wished them to believe. When after two years we set cash targets, and quantified precisely the expenditure figure which complied with the targets, the Tories at once grasped what was required of them and in most cases quickly delivered.

By 1982, if the achievements of Tory-controlled local government had been reflected across the country, rate increases would have been at an average of 11–12 per cent. In fact, Labour-controlled councils averaged 30 per cent. The Greater London Council, extravagant as always, wanted a 90 per cent increase.

Again, if all councils had matched the Tory councillors' efforts, numbers employed would have come down by 1982 to the levels from which they had soared since the time of local government reorganisation, and the Treasury's public expenditure targets would have been achieved. But the consensus within which local government had worked to rising expenditure targets up to 1979 had gone. The constitutional relationships between central and local government were at the centre of the stage. Labour-controlled authorities called in aid a conflicting mandate, and the ratepayers paid the bills. It is rare for government departments or local authorities to lower their expenditure. One man's cut is another man's opportunity to expand. In practice the scheme sacrificed by one department usually ends up as more resources absorbed by another. They all know this, so they all fight every battle step by step, fearing that a more benign attitude will leave them with no budget at all.

The other weakness of local government, which was

revealed in every negotiation I had, was its vulnerability to pressure from unions determined to preserve the numbers of their members employed. The unions' success, with weak management, in keeping their people in jobs ensured that Labour's expenditure cuts in 1975 and 1976 and their big cut in rate support grant the next year fell heavily on capital programmes, especially council housing, while revenue spending increased. The long-term social damage is immeasurable: the chief reason for the poor condition of the public housing stock today can be traced to local government's failure to contain its labour costs and a Labour Government's unwillingness to keep council rents moving in line with money values.

By 1979 local government had become a barely controllable free-wheeling employment machine which for year after year had been run largely for the benefit of the machine-minders.

It would be unjust and pointless to place blame on any group of people for the wastefulness in both local and central government which over several generations had become endemic and gross. I am more inclined to blame management than unions, and those who are elected than those who are appointed. Defective management structures become harder to change the longer they last, and any group of people working as a team will acquire habits of thought which resist any challenge from outside the circle. Habits of thought in Whitehall are cautious and defensive; but that is because ministers have long expected civil servants to protect them from error and political embarrassment. Ministers too, in their way, had become machine-minders.

If the Civil Service is imperfect then its shortcomings are of long standing, and all of us – governments not least – can conveniently blame our predecessors. My repeated critical comments on the Civil Service must be reconciled with my declared admiration for the many officials with whom I worked daily for nearly seven years in Cabinet. There is no contradiction: the performance of the institution does not begin to match that of its best members. Its performance is influenced far more by the rules, expectations and machinery within which civil servants operate than by any innate ability in the people themselves. I know of no more intelligent, industrious or public-spirited group of men and women than those at the top of the British Civil Service. They are by no means as highly paid as people of comparable ability in the private sector. They are cossetted only in the sense that they act with incomparable personal career security and invisibility. If in the longer term the continuing loss of some of the best Whitehall talent to other fields persists, this will prove most worrying; but it is remarkable that the outward flow is not greater because if, as I believe, the Whitehall machine is no longer adequately meeting the needs of the public it serves. neither is it worthy of those it employs. As the differentials in the private sector have widened in a world hungry for talent, it becomes increasingly urgent to find a framework where the talented civil servant can enjoy a career properly rewarded and properly appreciated. He will have to accept change to bring this about, but so will we.

What then should be done? There can be few sensible proposals for change in the Civil Service which have not been made before and usually ignored or abandoned. Many determined reformers have passed this way only to leave their footsteps in wet sand.

The Fulton Committee in the 1960s laboured harder than most. Its chief monument, the Civil Service Department, lived for little more than a decade before being abolished in 1981.

Another much-precedented technique to bring new experience to the public sector is the secondment of private sector managers. At its best this yields high dividends. It cannot automatically be assumed that private sector companies will always offer up their most talented people, or that their secondees will thrive within the Whitehall culture, but I am an advocate of many more exchanges and secondments.

I introduced three exceptional men into the world of Whitehall to help us in specific policy areas for limited periods. Tom Baron, Peter Levene and Ed Berman had each experienced the effect of Government policies on their daily work in different areas. They knew the limitations of the official mind, the timidity of politicians at national and local level, the weaknesses in the Whitehall systems.

Tom Baron had a lifetime's experience of building houses on a big scale. He formed the Volume House-Builders' Group of half a dozen of the biggest building firms, who had special problems and combined to make sure that these were known to government. They invited me to a lunch and it was thus that I first met an entrepreneur from the sharp end of wealth-creating activity who could think as effectively as he could act.

It was clear that Tom would meet my first precondition for successful transplanting: he could hold his own intellectually with the civil servants. He also possessed the power of decision and was used to taking responsibility and not to passing the buck. As for ideas, he was like a catherine wheel: for every problem he had ten solutions although, since he was also human, not all were practicable. In the Civil Service this quality is beyond price. When you express ideas, you risk criticism and rejection. Whitehall ladders are most easily climbed by 'sound' men of high critical intelligence, but too often without creativity of any practical kind.

I was attracted by Tom as someone of energy to support John Stanley and me in our efforts to stir up new ideas in the field of urban housing. At the end of a most valuable lunch I asked my permanent under-secretary to see if Tom would come and work for me. To my delight he agreed.

Peter Levene was different in that I had heard of his reputation before meeting him. When I moved to the Ministry of Defence I inherited the problem of the Procurement Executive, a bureaucracy which was spending £7b a year on weapons systems. The Procurement Executive was the brain-child of Lord Rayner, one of the most talented private sector managers to give time to public administration. He set up the right machinery but, as is so common in such cases, he was not able to stay long enough to see the full implementation of his reforms through. I was determined to secure better value for money by instituting competitive tendering wherever it was feasible.

The resistance to my suggestions was entrenched. I listened to grandiose presentations designed to convince me that competition would be unfair, would not bring down costs but, on the contrary, might even increase them.

We spoke different languages. It was clear that no directive from me could have a permanent effect, because it went against the grain. Only the right person could do what had to be done, and I had to find that person.

I made inquiries and Peter Levene's name was mentioned. I was told that he had built up a small company dealing in second-hand armaments and turned it into a major manufacturing business. I asked him to lunch and realised at once that he would be able to help me. He thoroughly understood my problems. He had dealt with the Procurement Executive as a major contractor and confirmed from his experience all my instinctive beliefs about its weaknesses. Here was the poacher urging on the gamekeeper.

Like Tom Baron, Peter Levene came to me as an adviser for six months, but before his time was up it became clear that there was a huge job to be done and that he was willing to do it. His readiness to become head gamekeeper full-time, as Chief of Defence Procurement, has yielded greatly improved value for money. In two years the value of defence contracts going to competitive tender rose from 38 to 64 per cent, and the savings of 10, 20, even 30 per cent as compared to our internal estimates exceeded the dreams of even the most optimistic advocates of competition. Peter Levene's appointment was in many ways indicative of what is wrong in public administration. He accepted a reduction in salary of £50,000 to leave the private sector and work for the public. In any language that is a sacrifice. In any other country it would be a matter for favourable comment. In Britain it was seen as a matter for criticism that he was earning so much money in the first place. There would, I suppose, have been less adverse comment if he had doubled his income by joining the brain drain and gone to work in California.

The Treasury came down on the side of value for money and firmly supported the Levene appointment; but the idea was unorthodox enough to arouse the opposition of many other forces, including the Civil Service Commission, and in the end only the Prime Minister was able to insist that we went ahead.

But he came and will have saved, by now, hundreds of millions of pounds for the Defence budget. If he has saved 8 per cent of the equipment programme – and he has said that he expects to save 10 per cent – he will have paid for the Trident programme single-handed. Not a bad achievement for one entrepreneur!

Of my third recruit to Whitehall, Ed Berman, I have less to tell because he came to the Department of the Environment shortly before I left it and before there was time for our relationship to develop as I had hoped. We first met at the city farm he ran in North London, and I was struck by the originality and persistence with which he was using his entrepreneurial talent to tackle problems of urban renewal and of employment which also troubled government. I hope the department learnt something from his energy and practicality and that he, too, felt that the venture was worthwhile.

I have no doubt that from time to time an individual with special talent, provided that he is given unrestricted access to the minister in charge, can invigorate a department. I also believe that if it were possible to establish a pattern of reciprocal secondments between Whitehall and the private sector, with civil servants and managers from industry and commerce exchanging positions for up to three years in mid-career, there would be great gains for both sides.

The career civil servant entering the fast stream on graduation has perhaps a 40-year run ahead of him. Against that background, it is hard to accept that he could not sensibly spend four or five years in industry in, say, two spells: one in his twenties, the second in his late thirties or early forties.

But although such exchanges take place, the difficulties in arranging them can be formidable. It takes ingenuity on both sides to devise jobs which will last only two or three years and yet be important enough to make full use of the talent and energy of a capable secondee. Unequal salary structures and rates of pension contribution can also create obstacles, as can problems over housing. The outsider coming in is often anxious that he will hinder rather than advance his career.

At the Ministry of Defence, Clive Whitmore and I both believed in exchanges, and we succeeded in arranging during one year – 1985 – for 50 managers from industry to enter the department on secondment and for 100 civil servants to take up positions in industry. I have no doubt that the participants on both sides will have gained valuable experience and that their performance will have improved.

One danger is that the public sector will lose too many of its better staff who will acquire too enthusiastic an appetite for the new environment. But if that would make the public sector improve its environment then it would be all to the good. It would be better, however, to ensure that public sector careers and rewards in the round are attractive enough to avoid the anguish.

The difference between Whitehall and the world outside in their attitudes to specialists is plainly shown in the relative standing of those who represent the big defence contractors and the officials who deal with them daily, speak the same language and, if the taxpayers' interests are to be safeguarded, must have comparable skills and toughness in negotiating. In the Ministry of Defence the contract area has not been seen as the place for high flyers compared with the glamorous 'policy' work reporting to ministers. In contrast, outside industry knows the importance of such work and recruits and rewards the staff involved accordingly. The Civil Service needs to put effort, rewards and status into those jobs at the forefront of the drive for better value for money.

My conclusion is that we must be bolder in planning for those changes in the Civil Service for which the need is increasingly recognised within the service itself.

In May 1986 Anne Mueller, the senior official in the Government's Management and Personnel Office, which is charged with promoting management reforms, described in visionary language, more reminiscent of political confidence than official caution, the changes which she believed were already taking place. The Civil Service was going through the most profound changes for over a century, Ms Mueller said. A new professionalism was being added to traditional virtues. The aim was better value for money for the taxpayer.

Ms Mueller said the new climate of cost-consciousness and efficiency called for additional qualities and skills. 'We now need more managers of budgets and more team leaders; more risk takers and innovators. We are looking perhaps for more robust and more pragmatic managers of resources undertaking a more positive role.' She added that, like the best American companies, the civil service was developing a 'bias for action'. Staff must get things done and not be held back by over-lengthy analysis and consultation which dragged on too long. 'We need to train and develop "doers" at all levels though, of course, they need to be able to think too.'

I hope she is right. But I wonder how many of her colleagues agreed with her, and how quickly that bias for action will become the norm. At any rate I cannot believe that a senior official would have spoken in such terms even two or three years earlier. It appeared to be a recognition that the culture of Whitehall must change, and will certainly put a new pressure on ministers to keep up.

That must be the guide to future action. The introduction of gifted outsiders, the efforts to increase posting in and posting out, are attempts to build bridges between the two distinct cultures which have developed inside and outside Whitehall. It would be better to fill in the dividing trench.

Another trench which could be filled at once by government is one which encourages a departmental culture. Officials do not often get experience outside their own departments, and this is a narrowing and polarising practice. It should be ended, so that officials could have a wider perspective of the many problems departments share in common. An effective personnel department in Whitehall would ensure more cross-posting between departments, as well as building on present experiments in posting between government departments and outside public organisations. As one might expect, the Treasury are ahead of the game: their officials do move out, but usually to colonise a department by appointing a senior Treasury official as permanent secretary.

I believe that one way to bring the efficiency of the best private-sector models into the public service would be to put much of the work now done by the Civil Service onto a contract basis. Where it is possible to find appropriate areas for autonomous management, managers should be engaged on specific terms and for specific but renewable periods. They would have agreed budgets to manage with full commercial freedom, including freedom over recruitment and pay. It follows that private management and the services of private sector companies would often be enlisted. Wherever possible I would go further and seek competitive tenders for whole areas of work to be contracted out. There would thus be every pressure to reduce the cost to the public purse.

If you look at the list of activities open to competitive tender, you will find that Whitehall is off-loading mainly the most tedious and lowest-value-added activities, such as cleaning, catering, driving, laundry services, guarding. Much more could be done, but the non-industrial civil service has thus far successfully resisted change. The transfer of the dockyards to commercial management is the signal for a sea-change in public sector practice as profound in its way as the present privatisation programme.

If many more activities were put out to contract, the central core of the Civil Service could be seen much more as an élite charged with the policy work that cannot be privatised and with the central administration of departments.

This is the heart of the matter. An overcentralised rigidity, a refusal to impose personal accountability, to associate reward with results, frustrates the talented and enables others to hide behind the system. The private sector has much to teach the public here. How do we achieve a more responsive, smaller Civil Service that offers the necessary incentives and satisfaction to continue to attract the talented men and women for whose high reputation the service is rightly renowned? The thrust of my proposals challenges the assumptions that we should have a unified Civil Service. The Civil Service has outgrown the power of official control from the centre.

It is quite wrong that responsibility for the service is shared between the Secretary of the Cabinet and the Chancellor of the Exchequer, two of the hardest-pressed men in Britain. Management of the Civil Service warrants the undivided attention of an official of the highest competence. The posts of Head of the Civil Service and Cabinet Secretary should be separated, as the Treasury and Civil Service Select Committee has recommended. A more flexible salary structure should be introduced in place of pay scales centrally determined and policed by the Treasury.

The Treasury's principal interest is to keep the cost of pay and conditions to the minimum, which is not to be confused with achieving value for money, and to enforce uniformity across departments.

The role of personnel manager should not be submerged under that of finance director. To expect the Secretary of the Cabinet to find time to become an expert in career planning and employee relations is to expect the impossible. There is no area more important for the good government of this country than the managing of so vital a workforce. It does not seem to me to be receiving the degree of attention that would be considered essential in a first-class private sector company.

When the new central organisation for defence came into effect in January, 1985, it was intended to be the beginning of a wider process of change involving increased delegation of, and accountability for, day-to-day management activities from the Ministry down the chain of command. Central determination of major resource questions was to be coupled with decentralisation of more routine spending decisions under accountable managers with their own budgets. A start had been made in giving all managers responsibility for staff and related costs in Staff Responsibility Budgets (SRBs). But we had also pressed ahead with a much more ambitious programme of Executive Responsibility Budgets (ERBs) covering the main executive operations of the Ministry. The system ran parallel with the four per cent annual reduction in manpower which I was still pursuing. This led to long discussions with Clive Whitmore, who was very keen to persuade me to give up the manpower reductions by arbitrary recruitment restrictions, and to use SRBs and ERBs to find economies on a more rational basis.

I understood his argument well enough. In theory he was right: it was not possible to say that we had delegated budgeting responsibility when we retained responsibility for manpower by requiring forced reductions; but in practice I had no doubt at all that, if full responsibility was delegated, the manpower savings would stop.

I acknowledged Clive's logic but I recognised also that the logic took us further. Civil Service pay and much else was centralised, and there was very little scope for anyone at any level to change, let alone terminate, a civil servant's employment on the grounds that his services were not needed. So long as this regime prevailed, the area of budgetary discretion was bound to be narrow in the extreme.

It is unreasonable to expect managers at any level to accept some degree of responsibility for costs in areas under their control, or to be properly motivated, when they are allowed

"I DON'T KNOW WHAT EFFECT HE WILL HAVE UPON THE ENEMY, BUT, BY GOD, HE TERRIFIES ME!"

It was not only CND that, in January 1983, questioned my appointment as Secretary of State for Defence

no say over either manpower or pay. Even that cautious observer, the Comptroller and Auditor-General, addressed this anomaly in his report on the Financial Management Initiative in October 1986, and questioned whether centrally imposed restraints over recruitment and pay would be appropriate for all time. This is hardly provocative language. They are a nonsense.

If permanent secretaries had the full powers of personnel management these central constraints would go. There would instead be a less tidy but more practical constraint: a department which maintained an inflated payroll or paid its staff more than they were worth would soon come to the attention of the National Audit Office and of the Commons Public Accounts Committee. Of course, permanent secretaries would only be appointed from those who had shown on the way up an ability not just to advise but also to manage. They could not be allowed to set their own salaries, which would have to be centrally controlled. In part they would be judged by their ability to preserve differentials in their departments.

They would start with budgets based on the expenditure levels which they inherited.

The concept of line manager budgets is one with which Clive Whitmore and I were experimenting in the Ministry of Defence but, as I have explained, it could never be reached as long as manpower targets ran alongside cash budgets, because the former took away the discretion implied in the latter. If the knot could be untied so that there was a strong correlation between reward and merit, penalty and poor performance, in place of central control, a different atmosphere would pervade Whitehall and a new breed of executive civil servants would be available to implant urgency into our national life.

Heads of departments, once freed from national terms and conditions of service and rigid grading structures, would be able to pay market rates. In all the offices and out-stations where the unglamorous routine work of the Civil Service is done, and where the wastage of overstaffing goes less detected, underworked and thereby overpaid middle-ranking staff would be thinned. The extra layers of management, which no private-sector company could afford but which multiply wherever pay is unrelated to merit, would go. One may well ask how it is that the staff inspectors do not detect this over-manning. Of course, they do – and moan in their beards about it – but they are under no personal pressure to enforce change. Indeed, they do not have the authority to do so: they advise. These are men who set their sights low, and miss. This is hardly their fault. They rely largely for training on the experience they gain on the job. They spell trouble for senior managers and expect little support. Long experience has stamped its message on them. A reinforced National Audit Office (with private sector help) should do this work. At the same time departments would have the freedom to pay market rates for the specialists who are leaving the service; not just for scientists and technologists, but for computer staff and accountants and anyone who cannot be recruited at present. Manpower changes in the Ministry of Defence, which employs more specialists than any other department, show the impact of uncompetitive pay for those with marketable skills. Those who are needed most have been going fastest.

So long as control over personnel policy resides in the Treasury this haemorrhage of high quality staff will continue. The answer, again, is to apply the private sector's proven methods. Bonus payments for those with special skills, or those who put in outstanding effort, should become a higher proportion of the Civil Service pay bill, and should be extended to more junior grades than those covered by the present performance pay experiment. Junior staff should be rewarded for acquiring professional qualifications: whether in accountancy, personnel management, purchasing or business management. The armed services know the value of such rewards in retaining the people they need; the Royal Air Force, for example, would be in severe trouble if flying pay were abolished. But then professionals have always understood the need to reward professionalism.

I do not for a moment believe that the Civil Service can be run on entirely commercial lines. Exceptional and non-commercial talents are needed among the men and women at the top. They must, I am equally sure, have a competence in personnel management and in financial management. They must also be able to set the pressures of the market-place against other less manageable pressures: the demands of Parliament and of public opinion, transient party political constraints, long-term national objectives, and the limitations imposed by European Community directives and wider international obligations. A rare combination of skills and wisdom is required.

Anyone appointed today as minister in charge of a Whitehall department can count on finding there a permanent secretary who will offer sterling service – someone of energy and fluency and high, perhaps brilliant, intelligence. A fortunate minister, and I was one, will occasionally find a paragon who, after years of work under pressure, still possesses originality and a flair for creative thinking. There may even be the willingness to take risks which Ms Mueller specified. That is a quality which not all ministers will appreciate, but then it is up to ministers to impose their own will in their departments. We cannot accept a culture that expects little initiative and demands little personal accountability below ministerial level.

I believe that our aim must be to seek wherever possible

to make the culture of the Civil Service less easily distinguishable from that of private industry and commerce. Whitehall should become a world where promotion rests entirely on merit and not on seniority; where the ablest travel fastest; where the failures are retired. As promotion opportunities decline with contracting numbers, ways must be found of rewarding outstanding service by means other than promotion. This would also help to cut down the almost manic drive to move people from job to job, skill to skill, to groom them for the next level.

If the permanent secretary of the future is to be in full charge of his department there is no reason in theory why his own future and salary should not depend on his performance. One difficulty, as I have indicated, would lie in placing a value, for example, on the quality of policy advice given to ministers. If advice is to be given fearlessly, the adviser's career must not depend on the minister's assessment. The most rigid checks must be put in place which will prevent ministers disposing of strong-minded civil servants, but which will not shelter the incompetent or the tired.

The difficulty must be faced and safeguards found. If the powers or the performance of even top officials fail they should be retired on generous terms, to create channels of promotion for their most capable and energetic juniors. There are methods to balance the interests of career stability with the injection of dynamism and accountability. The military have a system that presumes retirement unless promotion to certain levels is achieved at certain ages.

There is no justification for paying all permanent secretaries the same maximum salary of £62,100 and all deputy secretaries the maximum of £43,500. Size is not the only criterion. The senior official at the Ministry of Defence controls a budget eighteen times that of the Department of Energy and a workforce nearly a thousand times the size of the Northern Ireland Office. There are special responsibilities on the shoulders of the permanent under-secretary at the Northern Ireland Office which would be hard to overstate. But the justice of extra pay for extra burdens is already recognised, rightly, by the higher salaries given to two officials, the Head of the Diplomatic Service and the Permanent Secretary to the Treasury, and the still higher figure paid to the Secretary of the Cabinet. It should not be impossible to carry this principle further. In practice there is a market out there and private sector top salaries are leaving public sector salaries far behind. This will have its consequences.

But I would be the last to underestimate the resistance to change of this kind, from Parliament as much as the public. The annual spectacle of the Government agonising in deepest secrecy about the Top Salaries Review Body seems to have become an essential element of our political life. The sums involved are trivial and dwarfed by the scale of the responsibilities of those concerned. We would all gain from a more balanced assessment of both pay and performance.

The pattern of Civil Service recruitment and training has drawn the fire of many critics. I have nothing to add except that I agree with those who believe that both are too narrow, and that the service could make better use of those with degrees in business administration, for example, as well as of engineers, scientists and accountants. But one must remember that those who have acquired specialist skills are likely to be attracted by opportunities where those skills are at a premium, in research or industry rather than public administration.

If Whitehall departments were semi-autonomous, more imaginative career-planning would be stimulated. The Ministry of Defence is taking small steps, through the creation of the Defence Engineering Service, towards a more active and discriminating role in the recruitment and management of a group which should be managed by its parent department, but this process needs to go much further. The often-criticised favouring of generalists for senior positions at the expense of specialists would be tested in competition between ministries. Once central control of recruitment and promotion stopped, there would be more opportunity for the specialist to reach the heights of the service which few at present attain.

The parallel career paths for generalists and specialists often mean that a task requires the attention of two officials instead of one − of the lay administrator to whom it is entrusted and of the scientist to whom he has to go for advice. This double-banking of generalist and specialist, which struck me as dreadfully wasteful of talent, would also come under pressure.

A newer awareness of these problems and of the opportunities they suggest exists in Whitehall. The people there want to play their part in Britain's recovery; they will accept more responsibility and take more decisions.

But if there are to be fewer of them, carrying more personal accountability in a climate of less certain careers, they will need and deserve pay to match that received by their private sector friends. They will expect Parliament, except in essential areas of national interest, to allow them to do their business with methods more akin to the best private practice, and they will expect political support in resisting the public sector unions who will certainly object. It would be cheap at the price.

In spite of my choice of the word élite, I do not believe that all the best talent in Britain should be in the Civil Service. Industry and wealth creation must not be starved of brain power, and there is a limited supply. I make no apology for anything the Government may have done to encourage the best and brightest towards the wealth-creating sectors of the economy. In the end those sectors pay the bills. Against this necessarily discriminatory background, it is vital for the Civil Service to remain attractive to and make the best use of the abundant talent it already contains. I strongly supported the government's acceptance of the brave but unpopular recommendations of the Top Salaries review mechanism in 1985. It is essential that the paths to senior positions should be open to the brightest, and that the topmost posts, the permanent secretaryships, should be open and attractive to the ablest men and women in the land.

3

Privatisation: From Tentative Steps To Irreversible Achievement

I have spent much of my political life fighting to contain, reduce and refine the State's activities. The State must do less and do it better. Its natural tendency as we have seen is to become larger and slacker, to do more and to do it with less sensitivity and at higher cost. Conservatives have long believed that better government requires less government, and that unless they are vigilant in preventing the State's growth, and in lopping off the new limbs that tend to sprout so freely, then the servant will quickly become first master then tyrant.

So having written about the Conservatives' efforts to improve the performance of both central and local government, I now turn to our experience, and of necessity my own, in first limiting and then reducing the public sector.

A hundred ministers, drawn from a kaleidoscope of occupations and experiences, touching gently the levers of power, can know little of what is being done in their names. Sitting briefly at the top of the pile and hiding behind such words as social ownership, public interest, accountability, they see little enough of the delays and inertia that surround the official who, ten layers of authority below them, acts on behalf of government. This sounds disparaging of officials, but it is not. It is in no way a criticism of the harassed clerk or the overwhelmed and often underpaid official. The system is too big, the tasks too ill-defined, the disciplines too remote, and the fine phrases have to be turned into indifferent compromises. Particularly one must beware that, wherever the torpidity of this system reaches as far as industry and commerce, its effect can be too slow and deaden not just the

public sector, where it invades it, but every outpost of the
wealth-creating private sector which it touches.

So for anyone in office the rule must be: what you must
do in the public sector, do with conviction and to the right
standards, but do it sparingly and question the need first.
Remember the human limitations in managing the large
scale.

I was first plunged into the arguments about nationalisation when I was at Oxford in the early 1950s. The legislation of the first Attlee government had engulfed the Bank
of England; the railways, waterways and civil aviation; coal,
gas and lastly steel. While I was at University, the Conservatives gave a first hint that the tide might be checked when
they denationalised steel in 1953; but it was an isolated act
of defiance and there never seemed to be any doubt that
renationalisation would follow, as it did fourteen years later.
Now, after a generation, the tide has indeed turned. The
Labour Party talks now of social ownership. Nothing so
indicates doubt about a product as when the name and the
wrapping are changed. A report from the National Economic
Development Office in 1976 concluded that nationalisation
has not satisfied customer, employee, union, manager or civil
servant. Today, as the Soviet Union tries to counter the
corruption in its society by legitimising small enterprise
activity, only a small rump of Britain's Left clings to the
outworn theories of nineteenth-century socialism.

My first parliamentary battle was under Peter Walker,
when he led the opposition to Barbara Castle's Transport
Bill in 1967. With Labour secure behind an overall majority
of about 100, there were few opportunities for parliamentary
victories. Steel had been renationalised the year before.
Beyond Peter's vigorous induction into parliamentary
warfare I had little in the end to show for my pains. I was
asked to be responsible under his direction to fight against
that part of the bill which was to nationalise private bus
operators through the creation of the National Bus
Company. But even as we fired a few sighting shots our
supposed allies in the bus industry sold out, accepting the
offered compensation.

As I stood and watched the fleets of private buses drive
voluntarily into Labour's garage I decided that it was wise

in politics not to be hasty in judging the motives or counting on the resolve of one's apparent allies.

Nobody could criticise that Opposition for lack of resolution. Peter Walker's tenacity was remarkable and instructive and I drew on what he taught me when, the following year, I myself had to lead the opposition to the Docks Nationalisation Bill. Parliamentarians know that the best and usually the only weapon in the hands of an Opposition facing a Government with a big majority is the power to delay legislation. We made the fullest use of the standing orders and rules of procedure to see that this proposal for nationalisation was thoroughly scrutinised. Our efforts were rewarded: when Labour decided to have a general election in June 1970 they had to abandon their bill, and the docks remained in mixed ownership. This Government has turned the majority of ports over to private ownership. The Transport Act 1981 provided for the sale of 49 per cent of the equity in the British Transport Docks Board, which owns nineteen of Britain's most profitable ports. 51 per cent of the shares in the new company, Associated British Ports Holdings plc, were sold in February 1983 with proceeds for the taxpayer of almost £22m.

After four years in Government I was back in 1974 in my now practised role, leading the parliamentary opposition to a nationalisation bill, this time a particularly doctrinaire and dangerous one, the Industry Bill. Labour's appetite for taking over industry was sharper than ever after four years of forced abstinence.

Anthony Wedgwood Benn, in charge of the Department of Industry, promoted the bill which he had spent his years in Opposition preparing from his power base within Labour's National Executive Committee. This became the Industry Act 1975, which included powers for the Government to acquire more than half the share capital of companies and to compel disclosure of commercial plans to trade union representatives. We did not know that Harold Wilson intended to remove Benn the next year and replace him with the much less ideological Eric Varley, who probably never intended to make use of the Act's wilder powers. Meanwhile, as we fought the bill in committee for week after week, our determination was stiffened by the rallying cry of my principal opponent.

One of the more potent political declarations of our time was the promise in Labour's manifesto for the General Election of February 1974 to 'bring about a fundamental and irreversible shift in the balance of power and wealth in favour of working people and their families.' Benn was credited with its authorship. It is unwise for a politician to say that he is about to do something which his opponents will not be able to undo: it offends the British voter's sense of fair play. The word 'irreversible' transformed a grandiloquent but legitimate claim into a threat which mobilised Tories of my generation. Both the phrase and its author, whenever they reappeared, confirmed our belief that our party was the only trustworthy guardian of the interests of 'working people', however they might be defined, and far more likely than Labour to spread wealth among poorer families.

Benn had a genius for contriving to be misunderstood. He was a master of the loaded utterance — the apparently plain words which invited his political foes and colleagues alike to read into them a meaning which he could disown before a sceptical audience but acknowledge to a partisan one. To the first he would explain in those days that he meant no more than that Labour would win the argument. For a time there were even some Conservatives who thought that this might be true. The country had accepted a large measure of Socialism; the terms of political trade appeared to have turned against the Tory belief in the individual spirit.

This mood of defeatism did not last long, and the hint of menace in Benn's phrase, which offended both Harold Wilson and James Callaghan with their shrewder appreciation of what ordinary people believed to be reasonable, helped to sustain the spirit of the defeated Tory Party.

During the Parliament of 1974 to 1979 we were encouraged to lay plans not just to stop the advance of nationalisation but to thrust it back and to begin in earnest the creation of a capital-owning democracy.

As well as the Industry Bill it fell to me in 1975 to lead the opposition to the Aircraft and Shipbuilding Industries Bill. My prolonged exposure to the attitudes of Labour MPs, and my obligation to probe the reasoning behind their nationalisation measures, rekindled my faith in the capitalist system as effectively as a journey in Eastern Europe rekindles faith in a free society. On Labour's Left, reason gives way to dogma. It is depressing but salutary to discover that the thoughts and actions of adult men and women can still be limited by clause IV of the party constitution, by the formula printed in their little yellow pocket books which requires them to pursue, though the sky fall, against evidence or experience, 'the common ownership of the means of production, distribution and exchange'.

The alliance which cost the country dear in the years after the war was between such intellectuals without intelligence, who abound on the Left of the Labour Party, and the thoroughly practical union leaders in State-controlled industries. The unions would say openly exactly what they wanted from nationalisation: the minimum change and the maximum investment, with the taxpayer's endless cheque book to underwrite them and their members' pay settlements, to cocoon the industry from any exposure to the market or to the wishes of the customer. Once the nationalisation measures were enacted, the unions were free to press their demands for more jobs and more investment, injected in a way that paid little regard to the expected level of demand or to the need for a return, with the inevitable result that huge losses were written off. Every write-off was a lost opportunity for profitable investment elsewhere.

Three Conservative MPs, Tim Eggar, Kenneth Carlisle and Michael Grylls, who have played a valuable role in stimulating the party's interest in small business, calculated at the end of 1983 that the capital written off in the nationalised industries to that date totalled £40 billion. It equals the entire cost of running the health and social security services for one year. We should not forget the enormity of this: the nation's scarce assets, invested for profit, produced only losses. The nationalised industries have been a huge sponge soaking up taxpayers' resources because, once moved into the public sector, they have been unrestricted by the necessary commercial disciplines.

The debilitating effect of this remoteness from the market place was aggravated when Labour was in power by naked political jobbery. In their raids on the taxpayers' savings,

nationalised industries were cheered on by Labour politicians, who often calculated that their electoral fortunes
depended on satisfying short-sighted union demands.

A strikingly cynical episode of this kind was the Beswick
review of the steel industry. Lord Beswick, who was Minister
of State under Benn, failed to look objectively at the arguments for modernising the British Steel Corporation to meet
its growing international competition. Instead a pretext was
found for delaying some of the plant closures which its
management knew to be necessary but which the unions
were resisting. Labour seats were at risk.

BSC's investment had fallen behind that of its rivals. Its
productivity was lower than that of its main competitors in
the European Economic Community and far below that of
the United States and Japan. The Corporation's plan,
endorsed by the Conservative Government in 1973, was to
invest £3b over ten years, and to end steelmaking at six older
plants.

Labour temporised. After two years' delay, they asked
Parliament to increase BSC's borrowing limit by only £2b,
and gratefully accepted Lord Beswick's suggestion that three
of the six plants recommended for closure should be retained.
By then American steelmakers, obliged to earn their living,
had already shed surplus labour and were building up their
strength.

When recession struck, BSC moved from after-tax profits
in 1974/5 of £73m to losses in 1975/6 of £255m. Labour's
political weakness had ensured that BSC's industrial weakness would continue until the Conservatives returned and
Keith Joseph, with great courage, saw through the required
changes to put it back on the road to profitability and
competitiveness.

If Labour had supported the necessary rationalisation
earlier, in more prosperous times, the industry would have
recovered its competitiveness more quickly, and the redun-
dant steelworkers would have found it easier to get other
work. The Government would have moved in sooner to help
small industry start-ups in the stricken steel towns, where
more diversified local economies would by now have become
established.

The lesson is that governments can too easily abuse their

responsibilities if they run industry; and that the consequence of Labour governments using their powers over State industries is to weaken them and, in the end, to hurt those who work in them and those communities which depend on them. They then send the taxpayer the huge bills for the damage they do. Labour's performance over steel mocks the claims of earlier generations of Labour politicians who believed, like Herbert Morrison, that nationalised industries would naturally wish to put the public interest first and would be allowed to do so, that they would be more efficiently run, and that labour disputes would be fewer. British Steel began to recover productivity and its labour relations to improve only after the Conservative Government obliged the industry to understand that it must compete in the world market.

In the last few years the best BSC plants have begun to close the productivity gap with continental plants, but we still have some way to go. In 1981, the production time per ton of crude steel was about 11 hours in Britain while it varied between 6 and 8 hours in France, Germany and Italy. By 1984 production time in Britain was down to 7.3 hours, but the other countries had not stood still: in Germany and Italy it had fallen below 6 hours, and France was down to 7 hours.

The general election of 1979 marked the end of the country's readiness to believe in Labour's ability either to distribute wealth or to create it. Since then the Conservative Party has shown Labour and everyone else how wealth can best be spread and how ordinary people, from being nominal owners of State businesses, can become instead the true and beneficial owners. We have proved that for the public sector to possess is for the citizen and worker to be denied.

The party's mid-term statement of aims, *The Right Approach*, published in 1976 when Labour was in full cry, was concerned with the efficient management of State industries. Its reference to ownership could not have been more tentative: 'In some cases it may be appropriate to sell back to private enterprise assets or activities where willing buyers can be found.'

By 1977 *The Right Approach to the Economy* was describing the Conservatives' long-term aim as being 'to widen the basis of ownership in our community' as well as to reduce the preponderance of State ownership. This was the first suggestion that denationalisation, as well as promoting efficiency, might also serve the cause of popular capitalism. But the 1979 manifesto did not echo this theme. In retrospect it looks extraordinarily unambitious. We promised to sell off, as circumstances allowed, the Government's temporary shareholdings in BP and other companies which were vested in the National Enterprise Board, and to interfere less with the running of those industries which remained nationalised. We also offered to sell back to private ownership the aircraft and shipbuilding businesses which had been taken two years before. Beyond that, the National Freight Corporation was the only State company in which we said we would offer shares to the public.

By 1983 there was no longer any doubt among Conservative politicians and our supporters that the best way to make the management of nationalised industries more effective was to require them to satisfy their customers. Our manifesto that year included a roll-call of shareholdings already sold – often to their employees – in Cable and Wireless, Associated British Ports, British Aerospace, Britoil, British Rail Hotels, Amersham International and the National Freight Corporation. There was a new confidence in the promise to go further, with Rolls-Royce, British Airways, British Shipbuilders, British Leyland and British Gas.

These changes of tone between 1976 and 1983 in the language coming out of Conservative Central Office record an historic change in the political development of the British people. We began slowly, and have moved further forward with growing public support only as we proved the effectiveness of our methods. The million new owners of their former council homes, the 3 million new share owners, the 400,000 who now hold shares in the former State businesses which employ them, are enjoying the fruits of a profound and wholly benign revolution in which there are no losers.

Only Socialism has been hurt. It is indeed a fundamental shift of wealth, and it has only just begun. The strength of this Conservative revolution is that, unlike Labour's compulsion towards nationalisation, it is not driven by dogma. It is hard to believe that Socialism in Britain will ever again be as assertive as it was between 1945 and 1979 – not, at least, if it hopes to earn a hearing from the electors. Equally I do not believe that the Tory Party will ever again be timid in proclaiming its belief in popular capitalism.

We have some way yet to go, all the same. In France and the United States a surge in share ownership has taken place as a result of generous tax incentive schemes not connected with any privatisation programme. Nigel Lawson's Personal Equity Plan does not show the necessary imagination or breadth. The main benefit of PEP is for investors whose capital gain in any year exceeds £6,300. The thrust is in the wrong place, because such people are already investors, The objective is to encourage wider share ownership and a deeper involvement of employees in their companies. What is needed here is the scale of generosity that lies behind the Employee Stock Ownership Plans (ESOPS) in America or the *loi Monory* in France.

ESOPS flowered in the 1970s when Congress was persuaded to provide for Trusts acting on behalf of employees to purchase shares in a company with loans raised from commercial banks. The loans are guaranteed by the company itself. As dividends flow into the Trust, the loans are repaid and the equity thus created is passed directly to the employees. Incentives to encourage the banks to provide the loans, and companies to set up the ESOPS, are provided through the tax system. In the United States the National Center for Employment Ownership claims that 8,000 companies now offer shares to their workforce, and that between 10 and 11m people – 8 per cent of the workforce – own shares.

In France, wider share ownership has been stimulated by incentives first devised by René Monory, Finance Minister in President Giscard d'Estaing's administration, then extended by Jacques Delors under President Mitterrand. Similar schemes exist in Belgium, Norway and Sweden. The principle is simple; in France a taxpayer can set 20 per cent of the cost of new shares against tax, subject to an annual limit of F10,000 per person or F20,000 per couple.

In advancing our cause of privatisation and choice against Socialism and direction we have won two political arguments at the same time, the practical and the moral. The moral challenge of those who advocate a Socialist society used to be that strong central power enables fair-minded rulers to dispense justice from the centre which the mass of people if left to themselves would never achieve. The belief is false. The State has no morality, and the Socialist system like the capitalist system is morally neutral.

The health of society depends on the widest exercise of choice by each man and woman, and not on a central authority which imposes decisions upon them. The prisoner in chains needs few moral constraints because he has no choice. The enlargement of human happiness depends on the individual's freedom to pursue it. Of course, every society must protect itself by setting limits to prevent licence; but the human instinct and need is to seek opportunities: the more a society encourages and allows individual freedom, and the more reluctant its rulers are to apply constraints, the more it will prosper. The generation of wealth characteristic of free societies provides government with the resources to discharge its responsibilities for those who cannot maintain themselves. The obvious caveat remains: our policy depends on public support; the new shareholders are also the customers and, in the conversion of state monopolies into private monopolies, the Government must be convincing in its use of its new arm's length regulatory powers if it is to convince people that privatisation does indeed promote the public good.

By the time of the 1979 general election I had, I believe, spent more hours on the Opposition front bench trying to slow or stop specific nationalisation proposals than any MP then serving. I was the more eager to take the offensive when we received our mandate from the country. The Department of the Environment had little responsibility for the problems of the State-owned industries, but there were plenty of other ways in which we could fulfil our campaign promises to push back the frontiers of the State, which we had correctly accused Labour of advancing while diminishing the role of the individual.

The more one considered where the energies and disciplines of the private sector might be applied to improve the public sector's performance and to spread wealth, the more possibilities appeared.

The hunt was on to substitute private for public management; for private funding to do urgent work for which public funding could not be found; for services in government departments and in local government which would be improved by exposure to competition from the private sector; for tasks which the public-sector workforce was in no position to complete unless private sector manpower was called in to help.

Privatisation, an ugly but useful word, showed itself capable of being stretched to cover large tracts of territory which private citizens and private interests had yielded to the State.

At the DOE, like our colleagues elsewhere, we set precedent after precedent. They are worth recording here to show their variety and as pointers to further advances. One area where we called in the private sector to shift a backlog of work was the listing of heritage buildings. It was an important task and was scheduled to take many years. The difficulties were aggravated by the constraints placed on recruitment. We needed a temporary increase in numbers to bring the work up to date, but there was the risk that if we had taken on more civil servants, someone would have found 'essential' work to justify retaining them once the listing was done.

We placed contracts with private firms with experience of heritage buildings. The decision caused some trouble with the Civil Service unions, but we went ahead. A monopoly was broken and the work prospered.

The breach of the monopoly was worthwhile in itself. Where the public sector procures a service from the private, it uses public money to establish an expertise. That private sector expertise will in the end have to sustain itself commercially. It will then offer competitive prices against which the public sector customer can check his costs. At the same time the capitalist company will have been enriched by its public sector contract and it will exploit this new experience as no public sector machinery is designed or allowed to do.

We used the same approach with the English House Conditions Survey, which works to a five-year cycle. The survey of about 9,000 dwellings was previously done by environmental health officers seconded by local authorities.

The heritage man

The Department of the Environment is the largest public – or private – patron in Britain

We brought in about 60 private surveyors to share the work with an equal number of council officials. On a larger scale the Audit Commission, which appoints auditors for about 8,000 local government bodies in England and Wales, now places about 30 per cent of the work with private accountancy firms. These firms are building up a body of experience to compete with and to complement the District Audit Service, as I had hoped when we drew up our design for the Commission.

I had two contrasting, surprising and in different ways stimulating experiences in my determination, as Secretary of State for the Environment, to fill two prominent holes in the ground in central London. The Queen Elizabeth Conference Centre opened in 1986 on the Broad Sanctuary site opposite Westminster Abbey. This prominent site had been cleared by Hitler's bombs about forty years earlier. It was more than a waste: it advertised to everyone who visited London an inability to make decisions.

The Treasury argued that the £40m needed to build the centre could not be found. It was suggested that the City might provide the capital cost. That proved simple enough but the backers, of course, wanted a commercial rate. The Treasury, in consternation, soon changed its tune and found room in the capital programme after all. The private sector withdrew in bewilderment.

The other equally prominent hole in the ground was in Trafalgar Square beside the National Gallery which, as is well known, wanted more space but could not afford to build. John Stanley, who was Minister of Housing and Construction, had the excellent idea of inviting private developers to submit designs for a composite building. They would include extra gallery space, which would cost the National Gallery nothing, and office space from which they would recoup their costs and make a profit. To stimulate the best design there would be an architectural competition.

It all ended, after a long saga, with the chosen building finding disfavour in high places. For the participants it proved a costly failure; but the potential for partnership between public and private interests for the public good was demonstrated. Now conspicuous private patronage has achieved what we set out to do. There will soon be one less vacant site.

A small but interesting act of privatisation arose when we transferred the Hydraulics Research Station, near Wallingford in my constituency, directly and finally from the public to the private sector. It was government-owned and staffed by civil servants attached to my department, and it did work for government and for private customers. It looked well able, if set free, to expand its non-government work, exploit its special skills and still meet the government's needs, possibly at increasingly competitive rates, as its commercial strength grew. We privatised it in 1982, and five years later our judgement is vindicated. Turnover has increased by 30 per cent and it now makes a modest profit – about 4 per cent at present. Its order books remain full and its services are in increasing demand from industry both in Britain and overseas. The next step would be to privatise its sister organisation, the Institute of Hydrology, which could also become a successful profit centre.

I have made plain in an earlier chapter my belief that private sector management is always likely to be more efficient than public sector management, not because the people are different but because of the twin stimuli of the profit-and-loss account and the workings of competition. One part of the Department of the Environment which I believe private sector management would transform is the Property Services Agency, the huge building and maintenance business responsible for the Government's estate.

The Agency has a turnover of nearly £3b and a workforce of 25,000, of whom 6,500 are administrative and clerical. It was formed in the early 1970s by an amalgamation, which was rational at the time, of the many separate works agencies of central government departments. We squeezed the PSA's manpower as hard as the rest of the department. It stood at 39,000 in 1979, so it has fallen by 35 per cent since then. Much of this reduction reflects work transferred to the private sector. A Treasury scrutiny in September 1986 found that in one area – new construction design – the recent introduction of competitive tendering had yielded savings in fees of between 10 and 26 per cent. I understand that the PSA already put out 100 per cent of their new work to private contractors. The PSA has very little to do with the Department of the Environment. The culture of a large building and estates department does not sit easily alongside the policy-forming instincts of the high-flying civil servant.

It could be divided into smaller units. Since we returned responsibility for the Foreign and Commonwealth Office estate to that department in 1982, my successors at the

Department of the Environment have not had to listen to the ceaseless complaints from ambassadors and their wives around the world: instead diplomatic answers have to be framed by diplomats.

The Defence estate comprises over half of the PSA's remaining responsibilities. One day it is likely to be returned to the Ministry of Defence which, using private sector project management and private contractors, will achieve very much better value for money for the Armed Services. A sizeable but much more manageable estate would then remain, which could be divided into smaller units along logical lines, grouping functions or departments into managerial units. I have mentioned the need to structure such groupings in a way that preserves accountability and competition.

I would myself now go in this direction and, as a matter of priority, adopt the commercial management techniques now being applied in the Royal Dockyards for the administration and maintenance of the Defence estate. I would also insist that specific contracts for capital and maintenance work were put to competition. The MOD would restrict itself to the smallest practical management unit.

The concept of large-scale commercial management had not been drawn to our attention until Peter Levene came to work in the Ministry of Defence. My eyes were opened by the burden on the defence budget of the two Royal Dockyards at Devonport and Rosyth, where there were clearly severe management problems. They are smaller than the PSA but they are large industries which together employ 19,000 people. Their joint annual turnover is about £400m. The strategic importance of the yards persuaded us that a straightforward sale to the private sector seemed on balance inappropriate. The reader will note the hesitancy, and I acknowledge it. It was a fine judgement whether to stop at this stage or to move to full privatisation. The urgent need was for effective accountable management and we decided the best way to achieve it quickly was to keep the land and assets in public ownership, and invite tenders for commercial management.

Several groups were formed to compete for contracts to take over the two separate companies and run them for seven years. The successful bidders are due to take over early in

1987. The contractors competed to undertake a significant proportion of the Royal Navy's business in their initial bid, with the opportunity to win more from the market place against the bids of outside yards. The hope is that commercial discipline will so improve productivity that the companies will be able to compete for extra non-naval business with other ship repairers. I have no doubt that the new regimes will prove themselves in both Devonport and Rosyth, that the Royal Navy, without whose enthusiastic support the proposals could not have been developed, will be better served and that the new competitive environment will stimulate the local economies.

Enthusiasm, I know, can sound like doctrinal obsession, so let me restate what I regard as overwhelming reasons why many organisations should be moved from the public to the private sector.

The first is that, in the public sector, there are few of the commercial challenges and comparisons which show whether the cost of a service, which may be only a routine activity such as building or consultancy, is properly competitive with what the private sector can offer. You cannot know that the price is not right unless there is competition and an arm's length relationship between customer and supplier. This the Government cannot have with its own limb, the PSA; nor until now could the Royal Navy with the Royal Dockyards, or the Army with Royal Ordnance. The clearest example of the weakness is again in the Dockyards. There was no budget of cost, only a record of what had been spent. Indeed, an awkward hurdle in the way of bringing in commercial management was the cost of introducing accounting systems. These were essential to enable proper comparison with the private yards, or pre-contract estimating, to be undertaken.

The second point is that, within such organisations as the PSA and the dockyards, there are skills which are directed solely to the limited objective of serving the Government's purpose, in these cases maintaining either warships or estates and offices. The scale of the job is defined within the limits of one programme and one purse. There is none of that thrusting for wider opportunities which is the natural activity and essential strength of the commercial world.

Plymouth's economy has been dominated by the approach

Advertisement in *Engineering* on 25 May 1888 by the War Office for a rangefinder.

When we extended competition in the procurement programme of the MOD, General, later Field Marshal, Sir John Stanier, Chief of the General Staff, presented me with this effective reminder that initiative is rarely without precedent

to business of the dockyards, whose role hitherto has been to supply a service at cost, without competition, to a fixed monopoly customer. There has been no incentive for the dockyard to expand its facilities, to serve wider markets, to seek jobs elsewhere or to create new investment partnerships with the private sector. The dockyard and its management have never lived that sort of life nor thought such thoughts.

For a measure of the inefficiency that has characterised at least this area of public sector activity, there is no need to look further than the figures for absenteeism. On average each employee in the dockyards was taking four and a half weeks paid, unauthorised absence a year. That reflects upon the management. The cost of the extra overhead falls on the taxpayer. The attitude to work which absenteeism on this scale reveals and engenders dramatically affects the quality of service that the Royal Navy can expect. It must also have set a style and approach which percolated into the wider local economy.

Private sector stimulus would long since have cured this. After the initial trauma of achieving acceptable levels of efficiency the private sector will seek to expand its business because that is its nature. The nature of the unregenerate public sector business is not to exert itself or change but to remain as it is, inefficient, inert and unenterprising. That is a burden on local society and the national economy which we can no longer tolerate.

The private sector cure has other benign side-effects. The successful private contractor itself becomes a local purchaser of goods and services, to the benefit of the local economy. In the dockyards and Royal Ordnance almost every service is supplied 'in house'. No commercial managers would imitate this because they would know that it was inefficient not to buy in the market the skills in which they themselves were inexpert. An expanding contractor will spread more widely the stimulus of public purchasing, and the small firms created or developed will themselves play their part in a virtuous circle of expansion.

The public organisation or employee who finishes an allotted task early does nothing more because there is nothing to be done. The private sector is driven to find more work. The stimulus goes wider because the private sector firm which develops special skills will seek to export them. I look forward to reading about the first repair contract for an overseas shipowner won for Devonport or Rosyth by the sales director who can boast: 'We do refits for frigates of the Royal Navy. You can imagine that we must be pretty good.'

There are many missed opportunities in unexploited specialist skills developed with public money which at present are locked into the public sector. Our water industries and airports authorities are just two examples that, once transferred to the market economy, could have every incentive to get out into the world and sell their experience and the nation's products.

Some of the least glamorous but most valuable savings have been found in the supply of basic services, either by competitive tendering or by contracting out, in both central and local government. At national level the Government's consistent and sensible policy has been to make new arrangements wherever sound management and good value for money require them. The Home Office, for example, has saved £1.6m a year and 760 posts by contracting out catering and domestic services at its residential training establishments.

At local level, a survey by economists at the London Business School and the Institute for Fiscal Studies in November 1986 found that competitive tendering for refuse collection in England and Wales had yielded savings of 22 per cent on average; and that about £80m could be saved without loss of quality of service if all 403 authorities instead of only 38 had followed this course. Nicholas Ridley and his colleagues at the Department of the Environment are more than justified in going to the rescue of ratepayers with their Bill to make competition for this and other services compulsory.

Ownership is theft, wrote Proudhon, and of course being a Socialist he meant private ownership. I am more charitable in my attitudes but, if I adapt the thought, would assert that public ownership is often theft; and that whatever is either taken or withheld by the State from the private citizen is indeed theft unless the State can demonstrate that it will use it properly in the public service and with the strictest economy and prudence.

So first, let the State be careful in its stewardship. Wherever

GOOD NEWS FOR COUNCIL TENANTS, NEW TOWN TENANTS AND SCOTTISH SPECIAL HOUSING ASSOCIATION TENANTS.

BUY YOUR OWN HOME AT BETWEEN 33% AND 50% OFF.

The Conservatives plan to give millions of people the right to buy a home of their own on generous terms.

Our new proposals will mean that if you've been a tenant with your present authority for three years you'll have the right to buy your home at one-third off the valued price. And if you've been a tenant for longer you'll get a bigger discount – rising to half price if you've been a tenant for 20 years.

Q. When will I be able to buy my home?
A. Within the 1st year of the New Parliament the right to buy will be created for tenants who've been with their housing authority for over three years.

Published by Conservative Central Office 32 Smith Square London SW1P 3HH
Printed by Quicksilver Offset 21 Curtain Road London EC2A 3DP

GE 24

central or local government or nationalised industry or any public body stretches out its hand to take or spend money, its agents must be watched and questioned more closely than has as yet become habitual.

And what of property withheld, for which the State has no overriding need? The Tenants' Charter gave a new deal to council and New Town tenants that enabled them to buy their homes on favourable terms and entitled them to proper standards and effective involvement where they remained tenants. I shall come back to this latter aspect later. Conservatives first saw what Labour politicians for so long failed to see – or if they saw rejected as an unacceptable affront to their municipal power-base – the justice of allowing tenants of council homes to buy them. Here indeed we see an irreversible shift of wealth in favour of working people and away from the State.

It fell to me in April 1979 to open the election campaign with a speech at Watlington in my constituency which committed the Conservatives to give council tenants the right to buy. Hugh Rossi and his team had prepared the exciting plans that I put to the Shadow Cabinet, where they were eagerly accepted. The transformation of many council estates where occupants have become owners is heartening evidence of a new pride in possession. The new doors, the painted windows, the extensions, the improved gardens are proof of how swiftly people will change, if given the chance, from dependence on the council to reliance on their own skills and pride. The change has revealed a willingness in people, frustrated before, to assume responsibility for a central part of their lives, to save for their futures and to create an inheritance to pass on one day to their children.

Our ambition was a million sales, and seven years later, on 4 September 1986, a family at Forres became the millionth purchaser. There are perhaps 2.5m people who today live in their own homes because the Conservatives gave them the right to buy.

Revenue from sales has yielded local authorities about £12.7b.

The implacable resistance of the Labour Party to our two liberalising measures (the Housing Act 1980 and the Tenants Rights (Scotland) Act 1980) and their repeated threats throughout the last Parliament to repeal them, showed extraordinary political blindness. Their later change of stance in no way reflects a change of heart. It is simply that Labour found at the 1983 election that they could not get a hearing on the council estates for their contention that Conservative policies were wrong.

In winning the argument the Tories have not only secured the spread of individual ownership: we have changed attitudes towards the management of council estates, and we have expanded the opportunities for partnership in public and private sector housing. This social revolution on the estates has opened up opportunities on a scale hardly perceived when we began.

The implementation of the right to buy will remain one of the most fascinating and worthwhile political experiences of my life. In John Stanley, a minister of exemplary energy and devotion, the Conservative Party found someone willing to master the detail of the legislation. It was well that he did. Our problem was that hundreds of local authorities, many controlled by Labour, were determined to resist the right to buy. We knew that it would not take the form of blanket resistance by every authority, but that the more determined would use infinite ingenuity and skill to try and find loopholes in the law. If one hole was found, a score of resisters would follow the leader through it.

With Michael Havers' help and encouragement we went to immense lengths to ensure that the legislation was watertight. Our officials had to advise the parliamentary draftsmen, but we wanted to leave nothing to chance. We therefore indulged in another piece of privatisation: we briefed a barrister from outside government to assume that he had been retained by a dedicated Marxist council, committed at any lawful price to frustrate the right to buy. It was a valuable exercise. Loopholes were found and closed.

As the Housing Bill went through Parliament legitimate anxieties were expressed by my Conservative colleagues, who understandably wanted exceptions made, for example, for special housing for old people. We did not dare allow these. We took the view, and it was right, that any exception would be open to exploitation as Labour authorities reclassified, converted, or adapted their homes so that ever-larger proportions of council estates fell into the exempt categories.

Once legislation reached the statute book, inertia overwhelmed the Labour authorities, as we had expected, while the Tory councils responded magnificently and proved how great was the latent demand for ownership. Week by week John Stanley patiently logged the complaints and the devices which were being used to frustrate us, and built up a formidable picture. We came under growing pressure from infuriated tenants and angry Tory councillors and MPs to use our

The artwork for the leaflet with which the Government announced one of the most profound social changes in the history of the Tory Party

powers to override obstinate councils; but we had to bide our time, to issue warnings to local authorities, and to build a cast-iron case. We would have to be able to prove that the law was being deliberately frustrated, not merely being observed at a speed inconvenient to ministers, so that when we eventually went to court there would be no risk worth the name that we would lose. There were tense days as we took the flak before deciding we could act. We acted against Norwich. We won, and resistance to the right to buy collapsed.

The Conservatives have not stood still after the triumphant success of the right to buy. We are now on the verge of another significant shift in moving the ownership of housing out of the public and into the private sector.

My own dedication to the taming of the State has both philosophical and practical motives. A Tory philosophy must build upon the individual. I believe that most people wish and need to exercise their own discretion and choice wherever they can. To go with that grain of human instinct, and to associate responsibility for decisions with the taking of decisions, I will always want to increase the opportunities for the individual to act freely. The more the opportunities the greater the satisfaction which personal accountability brings but which is denied when decisions become second-hand, remote and dissociated from their consequences. A society of free people is a richer society, better able to sustain those who have not the strength to survive unaided.

I recognise the duty of government to regulate and preside but not to dominate. Let people push down their own roots, establishing their own stability and security, and society will be the stronger. If the many own, decide, risk and share, then power will be diffused and the State less overbearing. The exercise of free will leads to that sophistication of judgement and maturity of experience with which individuals learn to fulfil themselves most completely, and in so doing enrich themselves and often society as well. The Left presumes the individual guilty until proved innocent.

My experience has confirmed my belief because I have helped to run the State machine, and I know that to sit at a Minister's desk is to see clearly the emptiness of the Socialist's vision of an all-wise State.

4

Industry: Who's For *Laissez Faire*?

There is nothing quite like starting your own business: the sense of independence, exhilaration and confidence that prompts you to the first steps, and the loneliness with which you return again and again to the bank manager. He knows what you are going to say. He has heard it all before. You do your best with arguments that have been rehearsed by others a dozen times that day and often rejected. He makes a judgement about you. Sometimes you are lucky.

Friday is crisis day, when the wages must be paid. The other six days are devoted to selling the product and collecting the cash. The entrepreneur lives on his wits, his nerves and ultimately his determination to see it through. It matters as few experiences can ever matter. There are many ways up but only one way down.

The rules are elementary. The bills can either be paid, or not. The creditors can either be kept at bay, or not. The product either works, or it does not. The scale of the thing seems huge because the stakes and the price of failure are very high.

It is not surprising that attitudes forged in such a climate engender self-reliance and a certain intolerance of advice. You come to believe that if you can survive in this jungle, you must have a destiny. Success creates intolerance of the slower-moving, orderly minds of bureaucrats or of anyone who lives in the non-wealth-creating parts of the economy. You pay the taxes; they spend them. You take the risks; they make it harder for you.

I remain deeply committed to the virtues of a private enterprise system. I have competed in the business world and I know the disciplines it imposes. There is no substitute.

Nothing drives an organisation to greater efficiency than fear of a lost order. The market place sorts out men from boys and entrenches power in the hands of the consumer, to whom the producer becomes servant. You work for your crust, or there is no crust.

In the early days of setting up a small business my views were simple and strong. I was convinced for a time that if only the Government would leave us alone, cut the red tape, forget the form-filling, get off our back, then nothing could stop us. I once went so far as to make a speech suggesting that the most constructive thing the Government could do for business would be to close down the Department of Trade and Industry.

That is how it can look from below, in the world of small industry and small commerce. From there one does not see the appalling complexities of the world in which many practitioners of larger capitalist enterprises have to struggle; nor the extent to which the fates of big companies and their smaller suppliers lie in the hands of government. One has no idea of the closeness of the partnerships between the large overseas companies and their governments. The leaders of British business have to compete with these partnerships for orders essential to the national economy.

In the Ministry of Transport I first encountered the magnitude of government spending. It is not given to many men or women to spend money on the scale that I have spent it. There are few programmes in this country financed within the private sector that approach in scale the road programme or the Concorde programme, and none approaches the annual expenditure by the Ministry of Defence of more than £9,000m on goods and services.

The remnants of my early entrepreneurial innocence vanished in 1970 on the day I took up my first government post. I began to perceive the decisive effect which the Government's market power could have on the welfare of key British companies. By the time I had completed two years as Minister for Aerospace and Shipping in the Department of Trade and Industry, my baptism had been one of total immersion. When I came to my last government post as Secretary of State for Defence I presided over a Department that is by far the biggest customer that British industry possesses, and the notion that governments did not require an industrial policy had become as untenable as the flat earth theory.

The Defence Department's responsibility towards its domestic suppliers, as well as to the taxpayer, was plain enough; but I was also working with defence ministers of allied countries, several like me the largest customers of their domestic industries, and I could see how great was our influence on the fortunes of our companies. Industrial strategic policies were weighed alongside defence strategic priorities.

Each of us sees the world from the background of personal experience, and I have been fortunate in seeing the world from both sides of the fence. What I now say and believe does not mean that I have forgotten my early experience of the entrepreneurial zest which drives the capitalist system, but it is not the whole picture.

When the Conservatives came to power in 1979 it was a critical time for the British economy. From Labour's policies at home, we inherited rising inflation and unemployment; from the world situation we inherited deepening recession. We faced, in a word, slumpflation.

Seven years later the Government has achieved an impressive double victory. Inflation has been cut to one-tenth of its peak rate; and in the longest post-war recovery period, output has been rising without interruption since the end of 1981. We have not had for a generation such low inflation combined with such fast growth as we saw in 1986. If Britain's output grows over the next four years at it has over the last five, real GDP wil have risen by 25 per cent in the 1980s – almost half as fast again as the 18 per cent growth of the 1970s and with inflation going down instead of up. This would be a famous achievement by any reckoning. But this victory over slumpflation has been won the hard way. No other government in the industrial world showed such resolve to stick to economic and fiscal rectitude in the teeth of the 1980–1 recession. The British example has now been copied elsewhere, ironically with the exception of Mr Reagan's America, which is now in all kinds of trouble.

The Government's resolve was tested time and again. Old battles were rightly refought, and this time won. It was not pleasant, as the miners' strike showed. Arthur Scargill divided the nation and broke the power base of his union. But, as a result, most of the private sector and much of the public sector have now had to come to terms with the disciplines of the world market place.

Nobody would pretend that the success so far achieved is absolute. Inflation is at bay, not destroyed. For an economy whose growth now outstrips that of many of its neighbours, interest rates are too high. Real rates have been at record levels for a considerable time. High rates do help to control and allocate credit at home, but today's levels also reflect a lack of confidence – in the financial world and abroad – in the sustainability of Britain's achievements. This nervousness has its causes: British pay settlements are still disturbingly high; inflation threatens to increase again; growth is at risk as the excesses in the American economy are brought under control. There is concern about the effects on the economy as Britain's reserves from North Sea oil and gas sales decline. Our manufacturing industry is not in a healthy state.

In politics you never reach the end of the road. As one problem is solved another takes its place. What is gained by hard grind one year can be lost through easy neglect in the next. Our competitors do not stand still while we struggle forward. The battle to catch up or stay ahead is unending. Britain's struggle, valiantly as it has been fought, has only kept us in the position to fight valiantly tomorrow.

One of the Labour Party's acute problems of credibility lies in its approach to public money and we make much legitimate political capital out of costing their programme. An electorate better educated than many of its predecessors just does not see how a future Labour government could get away with expenditure proposals here when Left-wing governments overseas have been behaving in much the same way as the present British Government.

One of the more intriguing conversations to which I once listened was that in which President Mitterrand sought to persuade Margaret Thatcher that he had lower income tax rates under a Socialist government in France than we did in a Tory Britain.

Few in government today believe it is possible to make a

short dash to freedom associated with significantly high public expenditure or borrowing. There is no mathematical formula to determine what precise percentage of GDP is a permissible Public Sector Borrowing Requirement. Nor is there a line on one side of which public expenditure is acceptable and on the other not. That is not to say there will be no new opportunities. Growing economies deliver choice as extra resources become available. There is the chance to switch within existing programmes. There is the opportunity to enlist the private sector.

Governments have more flexibility than they care to reveal. The same Iron Chancellor who is found during every Autumn's public expenditure survey, scraping at the bottom of every barrel with his back to the wall, is the beaming distributor of largesse and tax cuts on that glad confident morning of his Spring Budget. Geoffrey Howe found the money to pay for the whole of the Falklands War with no overall increase in public expenditure. Nigel Lawson reduced the target PSBR by £500m in his 1986 Budget, and announced increased public expenditure programmes of over £4b in the Autumn of the same year.

The priority must be to promote the creation of wealth rather than the current consumption of it. As a nation we are growing older. There are more workers today, but there will be more pensioners tomorrow. If in putting short-term considerations first we consume now, while neglecting the maintenance and improvement of our industrial infrastructure, the state of our cities, our social capital, and our environment, then our sons and daughters, fewer in number than us, will have not only to pay for their own living standards tomorrow but make good the defects that we ignore. For the same reason, we should not allow resources to stand idle, nationally or regionally, which with a little effort could be put to productive use, among other things in preventing that dereliction.

It is commonly accepted that Britain's industrial performance has for several decades been falling steadily behind that of comparable industrialised countries. Disturbing comparisons are often made between the relationship of the British government with British industry and the relations between the governments and the industries of our competitors. I believe that these comparisons are worth exploring and that they hold a lesson for our country which we should learn sooner rather than later.

Britain's steadily falling world share of exports of manufactures is only one indicator and, although too much can be made of it as evidence of general economic deterioration, it vividly shows how long the country has been in retreat, and is still retreating, from one important field:

1899	33.2%	1960	16.5%
1913	30.2%	1970	10.6%
1938	21.3%	1980	9.7%
1945	20.0%	1985	7.9%
1948	29.3%		

The first figures in the table simply illustrate the dominance which Britain achieved as the first industrial nation. Nor is there anything discreditable about the overall trend, since it reflects first the post-war reconstruction of industry on the Continent and then the outward spread of industrialisation, from the United States and Europe to Japan and the newly-industrialised countries of the Far East; but there is no reason why Britain's share of this trade should have continued to fall in relation to that of our closest competitors, especially those that are roughly similar to us – France, Germany and Italy. All four countries have roughly comparable populations and started at similar levels of wealth after the Second World War.

Germany, as we know, was the worst off after the devastation of the war. Italy was certainly not rich and, except for the industrialising north, had large areas of poverty and deprivation. France, which until 1939 was largely dependent on agriculture, had also suffered damage to her industry from the war and did not have Britain's industrial prowess and wealth. Britain suffered less devastation, but the war effort left the country much poorer. All four countries had to struggle to recover.

By the sixties all four had booming economies and all felt that they were on the road to success again. But in Britain's case it was a sad delusion. In retrospect we see clearly that our sixties boom was false: it merely masked our continuing economic decline, while that of the others was based on a strengthening of their industrial base for the future. Our boom reflected increasing consumer spending but not an improved production base. Germany made enormous strides in rebuilding her industry, and 40 years after the war has become the most prosperous country in Europe and a world leader in manufacturing and trade. France, a country with which we have had a long-standing rivalry, has also done impressively well. Italy has become a major industrial power.

In 1960 Britain was still the most prosperous European nation. By 1965, the four countries – three of which had become leading members of the European Community – all had roughly comparable standards of living, with income per head (based on purchasing power parities) varying between about $3,000 and $4,300, with Britain and Germany roughly equal first. Within 20 years Germany had passed the $6,800 level, with France not far behind at $6,536, while the United Kingdom was at $5,735 and Italy at $4,921. The comparison with Japan is even more striking; it was the poorest country of the group in 1965, but by 1984 it had reached the same level as France.

The standard of living in Britain has certainly improved dramatically since the beginning of this century, but it has not kept up with the advances in other industrial countries. Our position in the league table kept, by the Organisation for Economic Co-operation and Development, for per capita income, has fallen from tenth richest in 1970 to thirteenth in 1984. This means that only Italy, Spain, Ireland, Greece and Portugal are poorer than Britain.

It is quite clear that for the past 25 years we in Britain have lived off our past and have moved too slowly to improve our performance. One reason for this marked difference to other countries is our poor record on investment, especially in the early post-war years. It has been well below the OECD average since 1963, although the gap has narrowed in recent years. Not only has the rate of investment tended to be lower in manufacturing but it has been less effective than in West Germany, France and the United States.

The House of Lords Select Committee on Overseas Trade was not thanked by the Government when they reported in October 1985 that British industrial decline threatened the nation's standard of living and its economic and political stability.

Before they had put down their pens their Lordships were sharply accused of special pleading; and in its considered reply two months later the Government, in rejecting the committee's verdict, said that there was no crisis which 'required a new departure in the form of an action plan'.

The Government's initial brusque reaction seems to have been occasioned not so much by hurt feelings at the criticism of economic policy as by the report's numerous suggestions for various forms of cash help for industry. The Treasury does not like to be thought an easy touch.

The Government in its reply was mainly and, in the circumstances, understandably concerned to emphasise the considerable number of steps already taken since 1979 to stimulate competition and to create conditions for enterprise.

But the Government's reply also said that ministers accepted many of the committee's conclusions. They shared its concern about the long-term decline in the relative performance of the British economy, and agreed that its competitiveness must be further improved.

The chief value of the Lords Select Committee's work was that they accumulated evidence from a long and representative list of witnesses who told of their anxiety at the shrinkage of Britain's manufacturing industry and at the perilous condition of much of what remained. Few of these experienced witnesses shared the Treasury's optimism about the extent to which service industries would grow or would improve their export performance to compensate for the weakness in manufacturing; and few agreed with the Treasury that, as North Sea oil production decreased, the balance in non-oil trade including manufactures would automatically improve. It is all too simplistic a view, ignoring for example the time needed and the cost involved for any economy to adjust to so fundamental a shift.

In the face of much eloquently expressed anxiety the Treasury's relaxed approach to present and prospective levels of British trade, and in particular the deficit in the balance of trade in manufactures which was the focus of the committee's enquiry, was striking. The committee's principal recommendation was that the nation's attitude towards trade and manufacturing must be changed if social and economic crisis 'in the foreseeable future' was to be avoided. To change the nation's attitude, to bring about what amounts to a cultural change, and to do so quickly, sounds an impossibly ambitious objective; but to change the attitude of government should not be impossible, and that in itself would be a worthwhile first objective.

All major industrial countries have seen a decline in their manufacturing in the last two decades, but the British deterioration has been greatest. British productivity, competitiveness and unit labour costs have all improved but still remain generally unfavourable in relation to major competitors. In spite of improvements in certain sectors, the Association of British Chambers of Commerce believes that manufacturing has suffered greater overall losses in recent years in Britain than in any other industrial economy. One estimate quoted by the ABCC suggests that as much as a sixth of Britain's manufacturing capability may have been scrapped and not replaced in the eighties alone. Again, there is no reason why we should accept the inevitability of this trend.

For the present, manufacturing remains the key wealth creator and, until other equally powerful engines appear, its health will rightly be a matter of serious concern. Despite the increasing importance of services in the national economy – they now provide 60 per cent of our GDP, as opposed to manufacturing which contributes only 20 per cent – they cannot simply replace the manufacturing sector. In most other major industrial countries services have increased their share of output while that of manufacturing has fallen; but in those countries manufacturing has continued to grow in absolute terms. We cannot expect services to sustain the country's economy without the manufacturing base to sustain them, especially since the value added by manufacturing is three times that added by services.

However the figures are looked at, Britain is not yet in any real way producing adequate alternative sources of wealth and employment. In these circumstances it would be complacent to assume that manufacturing can be allowed to decline further without undermining economic recovery.

The Lords Committee has been taken to task by some critics for making too much of the importance of manufac-

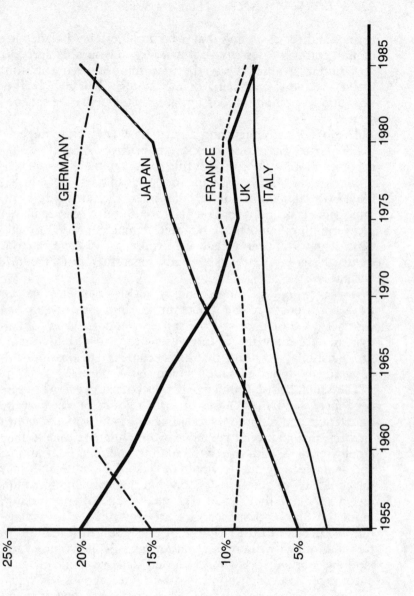

Percentage share of World Trade in the export of manufactured goods

turing, and for assuming that a favourable trade balance in manufactures was essential. But a large favourable surplus in manufactures has always been an important contributor to the economic well-being of the country. Not only has it now disappeared, but it has not been made up by the service sector.

The loss of manufacturing capacity leads in turn to further losses. Once an industry in a competitive sector fails, it becomes more and more difficult to contemplate its revival in future years. The gap in the market is likely to have been filled by a competitor country. Dislodging it can become an impossible task and the market is lost for ever. When demand picks up, more imports are required to make up the national deficit. Importing more than we export, as we have started to do in recent years, then leads to further fundamental weakness.

It weakens not only our economy but also our self-respect. British citizens become reluctant to buy British goods, whether good or bad, and the spiral of imports grows. In a dynamic economy the country can afford to pay for these products; in an economy that has become fragile the imports dangerously drain the nation's financial resources.

The Think British Campaign suggested that, if every household increased its purchases of British goods by £3 a week on average and reduced its spending on imports by the same amount, the balance of payments would improve by £900m, employment would rise by 350,000 and £2,500m more personal spending money would be created. No one can force the consumer to buy British goods but there are innumerable instances where they are of high quality and offer value for money. Marks and Spencer are probably unique in buying only 10 percent of their clothing from non-British manufacturers although Britain as a nation buys 30 per cent of its clothing abroad. M and S adopt positive policies and encourage domestic suppliers to produce goods of high quality and design for them, where necessary giving their suppliers practical support, with of course the incentive of the large potential market which they command.

No one should be expected to buy the second rate or the overpriced, but as a society – and that includes government as the largest customer – there is too little attempt to encourage a national response to the legitimate disciplines of the market place. Not enough people try to find a British solution, or help others to do so.

The capitalist economies with which we have to compete do not operate on the theory held in Britain that government is an onlooker in the industrial game or at best a referee. In most of these countries there are partnerships of one sort or another between the government and the industrial world. The partnerships are of varying kinds, but in most cases there is a common attitude and approach which is more mature, less adversarial and demonstrably more successful than ours.

In some respects the American economy operates from the same set of free market assumptions as ours. But its scale is unique, and the size of its domestic market gives to those who emerge within it an advantage with predictable consequences. They can buy their way out of trouble. The positive cash flow year on year generates wealth for investment that no other economy can match. The big get bigger. A continual challenge from the new and small keeps the big on their toes. If one adds to that the scale of the American Government's procurement programmes, especially for the defence and space budgets, and the determination of Congress to protect not only the consequent technological capability against all comers but other industries as well, the idea of a free market loses some of its certainty and simplicity. The scale of the American taxpayer's support for companies at the frontiers of technology is as impressive as that of the consumer. The fact that in this field of technology it is probably the most protected economy in the free world adds to the in-built strength of its more advanced industries.

The American system is, of course, highly competitive, but that is made possible by the internal scale of its economy. In Britain we may sustain one manufacturer at the frontiers of one technology, provided that the domestic environment is not competitive, but the Americans can have three or four contractors at the frontiers of the same technology and thus in competition.

The nearest thing in scale, although only half the size and utterly different in character, is the Japanese economy, which is a brilliantly orchestrated and managed partnership between the industrial and governmental worlds. Nobody would pretend that you can take that model and adapt it for use in this country; but its strength is undeniable. Its capacity to achieve excellence and to promote harmonious relations among government, banker, shareholder, manager and worker in pursuit of common objectives is renowned. Government support for industry in Japan has been targeted much more to products with a visible pay-back in the medium technologies rather than in the glamorous but risky areas of high technology. In other words, they have done the very thing which we pretend no government can do: they have targeted the world's market place and, with a combination of domestic competition and taxpayer support, they have come to capture an increasingly large share of it. Do we really think our companies can win without the backing of our government when the consumer appetite in Britain is so eagerly fed by imports from a country whose economic and industrial effort is so single-mindedly directed?

France and West Germany share with Japan the sense of national purpose which so many observers note in our competitors but do not find in Britain. Each country has institutions which embody and strengthen this national purposefulness, and foster a partnership of the different elements whose well being depends on industrial harmony and success. In the Federal Republic, the system of two-tier boards for companies, with employees represented on the supervisory board, ensures that the interests of the employee and therefore of the locality have a strong and often decisive influence on each company's development in a way that has no modern equivalent in Britain. The fact that pension funds are invested in the employing companies not only provides cash for investment which British companies hand over to outside funds; it also focusses the minds of employees as to where their long-term interests lie. At the same time the federal structure encourages competition for industry among the German *Länder* and creates political pressures which tend to support prosperity in the regions.

In France, although industry found the intervention of the last Socialist government burdensome, the closeness of co-operation between government and industry is a traditional strength. The French performance benefits from the interdependence of the two, and from the freedom and frequency with which senior executives move back and forth between the private and public sectors. In many of the high technology fields, the role of the government is a manifestation of French will. In areas where France has been determined that there will be an individual French capability, or a European capability which is French-led, European industry as a whole has gained. We would not have a major civil airframe manufacturing capability in Europe today if it were not for France. We would not have a launcher capability in the space field but for France. The French recognise more clearly than any nation in Europe that, if they are to maintain for themselves a destiny in the more sophisticated industrial field of tomorrow, government and industry have to work together. It is no accident that, while the Strategic Defence Initiative programme pushed forward American technology, it was France that proposed the European civil programme EUREKA.

For many years the British nation has fallen steadily behind as rival economies have prospered. Today, after remarkable exertions by Government and people, our decline has been slowed, although not stopped. If we do not change there will come a time, perhaps when the oil runs out, when the British will discover, like others, the primacy of profitable industry in a thriving modern economy. Whether we travel abroad to see how our neighbours live, or whether we learn it from the expansion of direct satellite broadcasting, we are likely to become more aware of their growing prosperity and of our relative poverty. If that does not rouse us, perhaps we may respond after further decline, when the loss of key industries will have deprived us of more employment and of the means to buy the imported goods which British manufacturers no longer provide.

No doubt at that moment a sense of national purpose will at last be born in us. Government and industry, owners, bankers, managers and craftsmen, will see the need to make common cause. But poverty is not the most satisfactory condition in which to start a fight for life.

5
Industry: A Strategy

Britain is in a competition for economic survival. Our relative manufacturing decline has been debated for decades, but not arrested; and its destructive effect on our economic strength today lies partially hidden from the public by the temporary flow of oil and gas from the North Sea and by sales of assets. This partial concealment makes it no less destructive and its correction no less urgent. Sooner rather than later, what seems to be a cultural defect in our national attitude to industry must be properly diagnosed and cured.

There is no question of sudden disaster, but rather of continuing relative decline in our material standards by comparison with those of our nearest European neighbours and, beyond Europe, with both the older and newer industrial economies. Relative decline is the more dangerous for being less obvious than sudden crisis. It does not provoke action or sharp debate. The Conservative Party has therefore two tasks: it must defend and attack; it must avert the catastrophic consequences of the Socialist threat to the very foundations of our economy, and, as Government, ensure that the concealed weaknesses in Britain's capacity and concern to create wealth are recognised and remedied. Success will need the continued pursuit of international competitiveness. It also needs a strategy to augment the status and achievements of British industry.

In a later chapter I shall make plain my view that Britain's commitment to Europe is an indispensable, indeed central, element in any industrial strategy. This chapter outlines the need for, and the essence of, such a strategy. It does not pretend to be exhaustive. It starts from the assumption that government cannot stand apart from a responsibility for industry's success. Sometimes supporters argue that this Government does have an industrial strategy: to keep their hands off industry and commerce because they distrust the business judgement of ministers and officials and because they have confidence in the working of the market place. The Department of Trade and Industry will deny that there is, or should be, any view from the centre of how British industry might develop and prosper. If all this were true, it would be a strategy: too simple to persuade me, but a strategy of sorts. However, these disclaimers persuade nobody. That is not how government is behaving. The truth is that the present Government, like all its predecessors for at least the last 50 years, is up to its neck in the business life of this country, stimulating this enterprise, stifling another and interfering at every turn. Commercial judgements are made across the whole range of government in every hour of every working day.

Such involvement is not a matter for shame. It is vital to the survival of the British economy. It is benign in intent, if not always in practice. It preoccupies the governments of most other developed industrial nations, and the nature of it has now to be at the top of our political agenda.

At the outset let me say what an industrial strategy is not about. It is not about planning, if by planning is meant targets to be set and achieved, rules to be laid down and complied with, forecasts elevated to a degree of certainty quite beyond the experience of anyone who has spent a moment of time in the executive world of either the private or public sector. We want no five-year plans here.

It is easy enough to say what strategy is not, but while Conservatives have a well-founded distrust of rigid, central Socialist planning, which I fully share, the truth does not lie at the other end of the spectrum. The averted gaze is equally dangerous because it delays the urgent debate about Britain's industrial future, which cannot be advanced until we accept that the health of British industry depends crucially, in many fields, on it having government as a partner.

When a Conservative government commits itself to a medium-term financial strategy, regimenting its public expenditure programme in precise quantifications for three years ahead, that is a plan. It implies, with the rigidity of its figure work, an ability to foresee the future, or to ignore its consequences as they unfold.

It is not my view that we should seek to introduce the rigidity that underlies our public expenditure planning into any sectoral, indicative industrial planning.

The debate should be concerned, as most people outside the Government know, not with whether a British government should have a strategic approach to industry but with what that approach should be. Once the Conservative Party recognises that, it will be seen as the only party able within its philosophy to attract a wide consensus of national support.

I have stated that commercial judgements are made by ministers and civil servants in every hour of every day. Conservatives are content to sustain a whole department of State guiding, subsidising and protecting agriculture. Regulated as minutely by this Government as by any of its predecessors, it has outperformed the rest of our economy for decade after decade. I know of proposals to change the emphasis of that support, but of none to abolish it.

The Department of Energy weighs and reviews the market judgement and the investment proposals of our energy industries; it approves their price structures. Ministers and officials could not undertake this if they were not supposed to think about the consequences, if they were ignorant of the commercial arguments, if they shared none of the responsibility for what followed. The Department of the Environment has teams of public and private sector employees appraising the commercial viability of urban projects before grant aid is given.

Government departments spend £3.5b a year on research and development programmes. Does anyone outside the Government believe that the Departments of Education and Science, Transport, Agriculture, Energy, Industry and Defence do not, and should not, ask questions about potential markets, about the expected return on public money, or about exploitation of property rights?

The Department of Trade and Industry determines, case by case, the creditworthiness of every overseas market we have and, company by company, product by product, whether to provide export credit above normal commercial judgement. It is not credible that this same department should protest repeatedly that governments cannot know about markets or decide which companies deserve support.

The New Towns, the development corporations and the regional offices of the Departments of Employment or Trade and Industry involve themselves in detailed consideration of the endless stream of grant decisions which have consequences for local industry and commerce. It could certainly be argued that they involve themselves too much in the detail, but it cannot be argued that they do not involve themselves at all.

The double-guessing of sponsoring departments is redoubled by the Treasury, which never hesitates to concern itself with the most nit-picking details. Are we seriously expected to believe that, when the Treasury sets out to impose this or that rate of return on an investment programme, its ministers and officials remind each other that they are doing so in some commercial vacuum? The dialogue in the economic committee of the Cabinet hums with an erudite exchange of fact and theory about the abilities of entrepreneurs and their companies.

The language of government relations with industry is littered with strange names, some British, some the acronyms beloved of our fellow Europeans. EUREKA, Alvey, ESPRIT all mean the same thing: the use of taxpayers' money to underwrite commercial, civil and industrial activity to keep Britain up there in tomorrow's competition. Our government spends it just as all our competitors do. Are civil servants just rubber-stamping private sector initiatives without judgement, knowledge or influence? Don't you believe it!

Given the minuteness of the scrutiny that quite properly is undertaken when these increasing sums of taxpayers' money are poured, year by year, into industrial support, platform slogans about getting off people's backs are vacuous. But the truth is too serious to be so easily obscured. Industry is clearly not left to its own devices in the market place, but pushed and pulled by anonymous officials applying countless forgotten regulations. It is subjected to constant battering by policies which are seldom brought to bear intelligently and systematically, but haphazardly and piecemeal.

What this Government has rightly done is not to withdraw

from industrial support but to cut out much of the subsidy that, under weaker predecessors, has been a characteristic of that support in the past. It is not intervention that is wrong: in the modern world, it is unavoidable. What was wrong before was the subsidising of losses and the cosiness and lack of professionalism associated with that. Intervention and featherbedding are not the same. The trick is to distinguish between them.

I would not pretend that strategic judgements about our agricultural, defence, energy or transport industries have always been right. But neither should anyone else pretend that there are or could be no strategic judgements at all. Often the closeness of the political/industrial relationship has fostered a cosiness when competition would have served us better. That does not mean that the concept of strategy or partnership is mistaken, but that we have pursued both in too amateur a way.

Governments everywhere acknowledge responsibility for creating a favourable climate for industry. This ambition is shared by the British Government. We are enjoying a period of relative growth and, in this role of rainmaker, we are now up with the best performances of our competitors. To augment this we must recognise overtly much of that which, in its relationship with industry, government prefers should be covert. We need a dialogue in which the voice of industry is sympathetically heard and its interests fully considered.

We know of the scale of government support, but the priorities are not co-ordinated and the disciplines ineffectively applied. We cannot plan the future, but we should understand how each party sees it, so that in the decisions that both industry and government must properly take themselves, each is at least informed of the other's views. Above all, we must discuss together what other competing economies are doing and determine what, if any, reactions are appropriate. There is a national interest wider than any one part of the capitalist system. The components of owner, manager, financier and worker do not sufficiently understand each other and too often work without regard for each others' interests. In all these things, which must in the end add up to a cultural change, government has an inescapable role.

The most serious industrial managers are now increasingly and articulately dismissive of a 'hands-off' relationship between government and industry. They want, and should be offered, a new partnership between those whose working lives are spent in British industry and commerce and the political and administrative machine. They want more certainty and stability in decision-taking and they want a longer-term view – not an apologetic 'help me when I'm down' affair, but a proud and visible commitment to a jointly conceived set of measures for the creation of wealth.

The capitalist system works best when owners, managers, employees and government understand a common interest and work as a team to that end. My perception of the capitalist economies with which we must compete is that they enjoy a relationship that is more cohesive than ours. That is not to say that all the interests of all these groups are the same. There will be different views of how the product of their joint labours should be divided, but there is entire agreement that the product should first be as valuable as they can make it.

Our bigger companies are largely owned by financial institutions which work within disciplines laid down by statute. It is right that those who are responsible for the assets of pension funds should see themselves in a different light from those who create the wealth in the companies they own. You can argue that the banking system must protect its own corporate entity and that its relationship with its customers lies in the letter of its contract. You can also say that it is the duty of managers to manage, as indeed it is, and imply that consultation with and involvement of their workforce is no part of their duty. You can argue that support for industry is not a government responsibility. You can argue all of these things and, if you argue successfully, you will find the British economy Balkanised: owners will be broadly concentrated in the City of London; managers will dwell apart from those who own their companies; the workforce will be a separate race, employed but not committed. You will also have what we in Britain have now: a capitalist manufacturing economy which performs less well than others of comparable size.

The Conservative Party has, of course, wrestled with these

problems many times before. Other generations of politicians
have understood these questions and tried to answer them.
Among the most profound influences on Tory thinking in
the second half of the twentieth century was that of Harold
Macmillan. Not only did he first describe new horizons for
our society, blown from our imperial past by the wind of
change into a future in the European Community, but in his
concern for the domestic economy he created the National
Economic Development Office (NEDO) within which to
conduct dialogue between government and the wealth
creators. He started also the National Incomes Commission
(NIC) in an attempt to reconcile the opposing forces which
determined the levels of pay settlements, in the hope of
moderating Britain's insatiable urge to pay itself more than
it can afford. NIC, like all subsequent pay policies under
all governments, has gone. It gave good sport to a society
intolerant of central regimentation, by providing it with the
satisfaction of leap-frogging over the never-ending series of
targets, norms, bands or ranges with which ministers sought
to make Britain stop squandering its inheritance. The pay
policies went and the nation continued to pay itself well
above what its Chancellor advised. Geoffrey Howe and Nigel
Lawson delivered 3 per cent inflation, a higher rate than that
of our competitors, but a remarkable gain. They must shake
their heads in despair as they now see pay settlement after
pay settlement erode the value of that achievement.

NEDO has survived through three decades as a Conservative creation which has never fulfilled its potential, but which
remains a proof of the Party's abiding commitment to an
undivided society.

Since the mid-1970s the economic climate has not encouraged consensus. I was a member of Ted Heath's Government
when the oil crisis of 1973 shattered a foundation stone of
the world economy. No government could have survived the
effects of so cataclysmic an event, although in February 1974
the National Union of Mineworkers and its leader Joe
Gormley nearly saved the Tories by the directness of their
challenge to the Government's authority. The years in opposition that followed understandably encouraged in the
Conservative Party an awareness of the huge effort that was
necessary to reassert Britain's industrial capability. Inflation

was rife, the unions wielded excessive political power and
the private sector was taxed to a point where taxation far
exceeded the point of confiscation. No warm-blooded
member of the Conservative Party could have been expected
to favour anything other than the swiftest restoration of
economic sanity, a climate of competitiveness and the
necessary rigour in economic management.

The battle against inflation had to be fought. Tax rates
had to be made competitive, an incentive society recreated,
the ill-disciplined subsidies to the nationalised industries
removed, a forest of forms, restrictions and government
impertinences removed. 'Setting the people free' is not simply
the most ringing slogan of modern times: it also describes a
real release of energy and enterprise into the economy. We
should not withdraw a word of our advocacy of these
objectives.

In these achievements the Conservative Government has
done great things for British business. The battle against
inflation has been bravely fought, while an unqualified
benefit conferred on business and on the whole country by
this Government, and a step of historic consequence, is the
passage of legislation which has made trades unions subject
to the law of the land. They now enjoy freedoms as other
bodies of citizens – no more, no less. Reduction of the highest
rates of income tax, from 98 per cent to 60 per cent, by this
Government has also removed a competitive disadvantage
which has long burdened business. Those who threaten the
limited number of high earners with punitive taxation fail to
recognise the extreme volatility today in the job market for
top managers. They are footloose and internationally trade-
able. They will not accept high taxes, but will go where the
taxes are lower. It is their companies which suffer, lose
export orders and initiate less as a result of their departure.
Tax rates, like products, must be competitive.

Many imaginative steps have been taken to stimulate the
start and growth of small businesses. The Government has
provided in grants, tax incentives and loan guarantees as
comprehensive a range of incentives as are to be found
anywhere in the capitalist world. By the end of 1986 new
businesses were being created at a net rate of 600 a week.
Enterprise allowances for unemployed people starting busi-

nesses were being paid to 2,000 new claimants every week. It remains true that small businesses in Japan, with their high potential for growth, account for twice the proportion of jobs which they provide in Britain. With roughly double Britain's population, Japan has about five times as many small firms. That is not a criticism of the present Government: it is a reflection of the more responsive and flexible industrial society Japan has created over a generation. It is also an indication of how we must temper our satisfaction with an awareness that there can be no let-up.

The Government has made notable gains and fought for them with tenacity. Our objective was to remove the obstacles placed in the path of enterprise either deliberately, through hostility to capitalism and in response to trade union pressure, or inadvertently, through mismanagement of the economy. For many companies, particularly the small, the innovative and those in growing markets, the creation of a sympathetic climate is enough. But the most interesting recent sequel to our work has been industry's response to Conservative freedom, for in November 1986 members of the Confederation of British Industry passed for the first time a resolution calling for a national industrial strategy. Many supporters of the present government, if they had been asked in 1979 what that meant, might have recited the Conservative agenda and talked of forms torn up, of red tape untied, of the Civil Service reduced in size and the Employment Protection Act amended. That would have been, in aggregate, an industrial strategy. All are measures with which I was in the fullest agreement, and my departments played their part in implementing them. There remains wide support for the message set out by the Secretary of State for Employment, David Young, in his white paper *Lifting the Burden*.

Yet, with all these things substantially done, the industrialists who have been set free in the market place, their taxes reduced, still want an industrial strategy. How should a Conservative respond? If he is wise, he will interpret this as a further sign of the growing awareness, at all levels within industry, of the necessary complexity of relations between government and industry.

There is no free or fair market for British business in the world beyond Dover, nor are there any regulations, be they

European Community directives or rules of the GATT, by
which we can rely on other trading nations to be unequivo-
cally bound, although some nations have more regard than
others for the rulebooks. Other national governments and
industries act together to exploit the rules with single-mindedness to ensure success. They prey on any country too weak
and self-deluding to do the same. The Italian government
bailed out Fiat, the United States government rescued
Chrysler, the French taxpayer gives Renault whatever
support it requires.

British governments, when under pressure, recognise these
realities and act in the same way. A Conservative government
rescued Rolls Royce in 1971. The market place had spoken,
and a purist would have argued that its will should have
prevailed; but no government could have ignored the fact
that Rolls Royce had two problems. It was over-manned,
and lacked effective financial control, and for that managers,
unions and shareholders deserved what they got. But the
rock on which Rolls Royce foundered was the competition
from an American engine, the development of which had
been funded from the American defence budget and only
adapted by private money at the margin for civil purposes.
Rolls Royce, with no defence requirement but with a determination to stay in the big engine league with their RB211,
was fighting not just the General Electric Company of
America but a product the cost of which had been largely
paid for by the American taxpayer. If Rolls Royce had opted
out of the big engine league, they would never have come
back in. The Government had to start from the reality that
they were the only large aero-engine maker outside the
United States. To let them go would have been to extinguish
not just a company but a most valuable industry. Some
industries must go; the market moves on. But they should
not go by default when it is the competition financed by
governments that is the challenge.

The story of Rolls Royce raises the next question: should
government wait for the crises to come, or by thoughtful
anticipation attempt to prevent them? Do you wait until the
Treasury, once a year, has completed its public expenditure
review and then consider how the industrial consequences
fall out? Do you claim the role of reluctant bride, dragged

by the interventionist policies of other governments to a purely reactive interventionism yourself? When you have to make a practical decision about public investment, do you treat it as merely a short deviation from the normal course of ministerial life?

No minister would dare to make such a claim in the hearing of anyone who had seen the submissions piled high on Whitehall desks, full of assertions about strategic aims, long-term interests, foreign competition, subsidy and support. All the trappings of a continuous relationship between government and industry are there. What is missing is the conviction, the consistency and the machinery to mobilise owners, managers, financiers and the workforce to work together within a coherent industrial strategy. There can be no such strategy while there is no centre for its formulation within government, which alone can draw the elements of our capitalist system together.

In spite of its name the Department of Trade and Industry is not responsible for the sum of government's relations with industry. No department and no minister is so charged, and that is an indefensible state of affairs. I do not suggest any weakening of the Scottish Industry Department or the Northern Ireland Economic Development Department; but where industrial interests in different parts of the United Kingdom have to be reconciled – for example, if the British taxpayers' subsidy to Short Brothers of Belfast endangers some of the operations in Lancashire or Bristol of British Aerospace – the primary responsibility in Cabinet for shaping policy must lie with the DTI.

To discharge this, the Secretary of State for Trade and Industry should therefore have within the Cabinet greater seniority than now, and he would need a markedly stronger department. Just as there is the Home Affairs committee of the Cabinet so the Industry Secretary should have the power base of a new Cabinet committee, of which he would take the chair, on which other Cabinet ministers whose activities have consequences for industrial policy would also sit. It is possible to identify a dozen 'inevitable roles' of government which impinge upon industry – roles which every govern-ment fulfils. At present these are distributed among several departments.

The 'inevitable roles' include: controlling access to the British market; obtaining access for British companies to overseas markets; placing orders on its own account; deciding for or against major construction projects, from the Channel Tunnel to power stations; taxation policy; the overall control of education; regulation, including law-making; macro-economic decisions such as interest and exchange rates; competition policy; the provision of infra-structure; the allocation of funds for research and industrial support.

No effective mechanism exists by which the industrial interests affected by decisions in these areas can be consulted. Nor is there any policy requirement that they should be consulted, let alone given favoured treatment. A strengthened DTI would be responsible for seeing that there was proper liaison between industry and each department of government charged with policy in an area of concern to industry. It would also itself ensure that industry's arguments and inter-ests were fully taken into account in all the 'inevitable roles', and – so far as possible – that these roles were efficiently performed.

The first task of the Cabinet committee would be to examine the flow of incentives in our society. In a capitalist economy, talent and activity will go where the profit is to be made, but tax policy can influence where that will be. I have argued elsewhere that the present pattern of taxation tends to favour the large, publicly quoted company at the expense of the family business, and to destroy local owner-ship and control. The Cabinet committee would be equipped to consider whether this bias is contrary to the national industrial interest and, if so, how it might be corrected.

There would be much else for the committee's agenda. As I have said, the Germans have a system whereby their indus-trial companies create pension funds by investing in their own industrial capability. There would be no question of directing pension contributions into schemes created by the contributors' employers; the question is rather whether tax incentives should be applied so as to encourage the develop-ment of what happens in Germany and not, as now, to prevent it.

Are we right to give pension funds the incentives of tax-free income, and thus help them to divert the savings of the nation into a profile of investment which is not directed primarily to wealth creation?

Has every last start-up incentive been designed? I have one that I would wish the Government to adopt. We have been over-taxed at 'entrepreneurial levels' for decades: high levels of personal taxation have made it hard for individuals to save, invest and start small businesses on a scale that would otherwise have been possible. The cumulative deterrent effect of high taxation on the starting of new businesses is incalculable but severe. The Business Expansion Scheme is a significant attempt to recognise the problems, but we could go much further. By way of apology for the overtaxation of many years, the Government could allow people anxious to start their own businesses to claim back past personal tax up to the total paid over, say, five years, provided that they added to that reclaimed amount whatever income they themselves had retained. In simple terms a 60 per cent marginal rate taxpayer investing £100,000 would be able to reclaim £60,000 in repayment tax. This concession would be available if he invested within certain approved categories of wealth-creating activity which are already defined by the Department of Trade and Industry. It would discredit the system if it were possible, for example, to start a private portfolio on the back of reclaimed tax; but that could be prevented. Many initial loopholes in the Business Expansion Scheme have been stopped up, and similar rules could be applied to a new tax recovery scheme. There are two dangers: first, marginal abuse, the risk of which would be worth accepting. The second is that claims for past tax repayment might be so large as to provide a significant cost to public expenditure. If that meant that the number of small- and medium-sized business start-ups increased precipitately, that is the sort of problem with which the Government would quickly find it could afford to live.

The Loan Guarantee Scheme has proved its value in bringing new businesses into existence, but the ceiling of £75,000 on each loan has not been raised since the scheme was launched in 1981. The Government should reinforce its success here and raise the limit to £250,000 or more. The taxpayer would see his money back.

The committee's overall strategic concern would be to survey the incentives working in our society. Where they are sucking resources from wealth creation, they should be neutralised or removed.

The future of British industry depends on policy in many different fields being framed to take account of its needs. The Department of Education and Science has been severely criticised for the failure of schools to produce in the past, and to be teaching even now, the skills which industry and commerce need. Welcome changes are now evident but, with the ministers in charge of this department involved in an industrial policy committee, there might have been constructive discussion earlier about why we have in many parts of the country large numbers of job vacancies for skilled people and yet more than three million out of work. This failure by the country to train the workforce for profitable work is one of the graver impediments to our industrial effort. It is a clear example of how major government departments over decades have failed to talk and work together to anticipate problems and changes that others perceived more clearly. The message has been spelled out over a century in report after report, but other countries have left us far behind in their determination to train and retrain their people.

Of course there are opportunities today within existing machinery for specific issues about industrial policy to be raised and papers prepared. But it is *ad hocery* and has nothing to compare to the driving force of political management which is the Treasury's never-ending round of book-balancing. The Treasury seeks targets years in advance, Parliament and Whitehall devote huge energies to limiting the deviations or excesses that all targets produce, and industrial policy is too often a drop-out consequence of all this.

The Chancellor's office is important and its occupancy long-term. The Department of Trade and Industry is, by contrast, a perching point with often very junior Cabinet ministers in charge. The views of the City are in the mainstream of policy: those of industry are frequently dismissed as little more than special pleading.

Political effectiveness is directly related to the ability to get resources. The Treasury's political strength stems from its historic relationship with Parliament as the department to which money was voted, and this pattern of power has not changed to match the steadily growing importance of the Government's involvement with industry.

Somehow we have to shift the balance. This cannot be done by the restraining or destroying forces with which the Left, given the chance, would threaten our financial institutions.

The Conservative Party has an obligation to direct policies to the creation of wealth and to set aside any dogma, whether inherited or acquired, which risks impeding this. Like the word 'profit' in the mouth of a Socialist, the word 'plan' has become an expletive in Conservative circles. It must not be whispered even among those who fully understand, for example, that, where industry and commerce are denied free markets in spite of international efforts to maintain freedom, a refusal to plan selective attacks on export markets may in these days be an act of surrender.

Conservative governments have planned or attempted to plan the supply of money and credit, the size of public sector incomes, the cash limits of nationalised industries, the expenditure of local authorities and, like all governments, the use of land and much else. We set targets and limits and restraints while persuading ourselves that planning for industry is foreign to our nature, oppressive to the human spirit and wrong.

So let us expunge the word 'plan' from our vocabulary. Let us agree that plans which governments help to formulate tend to be rigid, and at the same time to raise false expectations of the subsidies and cosiness which suffocate the spirit of enterprise.

Let us not say that the Japanese plan to target our markets. Let us just say that they target them. They do not do this overnight but over decades. They do not use vague generalisations. They co-ordinate every strength of a formidable capitalist economy to produce the increasingly sophisticated products of an efficient and competitive industry. It is not done at the whim or judgement of a free-standing capitalist company alone, but with the active involvement and support of the Japanese taxpayer through his government. Some may think that it is a market place in which Britain's industries have only to set up their stalls and start counting their takings. A walk down the high streets or round the offices or factories of Britain will reveal a different and disquieting reality. Is it not time that we began to acknowledge the way in which the world's market is organized, to believe what we see even if it conflicts with the textbooks, and to behave accordingly?

The emerging economies of the Pacific basin will copy the Japanese method, not ours. The competition is getting tougher, not easier.

Some industries which have been staples of the British economy will sicken and die; others will recover if helped. Some industries promise to grow fast and to compensate in wealth and revenue for what is lost elsewhere. Of these potential growth industries some may grow spontaneously; some will grow only if helped; some if helped will grow much faster than if left to their own devices.

If these are truisms, it should be a truism also to say that the Government should use all the skill available to it, with the help of those who work in industry, to enable it to judge where the weight of public support, already spent on a vast scale, can best be applied. In a competitive world, where other governments work closely with their leaders of industry to decide where the effort should be made, Britain has no choice.

Some industries, including several defence contractors, are vital to Britain's national security and for that reason alone must be sustained. That responsibility is the Government's, but it goes far wider.

Government cannot pretend that it is not involved in decisions about the future of the key 'platforms' of industry, or that it is up to the companies alone to ensure that they are able to compete effectively in the managed market place of the world. There are industries, such as the steel industry, the car industry and the airframe industry which cannot be allowed to fail if Britain is to remain an advanced economy. Ideally the Government should not own them but it has an ultimate responsibility to determine if they have a role in the economy. These are the industries at the heart of the economy from which blood vessels run in all directions; to suppliers of raw materials, semi-manufactures and components and to dependent service industries – all the countless life-forms which are put at risk if the blood supply stops.

A classic example is provided by the motor industry. Governments throughout the world, and especially in Europe, are heavily involved in giving financial support to their motor industries. This support comes in many shapes and sizes, and for a variety of purposes. The French government regards the motor industry as a key plank of the nation's economy, to be helped in any way necessary. In 1985, for example, Renault received F3b in capital grants and a further F2b in soft loans from the government. Further capital grants and loans were given in 1986, and estimates suggest that the State will support Renault to the tune of F20b during the three years, 1985–7. In spite of losses (around F10b in 1985) which have dwarfed those incurred by the Rover group, there is no question of Renault continuing to be anything other than one of Europe's largest car and commercial vehicle producers. Also in France, Citröen (part of the private sector Peugeot group) has recently received a large soft loan from the French government's industrial modernisation fund to launch the new AX model, which is scheduled to enter the United Kingdom market in 1987 and to provide competition for Rover's Metro.

Fiat has been accused of being the most subsidised car manufacturer in Europe because of the Italian government's *cassa integrazione* policy which effectively enables a large company to rationalise its workforce at the expense of the State. Meanwhile, each of Spain's five car producers has negotiated with the country's Ministry of Industry for a package of state aid in the form of investment subsidies and soft credits. So it goes on.

Faced with these realities, it is simply not an option for the British Government to tell the country's motor industry to make its own way in the world. Already there has been a dramatic decline in its fortunes: a loss of volume, with car production almost halved in fifteen years and trucks down by two-thirds in less than a decade; and an increase in assembly operations, with Vauxhall now an assembler of Opel kits and Talbot (formerly Rootes) an assembler of Peugeot kits.

An ominous development has been an increase in foreign

ownership and control. Foreign investment and interest is, of course, to be welcomed, but control has its dangers. For the major parts of the British motor industry to fall entirely into foreign hands would leave it a hostage to decisions in Detroit, Paris, Turin and perhaps Tokyo. Experience shows time and time again that, when the going gets rough, as it always will in such a cyclical industrial sector, foreign subsidiaries (which in this case means subsidiaries in Britain) will bear the brunt of the cutbacks. The skills in research and development tend to be lost. That is why the future of the sole remaining British-owned and British-controlled motor manufacturer, Rover, will continue to be a matter for the Government. Otherwise the British motor industry will find itself further down the cul-de-sac to extinction.

Collapse, almost too dire to contemplate, would mean a loss of employment at the vehicle manufacturers; a further rise in the UK's motor industry balance of trade deficit; a knock-on impact among the component suppliers, and in turn on their suppliers; a loss of credibility for the component suppliers in valuable export markets; and a serious loss of skills.

The expertise that has not come easily to government is that of combining ultimate responsibility to preserve the capacity of our industry with the introduction of effective management and market-oriented skills. The original British Leyland rescue was a notable example of the right decision in principle being executed with minimal regard to the realities of commercial life. Managers who run a company into the ground must play no part in its rescue, and over-manning and out-dated or restrictive practices cannot be supported. Ian Macgregor's management of British Steel and British Coal, or Lord King's management of British Airways, show a much more encouraging pattern for the restoration to fortune of large enterprises on their way back to the private sector.

Every worthwhile company has a plan and anyone with any experience of those plans knows exactly what their value is. In the best companies planning becomes ever more sophisticated, but even the best plans are usually treated with scepticism. They are indicative, giving broad outlines of possibilities. They deceive none of the managers, but no management would be without them. They make the company think about tomorrow, ask the uncomfortable questions and project forward the consequences of the decisions taken today. They serve an essential purpose.

The classic example of the Left's failure to understand industry was Labour's idea of planning agreements, which was broadly to take the corporate plans of large companies, sanctify them and make them rigid. No company can commit itself to doing business on the basis of its forward projections, which its experience is continually revising. The idea that you can aggregate them and call it a strategy for the nation is fantasy.

The art form which we must practise, though we can never perfect it, will bring government and industry together in the fullest possible dialogue about the future, in the closest possible agreement but with limited commitment, not to make blueprints but to know and understand each other's attitudes before decisions are taken, in the knowledge that each party is becoming more vulnerable year by year to the other's mistaken decisions. Sometimes the most valuable role of government to emerge will be the use of its procurement power to intensify competition, as we found in the Ministry of Defence.

If the Department of Trade and Industry is to increase in influence the Treasury will see this as a threat. So it should. The question of whether the Treasury has too great an influence on policy is always at the centre of discussion among spending ministers and among the familiar hordes of special pleaders for the outlay of public money. The Treasury bastion has survived every attack unscathed, and the failed attempt by the Labour administrations of Harold Wilson in the 1960s to establish a rival Department of Economic Affairs discouraged later assailants.

Labour's short-lived DEA, which had much to do with the Party's internal rivalries, was conceived as an opposing centre of macro-economic management because of the party leadership's fear that Treasury caution might frustrate the planned expansion. It was overwhelmed by the financial waves that flowed from that Labour government's economic mismanagement.

The serious question remains of whether the Treasury's

economic thinking should be decisive in all considerations of policy towards industry. The DEA's defeat by the Treasury has, for twenty years, prevented governments in Britain from thinking in strategic ways about the future of industry. The Treasury's outlook is much like that inherited from the days when Britain was a major colonial power. That imperial opportunity was one in which it was easy to suppose that Britain's excellence was the excellence of a *laissez faire* economy. The fact that two-thirds of the world's surface, painted red on the maps of my childhood, was controlled by British governors or district commissioners, or was in the protected spheres of influence of large British companies, is easily lost to sight. But that political dominance, added to our industrial capability, gave us an overwhelming advantage. It was not just a free market in the sense in which the words are used today. It was our market. The illusions were slow to fade and have not yet been exorcised from Treasury Chambers.

The Treasury is the leading advocate of the belief that if you get the economic climate right then industrial success will follow. The macro-economic disciplines are all-pervading. Every year in season the public expenditure round decides the allocation of resources. For three months of the year Whitehall is plunged into turmoil as the Treasury seeks to square the circles and its books. So long as the national books balance it is assumed that the benign climate will follow. The Treasury gardeners do not think they need to plant seeds: they prepare the soil, then stand back. Politics in Britain panders to consumers, so investment has to suffer. Political commitment and indexation and every manner of benefit, tax allowance and pension, increase the pressures on capital programmes. On them, therefore, the axe falls: the appetite of consumption has been fed, the public sector machine has protected its own and the cuts in capital programmes are felt first in the private sector, where engineering or building contractors lose the expected government orders and lay off their workers.

The Treasury does not, of course, deserve the whole blame for our national habit of consuming what we should invest. My concern is that the distribution of power within government, and the hallowed method of bilateral haggling, prevent adequate and regular consideration of the consequences of decisions about expenditure for industry, for the wealth creation upon which in the end the freedom to consume depends.

What is interesting is how often the Treasury can fail to see the big defects in its conduct of affairs, because of its close pursuit of the detail. The Treasury's distribution of resources by volume under the Plowden system was not replaced by cash planning until 1976. Some of us found Plowden's divorce from reality almost unbelievable in its assumptions that the world just went on, without regard to enhanced efficiency or to the need to contain inflation. The shift to cash planning, which came five years later than it should have, is the only possible way of imposing discipline in Whitehall.

Everybody knows the dominant role of the Chancellor of the Exchequer, and all follows from this. You only have to be a minister to understand the frustration of officials in spending departments when they encounter their Treasury colleagues. Any deviation or resistance to the pressure is a threat to the department's relationship with the Treasury. The public expenditure round is based on the tested principle of divide and rule. One by one departments are picked off and their programmes attacked. Nobody dares resist on behalf of a colleague: to do so is to invite the attention of the Treasury and its supporters, who will suggest that your programmes should be cut to make room for your colleague's needs. Your officials do not need to remind you what a pity it would be to sacrifice your department's interests to a cause more closely and personally identified with another Cabinet minister. The management of Britain's affairs and the planning of our future is too serious a matter to be disposed of by such primitive methods. No one questions the need for the Treasury to play the central role in the macro-economic management of our affairs. The weakness is that there is not sufficient challenge to Treasury judgements which may frustrate the strategic industrial objectives of the Government and the work of the DTI.

So how do we proceed? Who calls the meeting? What is on the agenda? How do you launch a national industrial strategy? The answer is, you do not. I have no wish to raise expectations which would surely be destroyed. There should be no drama, no gimmicks; there can be no miracles. There must be the beginning of a long grind to make our society work together more effectively. Comparisons of relative performance show that the task is very great. The long duration of British decline suggests that cures will also take a long time to have an effect. No change of policy or programme could have an immediate influence on the many factors which impede or weaken the British effort. As we have seen, we have underperformed against our principal rivals for at least 40 years. Even to stop the continuing accumulation of that deficit will be hard; to begin to reduce it steadily and to restore our former position will require extraordinary effort and skill.

The effort does not require new machinery, but I would make three adjustments to existing machinery, of which the creation of an industrial policy committee of the Cabinet would be the most important. It would be charged with the promotion of Britain's strategic wealth-creating interests. The Cabinet Office staff that serviced it would have to be of the highest quality. Membership of the committee would be drawn from the Treasury and the departments of Employment, Education, Environment, Defence, Energy, Transport and Agriculture, as well as the Foreign Office and the Scottish, Welsh and Northern Ireland Offices.

The present role of the Foreign and Commonwealth Offices is unsatisfactory. Diplomats are now responsible for British commercial representation abroad; as well as being our eyes and ears, they discharge British Government policy in relation both to governments and to industries overseas. But in Britain they simply report to domestic departments and to industrial and commercial organisations and wait, sometimes in vain, for a response. The logic of their present responsibilities should be followed through, and they should become more involved in the domestic planning and implementation of Britain's overseas industrial objectives. Such a changed role would naturally require considerable changes in the training of diplomats. The Overseas Development Administration would also need representation on the industrial policy committee. The competitive use which the ODA makes of its budget for mixed credit (the Aid Trade

Provision) and the importance of its decisions for British businesses, make the closest liaison with the DTI essential.

No one can say with assurance what trends will be dominant in twenty or even ten years' time, given the shortening life-cycle of many high technology products. But the evidence is that there will be continuing development and growth in, for instance, aerospace, robotics, telecommunications and biotechnology. These are all areas which Britain's competitor governments are supporting. Government and industry in Britain must talk together about what markets exist, could be created or are under threat. They must consider if either or both, alone or together, can achieve more, and if so, how.

The Government has long since accepted the principle of such behaviour with its support from public funds for microprocessors, information technology and other innovative projects. The novelty would lie in applying the principle rationally and on a scale comparable with the efforts of our competitors.

I talk of a forum, not of controls; of an intelligent partnership of national self-interest, not of rigidity or bureaucracy. If British standard measurements of quality are too low for world markets, is the remedy in the hands of industry alone, from a background of minimal standards? Or should British governments lead their companies, as the German government does by the centrally-imposed DIN standards system? If our marketing is indifferent, should more university or polytechnic courses in marketing be encouraged? If a major strategic company is ailing, should shareholders act sooner or leave it to government to be forced to act later? Should the private sector be encouraged to follow the government's lead in import substitution? Some, like Marks and Spencer, do. Should someone ask the others?

The rapidity of technological change argues that British manufacturers, although left behind in some fields, may be able to start on even terms with new inventions and applications. You can never be counted out of a race with no end. Britain's geographical position and the liberalisation by the Conservatives of the telecommunications market are promoting rapid expansion of that industry. Both our geographical position in relation to the continent of Europe and our language have made us attractive as a point of entry for inward investment to the European Community.

My second change would be to make the Secretary of State for Trade and Industry chairman of NEDO in place of the Chancellor of the Exchequer; and my third change would be to carry through to NEDO's sector working parties appointments of those who could reasonably speak for the interests of owners, in addition to the managers, trade unionists and civil servants who at present attend.

These two steps would be complementary. NEDO's potential value is high, as the one forum where ministers regularly meet senior representatives of industry, the unions and the City. So long as the Chancellor is in the chair the monthly discussions of the NEDO council reflect the Treasury preoccupation. In his person the Treasury opens and closes each discussion. Other ministers present are politically acute enough to know that any broadening of the debate in the semi-public theatre of the council, the least deviance from the Treasury line, will be reported as a split in government ranks. Like most formal discussions, the proceedings are for the most part prodigal of the valuable time of the busy people who attend.

The organisation needs more of the language of the factory floor and less of that of the Treasury. The Secretary of State for Industry, with the more specific remit that I have outlined, would use the council much more to give purpose and consistency to the grassroots activities of the sector working parties.

If government showed that its policies might be affected by these deliberations they would assume an importance to the industries concerned. It is a question of leadership: if government were seen to be ready to listen and respond, the word would quickly spread and the exchanges would increase in value. The Ministry of Defence is a huge customer. I found as Secretary of State what I expected, that it has no difficulty in holding constructive discussions with captains of the defence industries. The benefits of these to the national economy are immense. In the negotiations over the European Fighter Aircraft, or the SDI contracts or the sale of Tornados to Saudi Arabia, the contribution of the industrialists and the partnership of national interest represented by them and the Ministry were crucial in the outcome of contracts which may prove to be among the most valuable that Britain has ever concluded.

As Secretary of State for the Environment, I was the first minister ever to go to a sector working party of NEDO – that dealing with the construction industry which my department sponsored. It says something about the willingness of government to use this machinery that this first visit took place some twenty years after the organisation had been set up. I found a forum to which both sides of industry habitually came to complain to the attending civil servants in language which placed the blame for everything that went wrong on government, and never seriously considered any change from within the industry itself. The official was not empowered to conduct fruitful discussion. He recorded the complaints. I never discovered if the record itself was ever read. After all, the complaints had been read the same day in the national press.

Since then, encouraged by Geoffrey Howe, the sector working parties have steadily grown more useful. Not all of them, but several, with Government encouragement, have begun to tackle some of the more difficult questions in their sectors of industry. It is another example of where the rhetoric of market forces is belied by the conduct of a Government that has forged in some areas an increasingly close relationship with industry. I advocate, therefore, a policy that is not revolutionary but evolutionary. There is no time for cosy chats between businessmen and ministers, nor for institutionalised talks which descend to banality or to special pleading. There is time and need for dialogue which both sides take seriously, where ministers will show no patience for self-seeking supplicants, where civil servants have the training and instinct to do more than take notes and pass on the complaints. As others have said, action must be on the agenda.

The weakness of the Government's dealings with industry is by no means the result only of the structure of power in Whitehall. Ministers know little about industry, since only a minority in any administration, and only a minority of MPs, have had industrial experience. Their officials have probably had less. Such knowledge as government possesses is lopsided. The position of government departments as sponsoring departments for nationalised industries gives ministers and officials particular knowledge of the State sector but relatively little of the private. It gives the publicly-owned industries an insider's start in Whitehall. Discussions within successive governments about the future of the steel industry, for instance, are held on the basis of fairly full information about the needs of British Steel but little about the difficulties or potential of the private steelmakers. How is this to be put right without the same quality of dialogue which every nationalised industry enjoys? A first step would be to divide, within the newly-structured Department of Trade and Industry, its sponsorship of any publicly-owned industry from its strategic role, so that there was no conscious or unconscious bias towards the public sector. As privatisation proceeds this problem declines.

Opportunities for anyone while serving in government to have other than superficial contacts with industry while serving in government are few. Ignorance in government of the views and needs of those who work in industry is therefore great and can turn to impatience and sometimes disdain.

The ignorance is usually mutual, and the disdain not unnaturally reciprocated. Sir Geoffrey Chandler, the former Director-General of NEDO, has recalled that there were occasions in the heyday of the Government's medium-term financial strategy when Treasury officials, sent by ministers to lecture senior managers, caused exasperation not only because of the inflexibility of the message they were asked to deliver but because their inexperience of industry disqualified them from grasping the equally forceful messages which their audience gave them to take back to Whitehall.

If there is a case, as I have argued, for some organisational change in government, to promote a more effective partnership with British business, there is also a case for business to reconsider with urgency whether it can better organise itself to the same end. I believe that British business, by pooling its strength, could do more both for itself and for the country.

At national level it is the Confederation of British Industry which most clearly articulates the views of business, although the Institute of Directors has sometimes appeared to speak more clearly for the entrepreneur. Their voice is not always heard, however, at constituency level.

When I first took an interest in our Chambers of Commerce, the impact of most of them on the political climate in the towns and cities where they were based was minimal. There were exceptions, but most had lost their former importance in their communities. It is different today, and there is a wider understanding of the need for business to make its voice heard.

Serious consideration was given in 1971 to a merger between the CBI, with its primarily national structure, and the Chambers with their separate local roots under their central umbrella, the Association of British Chambers of Commerce (ABCC). A committee under Lord Devlin recommended that they should merge but the advice was not taken. It is for the organisations themselves to decide whether by coming together they would make the voice of business clearer and more persuasive, and my guess is that they will remain apart, more anxious to retain their distinct traditions than to make common cause. That is the easy thing to do, and their doubts are understandable. There are dangers in over-centralisation and in rigid structures that may not suit the great variety of businesses in the country, large and small.

A possible pattern for rationalisation that seems much more attractive would be adaptation of the structure that exists in many Continental countries. Every EEC country except for Belgium and Ireland bestows public law status on its chambers of commerce. Each is required to act on behalf of all enterprises within its locality and all companies are required to join. The collective voice of business is thus regionally and sectorally representative and so the more powerful in its dealing with government. In return for State funding, through a special tax mechanism, the chambers provide a number of facilities for local business, in such matters as apprentice training, aspects of vocational education, technical counselling, or legal advice.

The constant increase in business activity across the frontiers of Europe also argues strongly for the development of powerful local chambers which can reach beyond regional and national boundaries. A number of Continental chambers have recognised that Brussels is an increasingly important source of funding and have opened offices there.

Once the concept of powerful local chambers is accepted, a new horizon opens up. Chambers of commerce could usefully play a more important role in training. The Manpower Services Commission now gives dedicated leadership in the training and educational field, but it is virtually all publicly financed and organised. On the Continent this is not so, and I am a convinced advocate of private sector activity in training as in much else.

Many activities vital to wealth-creation – such as small firms' consultancy services or export advisory services – are provided by the public sector; yet the people who need and use these services could organise them more effectively themselves and adapt them to their own purposes. This should not require extra money: companies already pay for these services through existing taxation.

The initial growth of the enterprise agencies, which I describe later, owed much to the ministers and officials from the Department of the Environment. My colleagues and I went from place to place urging industrial and commercial managers to come and help. The response was magnificent but the initiative should have come not from government ministers but from the business community. The chambers are now deeply involved, and we could build on this.

There could be great gains if every local wealth-creating community formed the habit of self-help and self-improvement. What the enterprise agencies are doing for small firms, a more ambitious programme could do for a great number of medium-sized businesses. Management and marketing standards are often low and recruitment and training programmes too unambitious. Import substitution, 'can-you-make-it' conferences, an environment in which local businesses joined to create opportunities instead of complaining about difficulties, could all be promoted by representative local bodies to the nation's great advantage.

One damaging consequence of the present gulf between the Government's two principal economic departments helps to maintain the debilitating division between the owners and the managers of business, who show a reluctance to talk to one another and an inability to understand one another which again seems unique to Britain. Dialogue goes on between the Treasury and the owners of capital, who are today found mainly in the City of London. A separate dialogue goes on between the DTI and other departments, and the managers of British industry. So long as the Treasury talks to the City about maximising its returns and about taking a world view of investment opportunities, without concern for the consequences for domestic activity and employment, this will continue to foster an attitude among the owners of wealth which is unlike that found in most of the capitalist economies with which we have to compete. Advancement of the DTI to become the Government's main arm of industrial policy would act to draw closer these two essential partners in industrial success, the owners and the managers.

There are no absolutes. Many financial institutions take an interest in companies in which they have shares, but it is not the norm and it is little co-ordinated. The norm is to see investment as simply a decision which can be reversed as quickly as it is made. The relationship which in a successful capitalist economy would be built up between owners, managers and the workforce is simply not there and is hardly understood. Managers are expected to take long-term decisions about investment without being able to count on anything but the short-term commitment of those who own the companies they manage. Managers must decide on the level of research and training to sustain the worth of the company tomorrow: owners can prefer the attraction of takeover bids which offer higher share prices by maximising profits in the short term.

Through two decades of weak investment in the British manufacturing industry the City institutions have steadily claimed that there was no shortage of available funds, while industry has reproached the City for being unwilling to lend long-term or to put money into new ventures, and has said that this creates difficulties for British manufacturers which their overseas rivals do not encounter. Both sides in this dispute are right. The difficulty is institutional: because banks cannot hold shares in companies, companies are forced to depend on costly short-term money, unlike their counterparts in West Germany or Japan.

There must be more effective dialogue. From owners we need commitment to the maintenance of quality in management and to the long-term success of the companies they own. The best entrepreneurial capitalist, if things go wrong, fights. Of course the right to sell is there and must remain; but the first instinct is to fight. Management in Britain has a legitimate anxiety that the owner today can be tempted too easily to sell. The dangers are clear. A short-term interest by shareholders in the balance sheet and the profit-and-loss account forces companies to prune expenditure for short-term purposes. Research and training, both vital, are at risk when managements are apprehensive of the takeover bid.

Institutional wealth, with its continued growth, has led to ever larger parts of British industry and commerce becoming the property of remote shareholders. The danger is that there will be a simultaneous growth in the industrial weaknesses and social ills to which the remoteness of a proprietor will always give rise. Where managers have only tenuous relationships with owners, where there is little commitment or understanding, how can managers know if they should maximise profits today and whistle for tomorrow? Do they look after the workforce, or do they send them down the street?

It is a legitimate criticism of our institutional shareholders that they have devised no adequate mechanisms to fill this vacuum, and it is unwise of them to tempt governments to fill it. In one respect the recent reputation of some parts of the City of London leaves them less time than they may imagine, and I would urge them to respond to the concern both of managers and of the public by creating their own machinery, to consider and express the wider national interest in a stable and productive pattern of investment.

Until they do, government should be more prepared to refer takeover bids to the Monopolies and Mergers Commission. Sir Gordon Borrie, the Director General of the Office of Fair Trading, has made the important suggestion that, at least where mergers above a certain size are proposed, the bidding company should be required to show that the takeover would have positive benefits in a wider national interest. He is right. The present criteria for reference to the Monopolies and Mergers Commission are concerned too narrowly with competition. The law provides for a wider reference.

In the world of business, auditors report to the shareholders, but they are effectively appointed by directors. No firm of accountants wants the reputation of being troublemakers. Some have to be pushed to a point where concern is acute before they will qualify a firm's accounts or take any action that might upset those upon whose goodwill they ultimately depend. I believe that healthier businesses might be promoted and the shareholders' interests safeguarded if an independent organisation, which the institutional shareholders could establish for their general benefit, were charged with appointing auditors to all publicly quoted companies. An alternative would be for boards to appoint auditors who, however, once appointed, would be responsible only to such an independent body and could be dismissed only by it.

Such an organisation would fill the need felt by our industrial managers for a forum with which to communicate. Ideally it would emerge from an awareness in the City of London that there are responsibilities arising from ownership which can only be exercised if shareholders have some means of combining to express a general view about their companies.

Another variant on the same theme would be the creation by statute of audit committees for public companies which would contain representatives of the companies' shareholders.

I would make one further suggestion in this field. Auditors at present are in a position to recommend management studies and have a very realistic chance that the work will come their way. Accountancy firms which also offer management consultancy, which is an increasingly valued and profitable growth area in the commercial world, ought I believe to be debarred from doing any other work for a company for which they act as auditors. In a number of other countries there are laws which circumscribe auditors in this way to prevent any possible conflict of interest. For the same reason in the United Kingdom the auditors of many public sector organisations are not permitted to offer other services to their audit clients. This discipline should be extended across the publicly-quoted private sector.

In the crucially important area of investment business, I believe that the Government is fighting a rearguard action to preserve self-regulation, and that the fight is not worth winning. I do not think that a British equivalent of America's Securities and Exchange Commission would prevent fraud. The Boesky scandal occurred in spite of the tightness of regulation in the United States. In Britain, the Lynskey tribunal of the 1940s uncovered corruption which had tainted goverment ministers. There will always be human villainy and frailty. But there is nothing to be gained by appearing to baulk at applying the utmost rigour if in the end, as I believe, a statutory machinery of regulation will alone meet public and political expectations. A Conservative Government would construct such machinery with the care it demands, and would be wise not to leave the task to the brutal relish of a government with a different set of motives.

There is yet another dialogue and partnership which is as crucial as any to the success of a business, but which too many businesses neglect. We must persuade British managers and their employees to strive for a closer and more profitable relationship. There are three obvious ways to promote this. The first is by schemes for profit-sharing or share ownership. Significant progress has been made in the incentives for such schemes and in the number of such schemes in existence. We should build on this.

One important area in which employees should be more directly concerned is over the control of their pension funds. In many good British companies employee representatives are appointed to the boards of pension funds. It would now be right to introduce a code of practice whereby employee representatives were elected by right to the boards of pension funds.

There is also the wider field of employee involvement in companies. I do not expect to see again a government elected in Britain on a mandate to put power back in the hands of the union boss at the expense of the union member, but in the recent past union leaders acquired their strength in part by filling the vacuum created by the absence of dialogue in industry with effective managers. The British people can work together and excel. As Secretary of State for Defence, I learned that our armed forces are the equal of any in the world not least because they understand the need to engage the foot-soldier, the aircraft mechanic and the ordinary seaman in a dialogue which explains what is happening and what is expected of them. You cannot translate a military environment to the shop floor, but the best British companies have maintained a quality of relationship which enriches the life and performance of the company, earns the loyalty of its workforce and enlists its support. The CBI has long urged that the laggards among British companies should catch up with the best.

Progress has undoubtedly been made, but it has been too slow; and if we are going to complete our conversion to an efficient entrepreneurial and capitalist society then the understanding of its advantages and disciplines by those who work in industry at every level is vital. The Labour Party still rejoices in its socialism. An understanding of socialism's emptiness and of capitalism's true potential begins on the factory floor. I would advocate legislation setting out a code of practice whereby publicly-quoted companies employing more than, say, 500 people would be expected to conduct a dialogue with their workforce. They could choose their own methods, but the aim would be to promote the highest standards of modern communication.

I would not try to put too precise rules into legislation. The mere existence of a requirement to report in the annual accounts the nature and scale of the internal dialogue would focus the attention of workforce, managers and shareholders on those companies which neglected this element of their duty and self-interest.

Good managers are already far ahead of anything that such a code of practice would contain. From the indifferent and bad managers there will be protests against interference and intervention. Governments are entitled to intervene to prevent social abuses or malpractices. Conservative governments have a special interest and duty to prevent abuses of the capitalist system which tend to bring that system into disrepute. We cannot afford to wait for the highest standards of employee relations to be imported with foreign control of British companies. What the Japanese will bring with Nissan to the North-east, British managers have got to bring to the West Midlands.

For all these reasons I urge the wholehearted recognition of the need for and the adoption of a British industrial strategy. Today separate pieces of policy dot the industrial landscape, some quite large and marked by flags, like regional development and innovation grants; and some small pots of subsidy money, half-hidden and often half-empty, like the Coal-Firing Scheme or the Small Engineering Firms Assistance Scheme. No government department is able to produce an exhaustive list of support schemes. The complete picture is known only to a few specialist academics and one or two top firms of management consultants or accountants. Different schemes spring up, mutate and die according to political pressures, to sudden crises or enthusiasms. Their life-cycles testify to the British genius for improvisation and a reluctance to anticipate even if it bears on the survival of our industry and the maintenance of our living standards.

It is time for the Government to thrust aside the notion that British government and industry can live at arm's length, like neighbours who cannot remember whether they have been introduced, and still remain secure in this rough world.

The present Government, like its predecessors, has for several years been doing what it knows it must do to help British business in those ways which are open only to government. It pays out large sums for research and development, although these should be larger; it helps small firms with start-up funds; it pays for industrial training through the Manpower Services Commission; it underwrites export credit. Sometimes a minister will make much of this support. More often the message is that we do not really need an industrial policy.

A year or two ago the Chancellor of the Exchequer offered the House of Lords the Government's opinion: 'It is industry's job to make itself competitive.' So it is, but the implication that it is not also in part the Government's no longer carries conviction.

6

Cities In Crisis: The Lessons Of Mersyside

An opposition must be alert to see that the great power of central government is not abused. A government has a different preoccupation; when to assert and when to withhold the power which it has been given to use for the public good.

Central and local government will similarly tend to have opposing views, especially when divided by party differences, of when the centre is entitled to take charge. Any minister who has had responsibility for an area of policy in which local government is well placed to resist him – such as education or housing, or the level of rate support – must have felt a twinge of sympathy for the Emperor Caligula's wish that all his enemies had but one neck.

When we created the first urban development corporations I was responsible as Secretary of State for the Environment for creating new centres of power to do what clearly needed doing but was equally clearly beyond the competence of the existing public authorities. I have no doubt that it was a necessary step.

Harold Macmillan told me that he approved of the UDCs, but he also thought it as well to repeat to me that sound political advice: 'Always consider the use that others will make of the powers with which you ask Parliament to entrust you.'

The maxim is wise, and the thought is never far from any politician's mind. Indeed mistrust of a shadowy successor government is a valuable restraint on any minister who may be tempted to make arrogant use of the strength which a parliamentary majority gives him. It may therefore be a healthy uneasiness; but it is also often a disturbing one, and it is continually roused by the deteriorating relationship between central and local government today.

Parliament cannot be equated with local government. Democratic accountability lies in Parliament, from which all the authority exercised at local level is derived. Central government is thus entitled, and seldom hesitates, to change local government's boundaries, powers and duties, to extend them or remove them, if it suits its purpose. Labour imposed comprehensive education; the present Government sold the council houses. But out of public view, beneath those head-line events, the supposed freedom of local government is minutely circumscribed, at least in theory, to a degree which astonished me when I became Secretary of State for the Environment. Through its manipulation of the controls on capital spending, central government has great power.

I found that the systems of control were suffocating; no brick in any plan could be laid in any local authority housing scheme which the regional officers of the department had not approved. It should be stressed that this power was negative. We could stop almost anything from being done; we could seldom enforce or require any positive action to raise standards or to improve performance. I sent for one of each of the forms we used, and had them stuck up on my wall to survey their full horror. Then we scrapped the lot, and brought in a simpler system.

Parliament is the centre of our democracy, but that does not argue for tightly centralised control. Conservatives distrust the concentration of power, both on principle and – as I have hinted – on the practical ground that it is just conceivable that the Conservative Party will not stay in unin-terrupted power, shall we say, beyond the end of the century.

There is, as I have said, an urgent need to improve the quality of public service in our country, at all levels. The majority of councillors and officials in local government know this, but not all; and the exceptions are increasingly found in the more deprived and distressed parts of our country. The loony Left in the town halls is a headache for Labour, and may indeed prove to be a fatal headache; for a Conservative government which believes in distributing power away from Whitehall, its activities create a quandary.

There seem to me to be four choices. We can stand apart

and let the deteriorating conditions worsen. We can move power back from local to national government. We can reorganise the electoral boundaries so that the irresponsible Left loses its tight inner urban constituencies. We can push power out beyond local government and into the hands of the people whom it is elected to serve. I prefer the last.

We cannot do nothing. No government can absolve itself from its responsibility for policy, or allow its plans for education or housing, covered by manifesto commitments, and endorsed by the country, to be maladministered or frustrated by local authorities. It has a clear duty to prevent local government, by the aggregation of the borrowings of scores of councils, from upsetting its economic management. There can be only one Chancellor of the Exchequer. Above all there is an obligation to intervene where a local authority's performance prejudices social conditions, the local economy or the stability of local industry. Central government must ensure that local authorities deliver adequate local services, and do not indulge in conspicuous waste and extravagance in order to provoke political confrontation with central government.

If we take powers away from local authorities and exercise them centrally, we invite the danger which Macmillan foresaw. Besides, there is no evidence that central government is more efficient than local. The public do not believe it, and more and more the courts tend to side in judicial review with the Davids who challenge the central government Goliath. While wealth and power continue to move towards London and Brussels, we should take care before we weaken any institution which resists this movement. The 400 authorities presided over by 20,000 councillors are a powerful, even if erratic and sometimes perverse, brake on the ambitions of central government. It is no bad thing.

The alternative which naturally appeals to Tory principles is to make local power more local still, by pushing it out to the people. It answers to Conservative instinct, and it fits with so much of what the present Government is doing. In much of what follows, this thinking will appear.

If housing estates are badly run, the cure is to give the tenants themselves more power. If public servants waste public money, let the private sector be called in to compete in saving it, while giving better service. If local authorities provide indifferent education, give more authority to schools and more influence to the parents as representatives of the pupils' needs.

When we created the first urban development corporations we had no doubt that this was an instance where there was a clear duty for the Government to assert itself, and use its greater power to do what had proved to be beyond local government's power. We did not, however, take any extra power into central government's hands. Drawing on the precedent of the New Town corporations, we took care to secure proper representation of local government on the new boards, as well as private sector representation.

My first encounter with urban decay on the grand scale was a view from an aircraft over the Thames below Tower Bridge in 1973. As a junior minister in Edward Heath's Government I had been responsible for the implementation of the proposal to put a third airport for London on the Maplin sands in the Thames estuary. I visited Maplin several times, often flying over East London.

At first I could not believe what I saw. The route downriver traversed some of the most valuable acreage in the world. Yet pressing close against the clamour of the City's square mile lay the emptiness and hopelessness of hundreds of acres of deserted docks, wharves and warehouses.

I should not have been taken so completely by surprise at what must have been painfully familiar to thousands of Londoners. But London docklands are out of sight of Westminster, except from the top of Big Ben, where few of us venture.

I could not understand how anybody could allow such desolation. There were all kinds of committees, reports, discussions, but beneath me stretched this appalling proof that no one was doing anything effective. The warring factions in local government and the nationalised industries had not the resources or the powers, even if they had the will, to apply themselves to the enormous task before them. Everyone was involved. No one was in charge. No structure existed where decisions could be taken instead of referred somewhere else for yet more consultation.

The shock of what I saw planted the first seeds that by 1979, when I became Secretary of State for the Environment, had grown into a conviction that we must find constructive solutions. As it happened, there was a secondary but important motivation, which first possessed me a year or two earlier. In 1970, I had had planning responsibilities as a parliamentary under-secretary, under Graham Page, which helped to open my eyes to a different sort of waste and impoverishment in the heart of London. It troubled me that so much new building along the river was of indifferent design and unworthy of the splendour of its site.

The Shell buildings beside Waterloo station seemed to be a typical product of the bureaucratic architecture which knows how to squeeze every last foot of floor area and pound of rental value from a site without regard to aesthetics. Our planning system encourages such mistakes. Just as the Englishman's home is his castle so his back garden is his development site. Planning permissions are granted or rejected for proposals that arise from ownership of land by companies or individuals. Very rarely does the public interest lay down standards for the development of a significant area. By and large we have left our most prominent sites to patchwork development, so that twentieth century urban Britain has little to show of scale or imagination. Many cities now show how thoroughly architects learned that their bread was buttered by impatient developers anxious to move on.

I told my officials that I could see no chance for imaginative design if it depended on the aesthetic values of property developers, with two tiers of local authority competing to impose a drab conformity under the disciplines of plot ratios. I argued for a single planning authority to take responsibility for the development of the banks of the Thames. My officials were receptive and did preparatory work on the framework of legislation. When I left the Department of the Environment in 1972 my hopes for the banks of the Thames were left behind. I could not have known then that I was to get a second chance.

In 1979, to my great good fortune, I took charge of the Department of the Environment, and one of the first things I asked the permanent under-secretary, Sir John Garlick, to do was to establish the means, through legislation, to create

The slaughter of over 60 of a department's quangos does not pass unnoticed

urban development authorities. I wanted them to have the same powers as the New Town corporations which, though successes in their own right, had drained away so much of the life of the old cities. In East London, the destructive work first of the Luftwaffe, then of the container revolution in shipping and of local councils without imagination, had created an opportunity that demanded action. The East End London boroughs had concentrated almost exclusively on the provision of public housing. As new generations grew up, often skilled and ambitious, their desire to own their own homes was just one more reason to leave the monolithic housing estates for suburban Britain.

In 1979 my concern was with London's East End. I had seen it. The Urban Development Corporation was designed to bring it back to life. Among many arguments deployed to prevent the establishment of such an instrument was that it would never reach the statute book because a proposal specific to London would need 'hybrid' legislation – a discriminatory measure which would give every private interest affected by it the right to petition Parliament. The delay can be interminable. There was a way through: we took general legislative powers to create urban development corporations in declining urban areas.

London's docklands were the first choice and the second corporation was established in one of the most acute areas of urban deprivation – Liverpool. My proposals still had a rough ride. For one thing, they offended against our commitment to the slaughter of quangos, although, when it came to quango-hunting, I was already up with the leaders. For another, the Treasury perceived a wide opening for additional public expenditure. The Prime Minister, however, overruled objections, sharing my view that the dead hand of Socialism should be lifted.

Our intention was to provide in two inner city areas of greatest need, along the Thames and the Mersey, the sinews to recreate the environment, the opportunities and incentives for reconstruction which had been so unhappily destroyed.

The London Docklands Development Corporation was to encompass 6,000 acres of land on both banks of the lower Thames; while Merseyside Docklands Corporation took in nearly 900 acres of polluted wasteland in the heart of one of Britain's great nineteenth-century cities. We also included two smaller sites in Birkenhead and Bootle. They were to have the powers, with the financial resources provided by central government, to own and acquire land, build factories, and invest in both infrastructure and environment so as to attract industry and commercial and residential development. They were to exercise planning powers. In all practical senses they were to be New Town corporations in old cities. The wheel had turned full circle.

Although neither body came formally into being until 1981, preparations began in 1979, two years before the serious rioting of July 1981 in London, Liverpool, Manchester and elsewhere alerted the country to some of the grave consequences of the long neglect of the cities.

Merseyside and its difficulties first claimed my attention when I took on the chairmanship of the Liverpool Inner City Partnership, one of the special instruments created by my Labour predecessor as Secretary of State, Peter Shore, for co-ordinating the use of central government funds in seven areas of exceptional need.

Each of these seven partnerships was to be chaired by a minister from the department. I chose Liverpool for myself because it looked likely to prove the most challenging. It was. The once-flourishing port for transatlantic shipping had found itself on the wrong side of Britain as trade with continental Europe grew, passenger liners gave way to aircraft, the unions obstructed every change, the southern ports offered generous discounts and the container revolution swept the

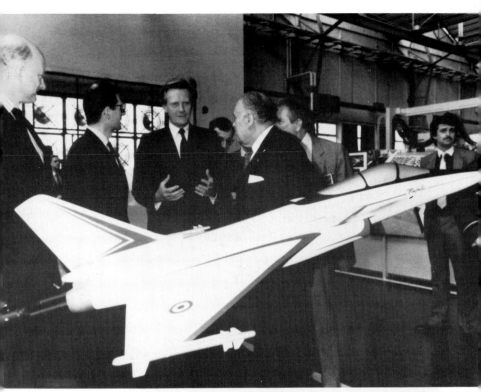

In an attempt to persuade the French to join the European Fighter Aircraft project on 2 April 1985 I visited the headquarters of Dassault. An ingenious local photographer portrays the British Defence Minister alongside the French alternative prototype

A visit to British Aerospace at Wharton enabled me to see the British prototype. Britain later successfully concluded the largest deal into which she had ever entered when we agreed with Germany, Italy and Spain to build a European fighter aircraft to enter service with all four airforces in the 1990s

Left:
With Cap Weinberger,
Defence Secretary of
our strongest ally, dur-
ing a Defence Planning
Committee meeting at
the Nato HQ in Brus-
sels

Below:
London, 26 September
1985: signing the
agreement to provide
Tornado and Hawk
aircraft to Saudi
Arabia — the largest
export order ever con-
cluded for a European
product

Below right:
Manchester Universi-
ty, November 1983: the
defence case had to be
heard, whatever the
difficulties, but it had
its lighter moments

Above:
Tri-service dinner, 12 July 1984, Royal Naval College, Greenwich, with (left to right): Back Row: Major General Jeremy Rougier, Lieutenant General Sir Michael Williams, Lieutenant General Patrick Palmer, Air Vice Marshal Anthony Skingsley, Rear Admiral Robert Gerken, Air Vice Marshal David Spottiswood
Front Row: Air Chief Marshal Sir Keith Williamson, Admiral Sir John Fieldhouse, Field Marshal Sir Edwin Bramell, myself, Captain Michael Pentreath, General Sir John Stanier, Vice Admiral Sir Peter Herbert

Visiting the Royal Highland Fusiliers on duty in Northern Ireland on 4 May, 1983
Below:
20 April 1983: flying the Hawk added a new dimension to my interest in ornithology

February 1984: laying a wreath in memory of those Welsh guardsmen killed in action in the Falkland Islands

shipping world. In the 1960s and 1970s it had lost a third of its inhabitants, and of those who remained 18 per cent were unemployed. This figure hid huge variations within the conurbation: of young blacks in Toxteth, 60 per cent were without jobs. The image built on the industrial relations record of two industries, the port and car production, frightened potential investors.

Liverpool contained some of the worst housing in the country: terraces built in the last century and dying of old age, and flats built less than twenty years ago which were already slums that defy description. Yet so great had been the cost of this recent building that the city had to levy, and often failed to collect, the highest municipal rents in Britain to meet the interest charges in the housing revenue accounts.

It was my responsibility to convince my colleagues in Cabinet of the true significance and extent of the multiple deprivation which my departmental ministers and I were able to study in the seven inner city partnerships, and to advise them on how it should be tackled. The seven, then as now, were Birmingham, Liverpool, Manchester/Salford, Newcastle/Gateshead, Hackney, Lambeth and Islington. They suffered and still do from wretched physical conditions and bad housing; from persistent long-term unemployment aggravated by low educational attainment and non-existent, outdated or unwanted skills. With the exception of the North-east they also had immigrant communities which had their own specific problems. Most of these cities suffered from a continuing loss of their vigorous populations and a relative increase in the numbers of dependent people leading cramped and difficult lives.

It was clear that we would have to rouse ourselves to offer new hope and opportunity instead of the palliatives being provided out of a thin trickle of taxpayers' money. I found in Liverpool, as my colleagues in the department found elsewhere, that whatever Peter Shore's intention, the concept of partnerships had brought little change. The partnership committees met to decide how to spend the funds. Government and local government representatives, members of health authorities and others all put in their bids, and any project which had been squeezed out of the main programme was squeezed back in again. If the building of a health centre or the resurfacing of a playground looked like being postponed, the partnership funds would revive it. The private sector remained shut out. It was a classic example of just throwing more public money at a problem without any attempt to address the problem itself. No serious analysis existed as to why the problem was so acute. Little awareness was shown of the need to rebuild balanced, socially mixed communities. The effect was likely to prove minimal, with the benefit restricted almost entirely to the local interest groups. It was clear that the right use of the extra funding would be not only to help the existing community but also to entice back, by improving the fabric and commercial environment, the more enterprising or fortunate who had left town and taken their skills and energy with them.

We set a new objective: to make the inner cities places where people would want to live and work and where the private investor would be willing to put his money. There would have to be greater reliance on private initiative and voluntary agencies; and people would not look to central government, as Labour had encouraged and continues to encourage them to do, to carry the whole burden.

The movement back into the cities began, and was led by the building of the first houses for sale in the depressed inner districts. As I write, some 2,000 houses a year are being built and bought by people in the London docklands area, which is a higher annual figure than the total number built there in the whole of the 36-year period between the ending of the war and the birth of the development corporation. This acted and is still acting as a magnet for those inclined to return as well as an incentive to others to stay. Those who did well in the cities and looked for houses to buy were now to have a choice between moving to the suburbs, which in the recent past might have seemed the only possible course, or putting down deeper roots in their communities by buying homes near their places of work. At last the successful were being courted, not driven away. Labour, of course, carped at the success of what we were doing, by referring to the 'gentrific-ation' of these areas – forgetting that some of the areas of greatest need (Brixton, for example) had once been favoured places in which to live and work, and stood every chance of being restored to economic health.

Then came the riots and with them my first opportunity of prolonged exposure to the needs of Merseyside. The riots in the summer of 1981, after the Bristol riots a year earlier, shocked the British people and Government. Riots are not an unknown feature of British history, as any minister who works in Whitehall may be readily reminded: the railings outside Admiralty House were put there to frustrate the mob's impatience with the authorities when ships of the Royal Navy failed to come home. It was 150 years since Bristol was set on fire during the Reform Bill riots; and 200 years since the Gordon rioters burned down 70 houses and four gaols in London. But memories are not that long.

The inner city riots of the early eighties took almost everyone by surprise. Politicians live very much for the day. Yesterday has gone and tomorrow can with luck be put off. The priority forty, thirty or even twenty years ago was to clear the slums. Few recognised the nature of the forces that were to bring a slide into physical and social collapse in too many cities.

Five years after the disturbances it seems to me that we do understand more clearly the causes but we have not addressed the dimensions of this collapse. I see no evidence that a response is being prepared on anything like the scale which will soon be demanded.

As the head of the government department most in the firing line I knew it would not be enough simply to call for reports and then propose some initiative without seeing for myself and making my own assessment, with all the first-hand evidence I could gather, of what had gone wrong and what the next steps should be.

As chairman of the partnership authority I already had some knowledge and, let me say it, some responsibility. I suggested to the Prime Minister that I should take three weeks off from other duties to go and talk, listen and become immersed in the problems of Merseyside.

Merseyside supplied me with one of those priceless forma-tive experiences from which every politician takes strength; it tested many of my deepest political beliefs and instincts and intensified my convictions. I dealt with six local authorities: a Labour metropolitan county, and two Conservative, two Labour and one Liberal metropolitan districts. They covered a conurbation that represents a social horizon of wealth and poverty as stark as anywhere in our country today.

Industrial excellence at the forefront of our technology thrives in a city the heart of which is haunted by derelict docks and by pollution in the river Mersey of a degree that would never be tolerated in the South of England. The comfortable rural fringes of north Cheshire and south Lancashire hem in a community whose post-war, public sector slums of Everton, Knowsley and a dozen others are a scandal of modern times.

I saw how an urban population can sink to a state where its political leadership is either impotent or predatory; but I also saw how swiftly life and hope can revive when the acrimonious dialogue of the deaf is replaced by constructive partnership between the agencies of government and the managers of capitalism, harnessed to the aspirations and energies of the communities concerned.

What I learned did not change my beliefs or approach, but it showed me how quickly we had to act and it greatly sharpened my appreciation of the scale and nature of the human and social crises with which the inner cities were struggling.

Any politician knows that you only have to go somewhere where there is trouble and say, 'I've come to look' and the first question from the hordes of journalists who emerge to watch you is: 'What are you going to do?' I knew that if, at the end of three weeks, I went away and said, 'Nothing' or 'I don't know' or 'I'll let you know' there would be no second chance. I would have missed what might be my one opportunity of galvanising those with the capacity to help put things right.

By descending on Liverpool at such a moment I was taking some political risk. More seriously, I risked further damaging the morale of local people by possibly raising and then dashing expectations that something might be done to help their city.

We had been in Liverpool for perhaps a week when I could no longer escape the dilemma of my own philosophical convictions. I had listened at great length to those arguing for this or that public sector initiative, for more government money. But I was all too aware that there had been government money. Indeed the assumption of it created a climate which compounded the problem. What had happened to this great city? What had happened to provincial Britain, to the modern inheritors of the energy and initiative of those who only a century before had stamped their names and their achievements indelibly onto their communities?

The top people, the decision makers, were not there. There were local bank, insurance and building society managers but virtually all of them were many rungs down the ladders of power which led to distant boardrooms. There were the names of national and international companies, but these were managers, no longer owners. I had to get hold of the chairmen and chief executives before anything would happen.

I said to my private secretary, 'Look, I think we must try and get some of the big boys up here.' There was a moment's pause before my civil servants said: 'Yes, Secretary of State.' Then they asked: 'How do you do that? Do you know any of them?'

I said that I thought I knew one or two, but asked for a list of the 30 biggest institutions – clearing banks, insurance companies, building societies and pension funds. This was done at once. It proved to be the easiest part of the exercise. 'What do we do next?' I was asked.

I said 'You must ring them up. We haven't time to mess about. If you write them letters they will all be away. Get them on the phone.' So the telephoning began.

The first day was a disaster. 'Who did you say you were? Merseyside? Liverpool? Secretary of State for the Environment? We only talk to the Treasury. It's nothing to do with us. It's a long way away.' Everyone was busy or away or on holiday. No one was available. So were we about to meet big success or big failure? There did not seem much doubt.

After three days they told me, 'We have two.' But by the end of the fourth day we had perhaps twelve responses, and the next day fifteen. On the sixth day the telephone rang and a voice said: 'I am so-and-so's personal assistant. We are one of the most important companies in the commercial field in this country. We have heard that you have a busload of our colleagues coming to Liverpool and you have invited six of our competitors. Our chairman was just wondering why these particular people had been selected.' We said, 'We'll ring you back.' We filled our bus. The sudden change of mood, I discovered later, began when my PPS, Tim Sainsbury, spoke to Robin Leigh-Pemberton, now Governor of the Bank of England, then chairman of National Westminster Bank. He at once said he would join us, and the word then spread.

Then followed the most extraordinary experience. I still had no idea what I had started or what would happen. I had persuaded a lot of extremely important and powerful people from the City of London, few of whom I had ever met, to come and let me expose them to the bleakest of Merseyside conditions. There was no way of telling what the local people might say or the Press write, what questions would be asked and, worst of all, what answers would be given.

There was nothing I could do to prepare the visitors for what they were to see; and even if we had thought of some way of lessening the shock that would have been to risk defeating our common purpose. We made no such attempt. We drove the bus to some of the worst housing estates. The passengers climbed out, the residents came to meet them and dialogue was opened. Distinguished and dignified City gentlemen mingled with an urban community whose material circumstances put them at the opposite social pole, leaving them with only one advantage: the fluency and force with which they could put their case.

There might have been trouble. At first I wondered if a single careless word and an angry response would leave me regretting the whole enterprise. But my initial nervousness did too little credit to my guests and took too little account of their sensitivity and of the impact on them of what they saw and heard. Perhaps I should have known that one or two of them knew more of Merseyside than I shall ever know.

The members of the bus party did not lack imagination and had not led sheltered lives. But they were all now in senior positions and for several the usual morning journey had become the short step from the company Rolls to the carpeted lift and straight to the panelled boardroom. I had brought them to see and smell the boarded, tenantless flats, the fouled stairwells, the vandalised lifts, the endless graffiti.

It is one thing to glimpse and deplore a slum from a passing car; it proved to be a wholly different experience for some at least of these distinguished men to find themselves standing beside putrescent housing, surrounded by its prisoners and victims, and compelled to consider what each of them could possibly do to help.

No one was unmoved. No one complained that I had wasted his time or that the visit had not shown him truths which no second-hand description could have conveyed.

As we came towards the end of a long day I could sense a rising anxiety in my guests. I suspect that the day had started for each of those chief executives with their personal assistants ringing them up to say, 'Look, sir, whatever you do, don't promise him any money.'

Now it was up to me. I had 30 people who had each given up valuable time to me and who were obviously greatly concerned about what they had seen. It was 3.30 and they all knew the London train left at 5 o'clock. So far I had given no hint of looking for some sort of commitment, but 90 minutes remained.

I suggested we might all have a cup of tea at the Adelphi to discuss what we had seen, and every face fell at my innocent suggestion. You could see that they were convinced that this was where the big touch came, although at that stage I had not made up my mind what to ask them.

I said, 'I have two things to say to you. First, I do not want any money.' The smiles had to be seen to be believed. Then I said, 'I want one thing: I want one of your brightest managers to come and work in my department for a year and to examine with us all the extremes of polarisation and the ineffectiveness of the public machinery which you have seen today.'

Thirty hands went up. It was the birth of the Financial Institutions Group, and the beginning of one of the most valuable experiments we have seen in co-operation between the public and private sectors.

It quickly became apparent in those first weeks that there was also a need for the efforts of the public sector to be more effectively concentrated. The Government therefore decided to create a Merseyside Task Force in which officials of three departments – Environment, Industry and Employment – came together for the first time to work in an integrated department.

The Task Force's first and highly energetic director was Eric Sorensen, who had been regional director of the DOE in Manchester. Its purpose was to advance any worthwhile project by speeding up clearance by the Government of applications for grants and to act as general trouble-shooter.

The representatives of the institutions made good their pledges within days, and in generous measure. They sent us middle-ranking managers, high-calibre enthusiasts, to work in the Inner Cities Directorate of the Department of the Environment. This team became the Financial Institutions Group (FIG) and for a year they did pioneering work with us, their salaries paid by their employers.

Their brief was wide: to review the practices of the public and private sectors as far as their policies towards urban areas were concerned, to devise new approaches and ideas for urban regeneration, to involve the financial institutions much more actively in the problems of the inner cities, and to find new ways of linking the efforts of public and private sectors.

From the start they worked well with the department's officials, the public and private sector brains stimulating each other. Soon the newcomers were largely directing their own activities, dividing themselves into specialist sections, the bankers looking at prospects for stimulating commercial and industrial investment, the building society representatives looking at appalling housing problems. They travelled across Britain and the United States searching for the best examples of success and opportunity.

Soon a series of reports began appearing on ministers' desks with fresh ideas. The most fruitful and far-reaching of their many proposals led to the introduction of Urban Development Grant (UDG) which was designed to secure the highest possible ratio of private investment in response to pump-priming with public funds. It was modelled on a pattern developed in the United States which laid the foundation of incentives that encouraged the private sector to rebuild parts of Baltimore, Boston, Minneapolis and other cities.

In the United States there are huge amounts of Federal

money, without which sites of the necessary scale could not have been assembled and cleared. In addition, American developers are offered tax relief unparalleled in this country. But we also need to appreciate that American cities are more entrepreneurial than ours. They have much greater financial flexibility. They often take an equity stake in the redevelopment, and they can offer highly attractive rate holidays which a local authority in this country would not have the powers to allow, even if it had the inclination. We need to create a less stultifying climate.

UDG was introduced within the year and began at once to promote economic regeneration in dead or dying urban districts. Private investment was introduced in project after project which, without the public element, would not have been begun.

The system encourages local authorities to work up capital investment projects in co-operation with private sector interests, which provide much of the investment, and submit them to the Department of the Environment for approval. The projects have to compete with each other for the available central funding, and the winning bids attract grants from government to cover three-quarters of the commitment of each local authority. To encourage imaginative ideas, any type of project is welcomed: plans for housing or shops or factories or sports grounds.

The notion of UDG had been nurtured in the department for some time, but the endorsement of it by the group was crucial. Almost all the group's members had been concerned in the world outside Westminster with development projects which had been abandoned because without an injection of public money they stood no chance of bringing their backers an adequate return. Our private sector practitioners were able to convince us that such a system of grant would work, and to show us how. In essence what the private sector managers brought with them was confidence. They were used to taking decisions. Too much of the Whitehall culture is about giving advice, and too often the advice is based on experience only of sectors of the economy that are in trouble.

For the same reason it made sense to put private sector experts on the team which was to appraise each project and advise ministers which would be worth backing. Experienced managers from accountancy and surveying practices put at our disposal a knowledge and expertise which would rarely have been found within government. The most lasting benefit has been in the change to the culture of the government machine. Civil servants were forced to enter into a dialogue with the business world. The cultural change probably impinged most on the department's regional officials. Traditionally they looked to local government; now they have to talk to Chambers of Commerce and the business sector as part of the assessment of UDG and Urban Programme projects. I made it a condition of Urban Programme approval that the local Chamber was consulted.

Urban Development Grant is now established as an indispensable element in the Government's urban programme. Throughout Britain private developers are using their ingenuity and raising funds to restore, rebuild and refurbish buildings and sites. There is the splendid £10m restoration, recently completed, of the Royal Agricultural Hall in Islington, London – which without the pump-priming of £2.85m of public money would certainly have continued to rot. In Dudley, Milking Bank Meadow was, despite its name, a moonscape of quarried and tipped land until Tarmac and Steetleys invested £12m on top of a £1.3m Urban Development Grant and built 600 houses on half of the 150-acre site, landscaping the remainder.

Over its first four years offers of Urban Development Grant have amounted to £105m. Matching investment, in joint development projects all over England, reached £439m, so that every pound of public expenditure in UDG is securing the commitment of more than four pounds of private capital. In cash terms that private sector enhancement is bigger than the entire Urban Programme of 1979. But it did not stop there. Broadly similar schemes have been introduced in Scotland, Wales and Northern Ireland.

I deviate for a moment to show how initiatives can founder. In 1979 there was no Urban Development Grant and Peter Walker's imaginative Derelict Land Grant was spent almost exclusively in the rural areas, greening old waste or spoil tips. We changed the pattern on which Derelict Land Grant was paid, both to increaase the proportion going to urban arras and to ensure that payment of grant extracted new money from the private sector. The experiment was an immediate success. The first £14m slice of grant set aside for joint public and private sector projects in urban areas attracted six times as much funding again from private investors – a total capital commitment far greater than the public purse alone could have afforded.

Over the next few years we created the concept of gearing: instead of just one pound of public money and only one pound's worth of expenditure on the ground, we used these grants to lever out private pounds. 'We clear the site, you build the house,' was the new understanding. Every pound of private money was pure gain. Up to that point it had been considered enough just to spend the public cash.

The Treasury never sleeps. The UDG scheme took a battering and some flexibility has been lost. The number of projects has grown each year, but not fast enough. Too much attention has been paid to detailed bureaucratic appraisal of each application, not enough attention to the risks being run by entrepreneurs. Investing in hard-pressed inner city areas is risky. If it were not, we would not be faced with the present scale of urban problems. We therefore need imagination and flexibility, adventurous investing institutions, and the minimum bureaucracy.

Among the institutions themselves the activities of FIG started ripples of new ideas which are still spreading outwards. The shock of the riots had made people ready enough to listen, and every business active in the cities had begun to think again about what they had been doing or failing to do.

Some of the liveliest members of the group came from the big building societies which were already stirring with new views of their role in the community. Traditionally their concern had been solely with housing finance, with finding the cash to help home-owners, but not with housing development. As one manager said, they all knew the word 'lend' but never used the word 'housing'. By the early 1980s the leading building societies were fully alive to the idea that there was a legitimate new role for them in using their large resources to help transform the quality of an area. They were pressing for legislation which would help them to buy, hold and develop land; and also for the crucial legal power to lend unsecured, so that they could expand their activities in housing stress areas where their help was so desperately needed. (They secured these powers in the 1986 Building Societies Act.)

The formation of FIG came at exactly the right moment to enable this new thinking to germinate. In return we received exciting support from the conspicuous leaders among the building societies. The bright and rising men from the big societies carried their experience in government back to their employers and, at the last count, three of the five managers who came to us in 1981 from big societies were running newly-formed housing development departments for the Halifax, Woolwich and Nationwide societies, with special responsibilities for work in the inner cities.

Changed attitudes helped to bring about one crucial change in the thinking of some of the financial institutions about the difficulties of the inner cities: the relaxation of 'red-lining', the marking-off of districts where both the housing quality and the prospects of improvement were so poor that a lender would not even look at an application for a loan. The expression comes from America. It means that the lender's surveyor, with a stroke of his red pen, will circle and condemn whole streets and terraces of habitable dwellings in districts which he decides are going downhill. The pronouncing of this financial death-sentence makes terminal decline of a district inevitable. The morbidity then spreads outwards.

In Britain the bigger building societies opposed the practice, and few societies would willingly admit to behaving in such a way. But the evidence of many disappointed applicants for mortgages told against them. (Equally, insurance companies were accused, and still are, of loading their premiums in bad areas, where indeed the crime risks tend to be above average, to a level which in practice denies cover to shopkeepers, householders or would-be householders of modest means.)

Judged by normal commercial criteria this practice might seem thoroughly sensible. When there was ample demand for loans on sound property in safe areas there was no reason for a building society to accept a bad risk. A more far-sighted and now much more common commercial view is that a policy which tends to destroy property values in ever-widening circles will also in the end threaten the purpose of the existence of the building societies. The societies now recognise, as one senior manager, Mr David Couttie of the Halifax, has said, that they have a vested interest not only in preventing their existing borrowers from finding their homes surrounded by areas of decay but also in securing their longer-term lending markets.

Several of the big building societies have since put their weight behind urban renewal projects with a will, going boldly into bad areas, investing and creating new confidence and new life. Several have 'special lending budgets' where funds are set aside for producing the houses which property developers would not build. Their aim is to satisfy the unmet needs of young single people, retired and frail elderly people and others for whom the market does not provide.

Of the £50m which the Halifax, for instance, has committed in London docklands, £15m is going into a low-cost scheme for 172 new houses and flats at Shadwell Basin, the biggest loan the society has ever advanced. Seventy of these dwellings are being offered for sale at only three-fifths of their market value, with a housing association retaining a two-fifths interest.

Insurance companies have found it harder to make pioneering and apparently riskier investments. Building societies have a co-operative structure and tradition and the profit motive is less strong. The head offices of building societies are still widely dispersed throughout provincial Britain. Other institutions owe a prime duty to their policy holders and depositors, and few will normally invest in a shopping centre in Bootle if a similar opening appeared in Haywards Heath, with its more obvious potential for growth. Pension funds are even more tightly confined by laws which prescribe their duty to their members.

Norwich Union is investing in Birmingham and the Prudential in Hackney in schemes where urban development grant has provided the decisive inducement. They are not alone.

It is disappointing, nonetheless, that during the eighties institutions have been moving out of property. Between 1981 and 1985, annual net investment in property as a proportion of all investment by insurance companies fell from 14 per cent to 9 per cent; and by pension funds from 11 per cent to 5 per cent.

I believe that there would be a greater readiness by institutions to invest in the rebuilding of the inner cities if they were given a strong lead by government. Without that lead, however imaginative and varied the initiatives, redevelopment will be an uphill task.

7

Cities In Crisis: New Towns In Old Cities

The malignancy which threatens government and society in some parts of British cities has taken so strong a hold because its roots were planted perhaps 100 years ago. It happened when those late Victorian families, whose fathers had helped to build the great wealth of the municipalities, began to move apart from the communities which had sustained them and drawn sustenance from them.

There was a weakening, later to become a rupture, of the bond between master and man, factory owner and factory hand, beginning with physical separation as the richer citizens moved from the city centres to the suburbs or the country.

I have always believed that England escaped revolution in the eighteenth century in part because, although there were some absentee landlords the privileged members of society were not divorced from their humbler fellows. They enjoyed very different standards of living, but they were closely involved and interested in the communities where they lived, and in general did not choose to desert their homes to attach themselves to the life of the Court.

With the coming of the nineteenth century and the explosion of capitalism in the Industrial Revolution communities still held together at first. Employers had to live where their wealth was made and close to the artisans and labourers. Neither the horse nor the canal offered the option of daily journeying between country home and city counting-house. So the rich, with pride in their communities, put up monuments around themselves in the splendid public buildings of provincial town and city centres.

Those endowments remain, but the descendants and

successors of the families who built them have mostly gone and taken with them their energy, commitment and concern.

Later in the century, the outward movement began with the great growth of the Empire and its demand for soldiers and administrators; and there were early indications that families who had prospered in the Industrial Revolution were anxious to lose their associations with industry and trade.

The train, tram and car arrived in turn to create and sustain the fashion for homes in the green suburbs and in ever more distant villages, away from crowds and smoke. The coming of the property-owning democracy encouraged more town-dwellers to buy homes, and the chance to buy them first in the nearer, then in the farther open fields.

This dispersal has marked our own century and brought with it a steady dissipation of municipal wealth and strength. The pattern has been common to Britain and other countries, but in Britain it has been aggravated by the actions of governments of all parties.

One more recent agency of dispersal has been the comprehensive school. The old pattern of grammar and secondary modern schools was thought to be socially divisive. But in the new world of comprehensive schools, many a parent with a talented child and the resources to move exercised a choice. The child was removed from the stress of the inner city comprehensive to the more socially relaxed culture of the suburban comprehensive. Many of the grammar schools or direct grant schools opted for private status, which again blocked off a ladder of opportunity for working-class children in the cities.

Social polarisation in schooling was not diminished: that between inner and outer cities was increased, and the tendency of talent to move to the periphery was reinforced.

London was unique in Britain. For decades the docks brought in immigrant groups with new skills and new vitality to settle in the East End, but when the docks died a yawning cavity slowly formed at the heart of a region of great prosperity. London did not suffer the double blow which fell on Glasgow and many English industrial cities: these were first made vulnerable by the flight of population from centre to suburbs, then steadily weakened by the movement of material resources to the more prosperous markets of the South and East.

Grave damage has been done by a tax regime which in some of its manifestations might have been designed to draw capital away from the provinces and from our manufacturing and trading companies to the City of London. Three forms of tax incentive in particular work against provincial Britain and therefore against the national interest. They aggravate the pull of the market and more than cancel the intended benefits of the regional policies which all governments have maintained in order to counteract that pull.

In 1985/6 the cost to the Exchequer of mortgage tax relief was about £4,750m. This subsidy to home purchase has helped to create the property-owning democracy which is one of the most profound social changes in the history of the Tory Party. But behind the huge growth of home ownership came the life assurance companies, riding on the backs of that subsidy to provide the life cover to secure the mortgages.

Annual cash flow into the life assurance market stands at £6,400m and, although the 1985 Budget removed tax relief for life assurance, much of the 'life' market is stimulated by tax relief afforded to the home-buying public. The subsidy was designed to spread home ownership and enhance local commitment. The life companies, rationally and prudently, invest their assets in ways not concerned with job creation or with strengthening Britain's regional manufacturing base. Half of the twelve largest are in London, and it would be surprising if the investment committees of the rest were far away. The result is that the savings drawn from the provinces are invested largely through the institutions of the City of London.

Of their total investments about 50 per cent are in British company securities, loans and debentures and these span the range of commercial, financial and property companies as well as manufacturing. But most of the rest is not used primarily for industry's benefit. About 20 per cent is invested in British Government securities and 14 per cent in property, and the rest in foreign stocks and a variety of other investments. It is therefore apparent that too much of this

Exchequer encouraged funding does not go towards helping to create future wealth by investment in industry.

The second huge subsidy affecting the flow of Britain's savings is that given to the pensions industry. Tax concessions to an annual value of £3,500m enable the pensions industry to attract the savings of company and worker alike, sucking resources out of companies to invest elsewhere.

The pension funds invest rather less than half their assets across the whole spectrum of British quoted companies; more than a quarter in foreign governments and companies; and about one-fifth in British Government stocks.

The Government's reshaping of regional policy in 1984 has led, as intended, to a progressive reduction in total regional support, which amounted last year to £168m for England and to £615m for Great Britain and Northern Ireland together. The Exchequer's left hand is now paying that sum in an effort to attract resources to the regions. Its right hand provides incentives to taxpayers amounting to around £8,000m a year in a manner which tends to pull in the direction where the market is already leading and on a scale that overwhelms any regional programme ever seen in Britain.

The third powerful pull to the South and East for which fiscal policy is responsible is the pattern of capital taxation on realisation of gains or inheritance. The family businesses, once the creators of provincial wealth and the basis of provincial power, have been taxed since the war into one-generation phenomena.

When owners have needed to sell and capital taxes increased the need, the remote, publicly-quoted company has been able to offer the attraction of paper shares with tax liabilities postponed; whereas the friends, neighbours or members of the local community who are interested in buying tend to offer cash. The choice is therefore to sell locally and pay tax at once, or to sell to the distant outsider and postpone tax. Tax deferred feels like tax saved. Owners are not philanthropists. There is no real choice. Governments made them offers they could not refuse. The diminishing stock of locally owned and managed businesses shrank further.

Recently Nigel Lawson has introduced welcome changes in capital taxation to give entrepreneurs with foresight the chance to perpetuate family ownership. With reasonable life expectancy, owners can now transfer to their intended beneficiaries, and tax on death becomes to some extent voluntary. But on disposal the in-built incentives for the takeover process by publicly owned companies remain, and must be corrected.

The most effective way to do this would be to end capital taxation on wealth-creating companies. Few things would so attract the potential entrepreneur. The Treasury will argue that abuse will follow as people shelter assets in artificial structures. Yet the abuse would be marginal, and so through timidity we destroy the whole for the sake of the peripheral. The ingenuity of the Inland Revenue must be subjected to the creation of wealth and to our political objectives and not given the power of veto. It must be instructed to attack the areas of abuse, not to so shackle the enterprise culture for fear of abuse that they destroy the culture.

As we change the tax climate to make the decision whether to sell for cash or publicly-quoted shares a neutral one, we should reconsider our assumptions about takeovers and the public interest, as I have argued above.

There is a well-established link between the economic decline of an area and the passing into outside hands of its businesses. A 1983 survey of regional policy prepared by the Confederation of British Industry found that in disadvantaged regions a relatively high proportion of firms were controlled by companies with their headquarters elsewhere.

In many cases the trend towards specialisation in industry is bound to increase to meet increasing competition, and some businesses will be forced to combine in larger groups, under proprietors more remote and detached from local needs and interests. But we should at least now be alive to the social and political risks which may follow when the economies of the provinces are subordinated to the metropolis. To prevent the bleeding will take all the skill of government: we cannot afford to make it worse by the use of fiscal incentives.

For three or four generations a great engine has been steadily impoverishing both urban and provincial Britain, its destructive potency only recently perceived and its momentum even now barely checked. It must be stopped, and the human and material resources drawn outward from the city centres must be encouraged back. We must do this as much to protect the environment of the South as to restore hope in the stress areas.

Only government can take the lead; and it will succeed only if it enlists in an imaginative and long-term programme for the inner cities the same energy and enterprise that first built what must now be rebuilt.

There can be no way of turning back urban decline that is not led by the taxpayer. The elimination of social stress and the eradication of urban dereliction are not the natural hunting grounds of the profit-seeking entrepreneur left to his own devices.

Solutions demand public and private resources. They will be founded on partnerships which recognise that there are some things that only governments can pay for, but also that the ingenuity and flexibility of the private sector is indispensable.

The first thing to recognise in shaping a policy to rebuild our cities is that we must speak to two communities. There is the community that remains in the inner city because it has no choice: the community of the elderly, the poor, the new immigrants and those whose only real prospect of being housed is on a council estate. It is a dependent community, sustained by the taxpayer, its members resigned to a place at the back of the queue for decent jobs and decent homes. For them competition is about a race for which they have neither the strength nor skill even to reach the starting line.

There is also the other community that is no longer there because its members had the chance to leave and grabbed it. They may have had skill or energy that set them apart, or just a bit of luck.

Our policies must address both. We must give hope to those who live in the stress areas, and persuade those outside the cities to look again at the opportunities which are now appearing within them.

The essential first step, with people as with businesses, is to halt the continuing flight and persuade those who emerge from the throng and find a measure of success or prosperity not to make a priority of departure.

The successful are an essential part of self-sustaining communities, giving hope and courage to the less successful and offering example and leadership. They also know about standards and have the will and wit to insist upon them. Here too is a bridge between the two groups, because what is needed to deter the fugitive will also draw back the exile: each must be able to take pride in what he does, what he owns, where he lives and who he is.

We must create new towns in old cities. We must put back green fields, replacing abandoned workshops and warehouses. We must deploy a scale of resource that will attract to the life of the inner city those with the ambition to buy their own homes, start their own businesses and live in a thriving, confident and tranquil neighbourhood. The attraction must be as compelling as the forces that first drove them to the suburbs or the dormitory towns.

It can be and has been done. There is now a green field in the heart of Liverpool where, in 1981, there was a growing dump of toxic waste which stood in piles up to 70 feet high. The wasteland of the Riverside district has been turned into an infant garden city which now stretches for a mile along the banks of the Mersey. It would not be Liverpool if all had proved plain sailing. A sad setback followed the liquidation of the company that took over the Garden Festival site, but it will prove temporary, for that site is now highly attractive and its use is assured. Further along the river the Albert Dock complex is home to the Maritime Museum, and will soon house the Tate Gallery of the North. Private developers are converting the buildings to flats, offices, shops and cafes. Granada Television has dramatically exciting studios in a restored harbour building, and the leisure facilities planned for the future could bring new life back to the Mersey. The Merseyside Development Corporation expect 4m visitors a year to the growing range of these facilities by the early 1990s. Any significant fraction of such a figure would have been laughed at five years ago.

This reclamation of 250 acres of despoiled urban land was the largest such work ever done in Europe, a triumph of private- and public-sector co-operation and a heroic achievement both by the management of the Merseyside Development Corporation and by the Liverpool workforce, all locally recruited, who took great pride in working to renew their city.

That workforce has in the past had something of a reputation for being difficult: in this task not a single hour was lost through industrial action.

The heart of the project and its inspiration was the 1984 Liverpool Garden Festival, the first ever held in Britain. Initial credit must go to Philip Goodhart, the Conservative MP who, when our party was in opposition in the late 1970s, sent me a leaflet describing how, after the 1939–45 war, garden festivals had been used on the Continent to restore both the fabric of bomb-damaged cities and the morale of their people. I had never heard of garden festivals, but I stored the idea away and when we took office I asked one of the ministers in the department, Irwin Bellow, to examine it with officials. He thought it might work, so we explored some suitable sites to see where the first festival might be staged.

By now Merseyside UDC was in being and its team under the committed chairmanship of Sir Leslie Young, a local industrialist, and its energetic chief executive, Basil Bean, was pushing hard to have the first festival on the banks of the Mersey. Stoke-on-Trent was the rival candidate, but before we had made our choice the Toxteth riots occurred, and it seemed to me urgent to dispel the sudden sense of failure and loss by starting something in central Liverpool which was new and would succeed.

I was sorry for Stoke. They were entitled to feel that my decision went against them because I was concerned for Merseyside, and there was an element of truth in their suspicion. I promised them the second festival, in 1986, and I hope that in the end they felt they were able to make good use of the extra time for preparation. German cities, I am told, usually take seven to ten years to plan their festivals. Basil Bean assured me that he could mount one in two and a half years from scratch. It was a bold undertaking and I backed him with some trepidation; but he and his team did it.

More than 3.3m visitors went through the festival turnstiles in the summer of 1984. The permanent benefit is less easily measured, but Liverpool has its new park which draws visitors and with the city's other attractions will lay the foundations for a permanent boost to tourism, to the hotel trade and to other service industries.

There was plenty of understandable mockery at first for ministers who thought they could solve Toxteth's problems by planting trees, but it was good to see cynicism turn to pride. A wider awareness grew that I was not preoccupied with Toxteth but with the wider condition of the city and others like it. The garden festival as a way of planting green fields in British cities proved itself in Liverpool and again in Stoke. Glasgow is now to apply the Mersey treatment to the upper Clyde, and work is far advanced on preparation of Princes Dock for the 1988 garden festival. This greening of central Glasgow is confidently expected to draw visitors in their millions, greatly help the climate for investment and tourism and reinforce the already notable success of the council and the Scottish Development Agency in marketing the city. Wales too is to have a Garden Festival, in Ebbw Vale in 1992.

I do not want to paint an unbalanced picture. My other ministerial colleagues too achieved good results in their respective partnerships. Tom King, for example, made great progress in Birmingham. Many exciting experiments started there as visitors to the revitalised jewellery quarter or those who benefited from the enveloping housing improvement schemes will know. The Aston University Science Park is a flourishing example of how to attract manufacturing growth. The determination that built the National Exhibition Centre, although it sadly failed in its bid for the Olympic Games, shows a strength in that city which makes the task of building anew encouragingly simpler.

The lesson of the widest general importance from the enhanced drive to improve the urban environment, whether through urban development corporations, urban development grant or derelict land grant, was and remains clear: that where urban land has become so severely degraded as to have a negative value it can be reclaimed only with public money; but that if public money is committed on a scale and within a timescale which means business, then the confidence and the cash resources of the private sector will follow, both sharing and ensuring the growth in value.

Sometimes the first private investor has to show more than ordinary imagination. Sometimes, too, he will take a considered risk to serve the public interest as well as his own. I have found that private capital, if encouraged by government, is willing to make great efforts to promote the well-being of its host community and to prevent the poisoning of the soil in which it grows.

In 1981 I telephoned Sir John Clark, chairman of Plessey, with a request and an offer. He responded to both in a way which I hope helped his own company but which established an experiment on Merseyside that I believe offers almost limitless opportunity for replication elsewhere.

The challenge was the 65-acre site of what is now the Wavertree Technology Park, a steadily expanding centre of high-technology industry and one of Liverpool's most visible beacons of returning confidence. Five years ago it was an appalling eyesore, mainly railway yards which had hardly been used for a decade, a great sprawl of industrial wasteland. Planners and developers had repeatedly examined the possibility of salvaging the land and finding a new use for it, but had given up in despair.

It lay within two miles of the city's commercial centre, a silent but eloquent rebuke to a society where it was always someone else's responsibility. Nobody bothered. You drove through Liverpool, you looked at this terrible place, and you drove on.

I was certain that because of its prominence the site must make the same daily impact on every other visitor to Liverpool that it made on me. It was as if a vast poster had been displayed with the message: 'This place is on its way down. If you are thinking of investing you had better try the suburbs – or the South-east.' I wondered what it did for the morale of workers at Plessey Telecoms on the neighbouring site, or what Plessey's visiting customers made of it. I knew that Plessey had been among those who had considered trying to do something with the site but found the job too demanding. British Rail owned the site but had little time or cash for a problem so remote from their main activities. I thought it might be worth having a word with Sir John Clark.

I asked him if he would join me in an experiment. I wanted him to become chairman of a trust to take over the derelict land, and we would use derelict land grant – taxpayers' money – to clear the site, eliminate the negative value of past dereliction and bring it up to the level which new investors would contemplate. We would then use the Government's development agency, English Estates, to put up advance factories, again with taxpayers' money, on whatever pattern the trust wanted. There would be a mixture of private and public sector people among the trustees.

I wanted Sir John's support and the psychological, not financial, commitment of his company. I also wanted him to find me a manager, and I suggested that he might be someone of ability who was nearing the end of his career with Plessey but would be full of experience. I said: 'We want someone who has a real contribution to make. Within the Plessey organisation I want him to use your muscle, ingenuity and procurement opportunities to fill those factories. No money is involved. I just want him to talk to people and have ideas.

'I want him to say, "You know those two bright young people you have in that laboratory, who have been saying that they want to start up on their own? We have room for them to do that." Or he might say to the printing division of a company, "Look, you don't need to work within the company any more. We will provide you with a factory for your own printing business and we will give you a contract to do our printing for five years." He can have any ideas he likes, but he must fill the place up.'

Sir John Clark and Plessey, to their immense credit, took on this challenge and responsibility. The Wavertree Technology Park is now a superb site, an outstanding success and a monument to Plessey's public spirit. It is not just another industrial estate but a fast-growing community made up solely of modern high-technology businesses. A recent survey of twenty science parks by the newspaper *The Electronics Engineer* found that Wavertree, with more than 500 workers, was employing more than any other except Cambridge, which was founded ten years earlier.

Wavertree is not linked formally with any institution of higher education like the typical science park, but its proximity to the University and to Liverpool Polytechnic with its excellent science faculty has brought mutually valuable opportunities for collaborative research, and the industrialists and academics thrive in each other's company.

The cost was £10m of public money in reclaiming and landscaping the derelict land and putting in roads, water and other services. The Park Company was formed with four equal partners – Plessey, English Estates and the Merseyside and Liverpool councils – each putting up £300,000 to acquire the prepared site, and then to market and administer the park.

The company was formed and work began in July 1983. By July 1985 site preparation was almost complete and the first instalment of 35,000 square feet of speculative factory and office units was finished and on the market. Within ten months more than four-fifths was either occupied or let. Last year a second batch of 27,000 square feet was begun and will be ready for occupation in the summer of 1987. Suddenly the wilderness is fertile.

Plessey Telecoms, from its 10-acre site next door, has been generous in providing the newcomers with financial and accountancy services on a consultancy basis at nominal rates, with advice on export procedures and technical standards, and with telecommunications and data processing facilities. They have also seconded two senior men of high calibre in succession as chief executives.

Those in charge have had difficulty attracting investment from far afield against keen competition from other regions and countries. Liverpool is a lively city and full of potential, but the city's recent difficulties and the well-publicised antics of the Trotskyites in the local Labour Party paint an ugly picture which the Wavertree promoters have had to struggle to overcome. Nothing frightens away new investors and new jobs so effectively as the extremes of Socialism.

Where the Wavertree Park now measures its success, with legitimate pride, is in the expanding firms long established on Merseyside which were reluctantly preparing to leave the region before the Wavertree opportunity was created. One early challenge was a sudden requirement from another Plessey division, Plessey Crypto, specialists in communications security, who had outgrown their old site in the city. In November 1983 it became clear that they would be leaving town unless someone could provide a new factory of 45,000 square feet within nine months. Wavertree met the challenge and the firm is there. Another employer who might have been lost to Merseyside is the leading biotechnology company, Powell & Scholefield, who had been in Liverpool for more than 100 years. Recently they moved into a purpose-built plant in the Wavertree park.

It is impossible to set a value on these first successes. Benign growth multiplies as fast as the cancerous growth which so quickly feeds on the physical fabric of districts where businesses are failing or leaving and people have lost hope. The employer who digs in is like the first planting of the forest which will stabilize shifting dunes, or the first groyne in a coastal defence system. Coastal defence is initially costly, but it is a desperately shortsighted community that grudges the cost.

Wavertree has shown how the rot can be stopped. The park experiment is a triumph, and therefore an experiment no longer. Rather it is an example to other imaginative industrialists to look for similar opportunities in their backyards. I was lucky in Liverpool to find the man and the company to match the hour, but Clark and Plessey are not unique. I had no chance unfortunately, before being posted to the Ministry of Defence, to prepare a list of cities and towns with similar tracts of debilitating industrial desert. I would have shown local employers what Plessey had achieved, and asked 'if they can do it, why can't you?' Every government research laboratory, industry-oriented university or polytechnic could look for private sector developers to help exploit the knowledge and experience employed there. I have no doubt that, in almost every case, there would have been a willing response to a clear lead.

The Wavertree success has achieved more. It has demonstrated several elements in British public life which Conservatives understand and which no British government can afford to forget: that leadership awakens a response; that the private and public sectors work best in partnership; and that British capitalists can show a well-developed sense of public duty. For me these propositions form a set of principles on which the rebuilding both of Britain's fabric and of its economic life must in part be based.

I have picked out Wavertree because I was present at its birth, but it is by no means an isolated case. The encouraging truth is that throughout the 1980s more and more businesses have come to see the value of forming partnerships with local authorities and sometimes with voluntary bodies in blighted urban areas. Scores of companies are sponsoring projects to provide jobs or training, giving practical support to people seeking opportunities for self-employment or bringing hope to those trapped in bad housing estates in areas of falling economic activity.

Business often takes the lead; and when it does government, with incentive, encouragement and help, can turn a first spark into a flame of enthusiasm. It happened with the movement known as 'Business in the Community', and the growth of enterprise agencies – a conspicuous example of caring capitalism.

Intelligent self-interest, although far from universal, is advancing across the country. It is widely agreed that the jolt given by the urban riots of the early 1980s provided the motive power, although the initiative to persuade business into a more active role was under way before the first riots. More leaders of big companies are now prepared to give their communities public-spirited help.

There have always been businesses whose shareholders allow their directors to act on the principle that social commitment should be coupled with economic attainments. Some even follow consciously in the tradition of those family-run firms in the last century (those run by Quakers such as Cadbury and Rowntree are notable examples) which distinguished themselves by an uncommon concern for the well-being of their employees both at home and in the workplace. Pilkington and Marks and Spencer are among those conspicuous in their adoption of such an approach.

Some would brush aside the suggestion that they may be partly moved by altruism. Given a few extra percentage points, they would rather endorse the sentiments of Lord Rowton who in late Victorian times raised funds to build some of the earliest hostels in London for single homeless men, and made his homes pay. 'Philanthropy is all very well, gentlemen,' Rowton would tell his backers, 'but philanthropy at 5 per cent is very much better.'

But many influential businessmen, without philosophising and without fuss, have simply decided that they must do something to help those around them; and this attitude, commoner until now in the United States than in Britain, grows by the month.

I first encountered an enterprise agency during a visit to Pilkington in St Helen's, not long after the 1979 election. Like so many companies facing technological change and the need to improve efficiency, Pilkington had to reduce its workforce drastically. In a town where it was the dominant employer, the directors resolved to combine their determination to keep their company at the forefront of the world market with an equal determination to temper the social consequences for the local people. At the suggestion of a senior manager, Bill Humphrey, they set up one of the earliest enterprise agencies. The concept was to draw together the local authority and local employers to advise people anxious to start their own businesses on how to find their way through the jungle of regulations that so inhibited them. They could indicate where premises might be available with appropriate planning permission, set up the basic books of account and inject that critical note of confidence. The premises of the St Helen's Community Trust were modest without being dilapidated. No flashy reception area or plate-glass window, but a back staircase and an upstairs room. 'This is where they start,' it was explained, 'not where they finish, but we don't want anyone getting big ideas.'

I was greatly impressed by the efforts of the first enterprise agencies, in which a number of big companies with local roots in areas of worsening unemployment had formed partnerships with local authorities and others to encourage the growth of small businesses. They lent their expertise and their staff to help plant and shelter the saplings.

I determined that we must do what we could to encourage the spread of this promising movement. Tom King took the lead and as Minister for Local Government called a conference at Sunningdale to which he invited leaders of local government, industry and commerce together with people experienced in similar problems in America. This led in 1981 to the founding of Business in the Community (BiC) with, at first, 30 member companies. The founder chairman was

Sir Alastair Pilkington, the deputy chairman David Sieff and its first chief executive Anthony Pelling, seconded from the Department of the Environment. We set a target to have an agency established in every town of 200,000 or more inhabitants.

BiC was begun as an experimental partnership of businesses, central and local government, voluntary bodies and trade unions. With the active involvement of the regional officers of the Department, it at once took on responsibility for setting up the network of enterprise agencies which we saw could play a vital part in local regeneration. The target of an agency in every town of 200,000 people was reached in a couple of years. By October 1986 there were about 250 agencies with more than 3,000 sponsoring companies. They are creating more than 20,000 new businesses every year and they estimate, I believe modestly, that they are either making or saving 75,000 jobs a year.

Six years after BiC's beginning it is still small but its growth rate is rapid. The value of its work, the effect of the agencies on the morale of communities where employment has been shrinking, is far greater than its numbers would suggest.

The importance of this life-giving work is that it is business-led. Businesses supply about three-fifths of the resources in skills, equipment and cash which the agencies need, with local and central government finding the rest. The Ministry of Defence supported the foundation of an agency in Plymouth where major reductions in the workforce were to take place in the Royal Dockyards.

Enterprise agencies began as partnerships of local interests whose objective was to increase the economic health of their communities. The initial purpose was to provide free counselling to those who wished to start businesses or whose existing businesses might expand if they could get practical help and perhaps extra cash. The best agencies, as they grow, have spread their talents into many fields and become enormously effective. They scrutinise land registers and find venture capital. Many support the Youth Training Scheme and concern themselves with other aspects of training and education. A logical first step is to encourage agencies to set up their own technology centres, providing accommodation and central services, accountancy and marketing at prices or rents designed for fledgling businesses.

About 60 per cent of agency directors and their deputies are on secondment from sponsoring firms, usually serving for up to two years. The help of secretaries and technical specialists is also freely lent to agencies. The total value of all these secondments is put at about £3m a year and rising. Sponsoring firms are encouraged to lend their best people, and secondment can be an excellent chance for the young high-flying manager to develop new skills of leadership and innovation. It can be equally rewarding for the experienced senior manager nearing retirement but still responsive to a fresh challenge. As for the agency and its clients, they benefit from the help of high quality staff whose services they could never afford to buy.

The Government is now helping small agencies in their first years with a grant scheme which supplements privately subscribed funds, and since 1982 cash given to agencies has been tax-deductible. It would be a small but generous gesture to allow companies to double the actual cash spent as an allowance against tax. The present cash payments by companies do not reflect the unquantifiable contribution of senior management which is fundamental to the success of the movement.

The Wavertree experiment proved that, where dereliction is far advanced and there is negative value to be removed from a site before anything can be done with it, public money is the essential factor that can produce the first growth. In 1979 insistent demands for public money seemed to be rising from every city in the land. We changed the guidelines on which the urban programme was directed so as to require a higher proportion of capital to current expenditure and an increased emphasis on securing contributions from the private sector.

So what choices do we have for the future? We must rule out the inaction that would allow the present deterioration to persist. One look is enough to show why government can no longer pass by on the other side. The growing pressures will create a political climate that will no longer tolerate stark deprivation in the midst of evident prosperity.

A half option might be to allow the present trend away

from city centres to continue and to pursue only minimalist policies of care and maintenance to alleviate the worst consequences. There is every reason to reject such a course. People will not put up with it. There will not be democratic consent for ever more development in the already overcrowded parts of prosperous Britain while land elsewhere, which was once developed and fruitfully used by earlier generations, becomes underused and unattractive.

It is necessary in any case to replace the infrastructure of much of Victorian Britain. It would be foolish to put new investment into inner cities, knowing that there will be dwindling use of it, while also putting new schools and stretching new roads, sewers, and other public services farther into the green fields. The cost of meeting the unavoidable demands in the South of England would at today's prices be prohibitive. In any event, minimalism would be self-defeating: the less we do to remove the causes of urban stress, the faster its frontiers will spread.

That is not to say that development on town and city fringes is to halt or that every southern field is sacrosanct. That is unrealistic: the demand for better housing, and the necessary demolition of parts of congested, sometimes high-rise estates, will increase the demand for land in cities. But the country as a whole is becoming increasingly concerned about the imbalances between North and South, and the same concern that demands the reconstruction of northern cities will in the South, as a corollary, increasingly require policies of planning restraint and environmental protection. These attitudes are now clearly perceptible in ministerial statements. The direction is no longer in question, only the pace of the journey.

If inaction is impossible and minimalism self-defeating, we have to advance a third course. I believe that there is one and that it is the right one: we must now move past the limited nature of present programmes and experiments. It was right to say in the early 1980s that throwing money at the problems might just repeat old mistakes, and it was right to examine and redefine practices and attitudes. But unless we believe that we learnt nothing we should now apply what we learnt, and with conviction.

There must be a new national commitment to bring life

The road to Wigan Pier led to decay and dereliction — now to
a restored confidence

I spent three weeks on Merseyside after the summer riots of 1981. In the worst
parts 40 per cent and more of the youngsters were unemployed

In October 1986 the Albert Dock in Liverpool was chosen as the most impressive preservation scheme in Europe by the F.V.S. Foundation of Hamburg

Below:
The Liverpool Garden Festival lasted for 6 months and was a symbol of recovery, the site a permanent improvement to the environment of one of our great cities

1970, and some of the 6000 acres of London Docks from which the heart had gone

Opening the Wimpey Showhouse in 1982. 2000 new houses a year are now being
built for sale in London Docklands. Only the Left protest

to the stress areas of Britain, beginning with an offer by central government to concentrate and increase resources within designated areas preferably agreed with local authorities. With the exception of some parts of inner London and some districts of Bristol, most activity will be in the Midlands and the northern part of what is now seen as the North-South divide.

In developing an enhanced programme, we need to understand our attitude to the relationship between local and national government and I have already alluded to this. But I believe we need a national urban renewal agency to promote, coordinate and drive forward the many local development initiatives in which the Department of the Environment is engaged. It would be best described, indeed, as an English Development Agency (EDA) since it would help to do for England what the Scottish and Welsh agencies have for years done in their own countries with great effect. At present provincial urban England and the deprived parts of London are denied, except in the two development corporations covering parts of the London and Merseyside docklands, the mechanism available to Scotland and Wales. There is no respectable argument that dereliction should be vigorously tackled by government with taxpayers' resources in one or two critical areas while less co-ordinated efforts are made in a score of other places in England which suffer similar hardship.

The EDA would not be the same breed of creature as the Scottish agency (SDA) which was set up as an arm of industry policy and which discharges several tasks which south of the Border are shared among a number of public bodies. In Scotland where a single ministry, the Scottish Office, is in charge of directing almost all economic activity the system of a single agency with a wide remit works well, but it is not necessary to transplant it.

The EDA would not have the English equivalent of the SDA's responsibility, shared with the Scottish Office, for promoting Scotland and attracting investment from overseas. It would however absorb English Estates, an arm of the Department of Trade and Industry responsible for advance factory building, whose Scottish counterpart was absorbed into the SDA in 1975. Restoring the strength of balanced communities cannot be dissociated from job creation in those communities. The present functional concentration on housing to the exclusion of work, recreation and environment is a mistake of the past.

The EDA would not itself possess the SDA's powers to hold land or to invest in, or subsidise, development projects. Its role would be to promote and enable development, not to undertake it. There is a great deal of work to be done. The EDA must be the starter motor, taking out of the hands of government the main initiative for bringing local authority, private and voluntary interests into partnership for joint renewal schemes which it can then promote on behalf of government. An enlarged urban programme would enable the Agency to distribute Urban Development Grant, Urban Regeneration Grant and Derelict Land Grant in much the same way as the Housing Corporation distributes central government support to housing associations.

No region of England has the benefit of a responsible minister in Cabinet to plead its cause as the Scottish and Welsh and Northern Irish secretaries plead for their countries.

I made a proposal once to my colleagues which did not command support but in which I still believe. The urban crisis is not the responsibility of one government department but of many. The Department of the Environment sponsors local government and the Urban Programme, but also involved are the Home Office and the Departments of Employment, Education, Health and Social Services, Industry and the Treasury, as well as the secretaries of State for Scotland, Wales and Northern Ireland.

The English provinces, each of which has its peculiar needs and difficulties, lack the advocacy in government that the other domains of the United Kingdom, each with its own department, can command. This is a weakness which could be rectified, and this is in fact what I proposed.

I believe that the fact that I was known to be concerned with the whole life of Merseyside, and not just those aspects which would normally have been the responsibility of the Department of the Environment, made for greater effectiveness. It certainly made me think against a broader backdrop. It is too easy at present for a minister to come to Cabinet meetings with his department's brief, argue his case and let it rest. When a minister visits the provinces, any question which does not concern his department can be deftly turned aside as the responsibility of a colleague. I would like ministerial responsibilities to be allotted so as to encourage horizontal as well as vertical thinking, with each region's welfare made the special, and additional, concern of a senior minister.

The EDA would do something to remedy this weakness, by both representing the needs of urban England as a whole and weighing the competing claims of its different towns and cities. It is important to be clear that we should not restrict the agency to activity in the dying hearts of the largest cities. It could usefully ensure the preparation of attractive sites in smaller industrial cities and towns.

Because it would work through both the executive arms of local government and the bodies which it helped to set up, it would require a small head office, based well away from London, of people experienced in public and private sector disciplines.

Its sponsoring government department would be the Department of the Environment since it would need the closest relationships with local authorities. It would itself have no planning powers and, like the SDA, would depend for its success on its ability to earn the confidence of local authorities who are sometimes wary of any involvement with the private sector as well as hostile to central government. A recent study of the SDA found that because it works at arm's length from the Government it has been better able to form constructive relationships with local authorities.

The EDA then would either enter into specific contracts with local government whereby, in exchange for central government funding, local authorities would agree the terms on which certain problems were to be tackled; or it would initiate the establishment of a variety of forms of private- and public-sector partnership, large and small, formal and informal, according to the size of a designated area and the type of task to be tackled. But to carry conviction and persuade the private sector that there is a long-term purpose and security for their endeavours any substantial scheme will need a distinct organisation and identity. Private sector interests must be represented in the decision-making, and bureaucratic formalities must be few.

It will be for the EDA to decide what shape and size of executive agency can best promote renewal in a derelict industrial site of hundreds of acres or a single blighted housing estate. The most powerful implement is the UDC, of which two are in existence and thriving, four are in gestation and more will very soon be needed and should now be in preparation.

The government announcement in 1986 of four new UDCs in Manchester, the Black Country, Tyneside and Teesside is another step in the right direction.

The choice of a site for a UDC is to some extent arbitrary. Trafford Park has been chosen, no doubt, because the local authority saw the opportunity and sensibly pressed its case. London by its scale and proximity to the centre had a self-evident case. Liverpool was a challenge at the other end of the spectrum. The EDA will gather the evidence, rank candidate cities in order of need and execute this aspect of urban policy on behalf of government.

An English Development Agency, backed by the Department of the Environment, would lead the campaign to restore the appeal of declining urban areas. The cities have infinitely varied needs. I have described Merseyside as a symbol, but in many ways it is special. Liverpool is a city from which the economic tide has ebbed, as it has from Sunderland and Middlesborough. There is no similarity here with Birmingham, Bristol or, in particular, London. Although these cities also contain the seeds of inner city decay, their road to recovery is closer and probably shorter, as the spontaneous release of energy in London's Docklands shows. Central Newcastle has experienced the decay of old docklands, but has virtually none of the problems associated with the new ethnic communities in Bradford, Hackney and elsewhere.

Sometimes the greatest obstacle to recovery is the enthusiasm of Mr. Kinnock's hard Left seeking to emblazon confrontation across their municipal standards. In practice, if the carrot is juicy enough, the EDA will no doubt secure more cooperation than might superficially seem possible, but there are now some militant local authorities which are concerned more to provoke central government than to cooperate with it. So wide is the division within the Labour Party that such confrontation would be as likely to frustrate a Labour as a Conservative government. There are too many authorities who see virtue in bankruptcy and political advance in visiting its consequences on their communities.

There are no charts through such waters, but there can be no acceptance either of no-go areas.

As local economies revive in areas covered by UDCs the alluvium of special government funding should be withdrawn and the renewed lands handed back to the local authorities with a rate base created or greatly enhanced. Boundaries will need adjustment so that the UDC may shrink at one extremity while expanding at another. At the present rate of progress tracts of London docklands will soon be secure in their new prosperity with no further need of special help. At the same time, along the Mersey I would advocate the extension of the boundaries further into the declining docks and into some tracts of the neighbouring bad housing. Such adjustments would normally be for the EDA to recommend.

The full-blown development corporation will remain the effective but drastic remedy of last resort. But the most promising of the instruments available to the EDA for medium-sized renewal projects is likely to be the non-profit-making private sector Development Trust.

These trusts would be locally-based single-purpose authorities, funded in part by existing forms of central government grant but drawing also on the private sector, with support from financial institutions and voluntary bodies. The full involvement of local authorities would be indispensable. In Scotland the SDA has been able to establish excellent partnership arrangements with Dundee, Leith and Motherwell councils.

The parallel is with the housing association movement and the hope would be that the trusts would harness the sort of local enthusiasm and skill which that movement has attracted. The EDA would have the task of putting together development schemes suitable for a trust to run and 'selling' them to local authorities and private sector backers. It would also monitor their work and be the channel and custodian of the grants committed to them. Such trusts would be eligible through the EDA to receive the existing range of government grants – derelict land, urban development grant and urban reclamation grant.

Private funding will provide extra resources. The government should empower the trusts to issue tax-exempt bonds to attract long-term finance at low rates of interest. This type of financing has been tried and found to work in the United States, where industrial revenue bonds have provided a powerful stimulus to job creation and to local economies. The idea requires only a political acknowledgement that this investment is worthy of public support. Trusts would then be enabled to raise bonds with interest paid net of tax. High tax payers would be attracted while the trusts would carry a lower interest charge than that currently available on the market.

Development Trusts are grounded on firm experience. They had their genesis on Merseyside, and here credit must go to Jim Lloyd, the Labour leader of Knowsley borough council. He had a daunting problem at Cantril Farm, an overspill housing estate designed and built by Liverpool City Council. Before it was even finished it was shunned by prospective tenants. When I first saw it in 1981, only 10 years after its completion, it was a disaster which looked beyond retrieving. It was losing the council £1m a year.

About 4,000 dwellings, a quarter of them high-rise flats, a shopping centre, six schools, six pubs and two churches had been built for 15,000 people from Everton slums which had been cleared; but the population never exceeded 12,000. There were now 400 vacant flats, many of them vandalised; 9,000 outstanding repairs; 800 tenants queueing up for a transfer. Crime flourished. The council had moved in scores of families whom they knew would never pay their rent, since the only other course was to leave flats empty to be smashed by the gangs.

Jim Lloyd, who had many other estates almost as bad, not unnaturally asked me – since I was now being described as 'minister for Merseyside' – what I proposed to do. I said: 'I'll try to find a solution, but I must have one assurance from you: you can reject any plan I come up with, but not on grounds of party political dogma. There must be no objection in principle to capitalism or profits or anything else.' His reply was: 'We have tried everything, and nothing has worked. I am in no position to argue.'

On that understanding we set out to put together a partnership of public and private sector resources. It was clear that huge sums of money had to be written off by Knowsley. Their books showed the cost of Cantril Farm, but Jim Lloyd and the council had to recognise that the estate was worth only half its book value, that they would never see their money back and that, if things went on as they were, they stood to lose much more.

A plan emerged to create a non-profit-making trust to buy the estate for what it was worth. Tom Baron, the builder whose recruitment by my department I have already described, was persuaded to run the trust. Abbey National Building Society and Barclays Bank agreed to invest. Lawrie Barratt then joined in and took on the risk of building houses on the edge of this disaster estate for sale to the private sector. To mark this new beginning Cantril Farm became the Stockbridge Village Trust. It was important to change both content and label.

The trust demolished 730 unloved maisonettes and built 1,000 new houses and bungalows for sale and rent; knocked down the shopping centre, which was laid out on a plan which might have been designed to cater for thieves, and built a new one; the council built a new health centre and a leisure centre. The place is transformed and house values have been rising steadily.

Mistakes were made in the hurry to get things moving. The estate changed hands for £7.4m, but this was £2.5m too much: the structural condition of the buildings was worse than anyone had realised.

Interest rates went up four points higher than expected. Three high-rise blocks intended for improvement and sale proved irredeemable and had to be demolished. Value Added Tax was brought in to push up repair and improvement costs at just the worst moment. A final unexpected and expensive obstacle was the decision of a local rent officer to reduce rents. The new trust found its rents £2 a week lower for improved houses than previously charged by the local authority for the same but unimproved houses, simply because they were in the private sector.

The lessons, however, have been learned. One obvious one is that there must be legislation to modify a rent control system which frustrates even non-profit-making development trusts.

Stockbridge is important because it has shown that solutions can be found. A no-go area has been turned into a place where people are choosing to live and buy homes. If it can be done there it can be done anywhere. Here again is proof that partnership between public and private sectors can save the day. The rescue entailed heavy public expenditure, but another five years of unchecked deterioration at Stockbridge would have left taxpayers and ratepayers meeting a much larger bill.

The Stockbridge story has had a sequel in East London, at Thamesmead. There a referendum held in October 1985 amongst local residents produced a majority in favour of a private, non-distributing company, limited by guarantee, to take over the management of some 5,500 tenanted flats and houses formerly owned by the GLC. Clive Thornton, who as Chief Executive of the Abbey National Building Society did so much to pioneer the Stockbridge Village Trust, became the first chairman. The 1986 Housing and Planning Act provides for other communities to consider the adoption of similar initiatives. The private development trust is another experiment which is an experiment no longer. It works. It is a model for future action.

8

Race: We're All British Now

In 1986 an American President was forced by domestic
public opinion to revise his policy on sanctions against South
Africa. Barclays Bank were so concerned by the drop in their
share of new bank accounts among students in Britain –
from about 27 per cent to 15 per cent over four years – and
the threat to their American business that they bowed to
pressure and divested themselves of their South African
interests.

In the last quarter of a century the world has become a
village and a profound change has taken place in the politics
of race. Britain is not alone as it considers the future of some
two and a half million people from the new communities
who now live here. The world over we have seen the emergence of large minority groups divided by colour, religion
and social habit, united by nationality. America, Russia and
France are only the most obvious examples. Germany,
without conferring nationality, now has about five million
Turkish and Yugoslav *gastarbeiter*.

People of Afro-Caribbean, Chinese and Asian origin have
lived in Britain for over 200 years. During this period we as
a people have had close links with their countries of origin.
They were part of the world's greatest Empire. It took in all
the major religions of the world, many racial groups and a
wide range of cultures. All subjects were equal and served
the monarch, and under the Imperial Act of 1914 everyone
born within the allegiance of the Crown in any part of the
Empire was a British subject by birth. Within the Empire we
also created a tradition of black, white and brown working
together.

People from all parts of the globe settled in Britain after the war, not only because they were looking for new economic opportunities but also because it was the mother country. No one then questioned that those who wanted to should come. Our laws, after all, provided for them to live, work and vote in Britain. When British industry, the expanding National Health Service and London Transport were looking for workers they turned to the Commonwealth.

By the end of the 1960s we had and will continue to have a multi-racial Britain. As a country, as a Party and as individuals we have to adjust to this new Britain. We need to know what we feel and believe about the issues of race. There will never be a time again when we can ignore them.

Throughout history, carnage has resulted from prejudice: racial, tribal and religious. The unceasing conflict in the world today is seldom the product of calculation.

Most of us act and react according to instincts of survival or self-interest. In that sense, prejudice is a natural human condition: we all have prejudices. Human beings are at their most secure in communities to which they can closely relate. The countryman is less happy in the town, the football supporter can develop an antipathy to a rival club, regimental loyalty has a proverbial strength; and in all these can be seen, however remotely, that sense of security we instinctively seek in the safe and familiar.

No one, after even the most casual of glances, can believe that racial prejudice is only about a distinction between black and white. I remember as a child that people pointed out the Jews, and when as President of the Oxford Union, I invited Iraqis and Iranians to the same dinner, there were several empty seats. Even in the great melting-pot of the United States, the Jews, the Italians and the Irish (among others) maintain distinct physical and cultural identities and attract criticism. Black and Asian communities are faced with a similar situation in Britain.

Majorities tend to stick together; minorities, feeling oppressed, cling together, which in turn provokes the majority into believing that they are reluctant to integrate or accept the values of the host community. It is difficult enough when divisions are historic and arise from close geographic proximity, as the tribal rivalries of much of modern Africa illustrate. Immigration on any scale can impose a further strain on the harmony upon which ordered societies depend. I do not seek to excuse prejudice, nor its consequences, but I like to know at the outset of a journey the point from which I start. The law, of course, is not concerned with prejudice: it is concerned to prevent the unjust discrimination to which prejudice can give rise.

I vividly remember my first encounters with flagrant prejudice and discrimination against the new arrivals in Britain, when I was part-owner of a small hotel in Bayswater and part-owner of a business specialising in recruitment for Britain's large companies. We had to handle application forms for positions in middle-management which came in from the potential employer with 'no coloureds' firmly written in.

I saw similar problems at the hotel. When guests arrived to find our hotel full, I discovered at first inexplicable difficulty in getting some of them rooms in neighbouring hotels. I would make a telephone call, reserve a room and send the visitor round. Five minutes later he would arrive to find, if he had a black face, that the vacancy was a vacancy no longer. After two or three such failures, I took a black guest round myself to see him register, but again the neighbouring hotel had suddenly filled up. It was explained to me that the other guests might be upset. The hotel did not wish to give offence, I was told, but they could not afford to lose business.

My contempt for this attitude was tested again when we put together a scheme to redevelop half a street of houses in Campden Hill. We had raised the money to take a lease, rebuild and sell the resulting flats; but when the draft lease arrived from the owners' surveyors, Chestertons, there was a provision to the effect that there must be no sub-letting to black people. I was 25 years old, and this was to be my first big break, but I was not prepared to do business on that basis. I went back to Chestertons. To their credit, they persuaded the owners to delete the offensive clause, and we went ahead.

By the time I entered Parliament, in 1966, the first Race Relations Act was on the statute book, but it was soon clear that another act would be needed to make unlawful the discrimination in jobs and housing of which I already had such unforgettable experience. To my dismay, the Conservative shadow cabinet whipped the party to oppose the new bill's second reading, on 23 April 1968. I was one of about two dozen Tories who refused to vote against it. We felt no little satisfaction and relief when the Party withdrew its opposition before the Bill's third reading.

On 20 April Enoch Powell had delivered his most infamous and unforgivable speech. The nation was mad, he said in Birmingham, to allow the inflow of some 50,000 dependents of immigrants settled in Britain: 'like the Roman, I seem to see "the river Tiber foaming with much blood".' The speech was important because it clearly demonstrated, by transgressing them, the limits to which senior politicians could be permitted to go in playing, it seemed to me deliberately, on the understandable worries of the host community so as to excite animosity, even hatred, against immigrants. In the immigrants themselves it aroused deep fears.

I know that in condemning the Powell speech some will say that I approved the unchecked flow of immigration into Britain. I did not. A policy of tight control is essential in the interests of all in this country. Primary immigration is now almost at a standstill. This is right and proper. Twenty years ago we had different obligations to many Commonwealth countries. Today we have continuing good links with them, but there can be no question of a relaxation of the present immigration controls; it would harm community relations here. The new communities should understand that this is not a racist view. Our obligations as a country today must first be to those who live here whatever their origins.

What was unforgivable about Powell's speech was its confusion of two related but different issues. He used highly emotive language, with consequences he must or ought to have anticipated, to create a climate hostile to the Race Relations Bill then before Parliament, which was concerned not with immigration but with the treatment of British citizens in Britain.

The political focus at that time was on the issue of how we should treat those of the ethnic minorities who were already here. The Powell speech had the effect of overshadowing this with the deep anxieties the country felt about immigration itself. It is difficult to imagine a more destructive intervention in what demanded the most constructive approach.

Fortunately, even more important than the speech was the response of Ted Heath, who at once dismissed Enoch Powell from the shadow cabinet. There could have been no clearer demonstration of the fact that the Tory Party, which Mr Powell later left, was and remains hostile to racial prejudice and to the inciting of racial hatred.

None of us who lived through the political consequences of that speech will ever forget the passions it unleashed, or the false expectations it aroused. Even today it is difficult to explain the mischief that lay behind it. From 1960 to 1963, when inward migration was at a peak, Mr Powell himself, as Minister of Health, had been one of its principal agents.

The reason why I was among the first Conservative MPs to disown Mr Powell's sentiments was that, by the time of his speech, many hundreds of thousands of immigrants had legitimately made their home in Britain. There was no question of persuading them to leave, as he seemed to imply. Britain had a new community in its midst.

In retrospect, some controls over immigration should have been introduced much earlier than they were. The Conservative Government brought in the first systematic controls in 1962, and it was in the interests of everyone in Britain that this should happen. The consequences of the new immigration were also felt widely throughout the Commonwealth, and perhaps still are. It is now clear that it was wrong to repay the huge debt which Britain owed to the loyalty shown by the Empire throughout the Second World War by creaming off skilled and talented workers so desperately needed in the countries from which they had come. It would have been far better to have repaid our debt with educational and vocational programmes in the new Commonwealth, and to have encouraged doctors, lawyers, nurses and technicians to invest their abilities in their own homelands.

We are still reminded of the scale of that debt today. Forty years after the ending of the war in the East, all of us in the Ministry of Defence were determined that Britain would commemorate it as we did so vividly the return of peace to Europe.

In the early morning of Remembrance Sunday, 1985, I

stood with the Duke of Kent and Field Marshal Sir Edwin Bramall – performing his last official duty as Chief of the Defence Staff and the last but one active British soldier to have served in the Second World War* – before the Kranji War Memorial in Singapore, listening to prayers offered up by priests of the Muslem, Buddhist, Christian, Hindu, Jewish, Sikh and Zoroastrian religions. I felt humbled by the knowledge that men and women of so many creeds and races had sacrificed so much for the British Empire, so many of whose values they had shared.

We have come a long way from the days of Mr Powell's warnings. To my mind this country has not only absorbed the changes brought about by the new communities remarkably well, but it has laid the foundations for a promising future for them in British society. We cannot be complacent about this but we have no reason to be pessimistic.

In considering their integration into society over the last twenty years and looking ahead to the future in certain key areas, I would make one generalisation first: we have been careless in allowing the language to be hijacked. We tend to accept with little question the polarised language of black and white. There is no such simple distinction, but it suits many people to pretend that there is. It builds up the numbers, heightens the confrontation and, by oversimplifying, obscures the truth of the great variety of cultures and attitudes. Our daily experience tells us that there is none of the polarisation that the extreme Left and the extreme Right would like to bring about. There is not a single black community in this country. Instead there are many different groups of people with different ethnic origins, assumptions and attitudes.

Given the swiftness of population change in Britain since the 1950s, and the daily possibilities for friction and misunderstanding, the mutual tolerance and friendship between our ethnic and white communities is impressive. It must not be put at risk, and this continual understanding is another important argument for taking some of the general steps which I have proposed to help the inner cities.

---

*The last, General Sir Michael Gow, retired as Commandant of the Royal College of Defence Studies in January, 1986.

The Commission for Racial Equality and its staff rightly highlight the injustices faced by the new communities. They have an important and often thankless job to do in making sure that the law of the land is applied consistently to all citizens throughout Britain – whatever their colour. I fully support their work, as should all Tories. By its very nature, the statutory obligation to promote good race relations must often focus attention on the bad. It is all the more important for others, therefore, to tell the other side of the story.

The good aspects of inter-community relationships in Britain should be proclaimed. There is much good news and it is easily obscured by the bad news, of discrimination and worse, which newspaper headlines so readily sensationalise.

In one generation, since the early 1950s, Britain has become the home of more than two million people who arrived, or whose parents arrived, from the countries of the new Commonwealth and whose darker skins at first marked them out as strangers. Their settlement has taken place with a minimum of disturbance, in spite of its being preponderantly in urban areas of the greatest social stress and in spite of increasing pressures in the 1970s and 1980s from recurrent recession and growing unemployment.

So the white, black and brown British have much to be proud of and thankful for. The children of those immigrants are in ever greater numbers taking the places in British society which were not open to their parents.

Today it is taken for granted that in business, as well as in entertainment and sport, ethnic British citizens are to be found among the most successful. The medical services depend heavily upon ethnic minority doctors, nurses and ancillary staff and the accountancy and legal professions have provided notable opportunities for many with ability and determination. It is not true to suggest that there is no road to the top. Many are embarked upon it. That it is usually a hard road, sometimes almost impossibly hard, I do not doubt, but it is easy to note the hardship and to miss the growing numbers who are overcoming it. This is not to deny that within the overall framework of success there are difficult, sensitive issues that we have to tackle, for the good of all in British society.

Employment is one area where there is always controversy

about the prospects for ethnic minorities. While it is encouraging to see that more and more individuals from the ethnic communities are employed in positions of responsibility, the overall picture is less satisfactory. The most recent Labour Force Survey by the Department of Employment showed that the average unemployment level among all ethnic minority groups in 1985 was twice as high as the level among white people.

The ethnic minorities unquestionably find it harder to obtain jobs, but provided that we recognise it and take remedial action we can put this right. The ethnic minorities earn less, but in the more prosperous parts of South-east Britain and in London the average difference in earnings between white men, on the one hand, and West Indian and Asian men on the other, is now of the order of 10 per cent and is diminishing. Sometimes this may be because of discrimination, but sometimes it will simply reflect the different qualifications, experience and fluency in English of different applicants.

In other cases, however, the persistence of discrimination by some employers is a matter of concern. The evidence gathered by the Policy Studies Institute in their survey published in September 1985, seventeen years after the 1968 Race Relations Act made such discrimination unlawful, showed that 30 per cent of employers still discriminated on grounds of colour and, more worryingly, that there had been little change over the previous ten years.

When a wrong has to be put right the pace of change is never swift enough. These ten years have been a period of increasing difficulty in the labour market, which is likely to have checked progress. It is worth reminding ourselves, all the same, that the vast majority of employers have begun to provide equal opportunities. An increasing number have made formal arrangements of a kind which they would not have contemplated or understood twenty years ago to prevent discrimination.

Some discrimination can be accidental or unintentional. Retiring employees in small firms, for example, will suggest replacements in accordance with long-established practice from the same street or even the same family. The same process is common in Asian or Jewish businesses. In small businesses this is inevitable, but in increasingly mixed communities, especially in the inner city areas, all employers need to be conscious of what is happening and concerned about the nature of the community in which they trade. As they grow, they should make the effort not to develop racially exclusive companies. There should be no room for doubt: the best person should get the job whatever their colour.

The code of practice drawn up by the Commission for Racial Equality, which came into force three years ago, encourages employers to check their procedures, to ensure that managers know the law and to discipline any employee who deliberately discriminates. The code is gradually having its educational effect, and is clearly a thoroughly sensible method of tackling both conscious and unconscious discrimination.

Employers at all levels, in the public service and in the commercial world, should dismiss from their minds the easy but often false assumption that, in filling a key post, there is no point in looking for a suitably capable and qualified black or brown candidate. In Toxteth in 1981 I found no job centre, few training facilities and few opportunities even for sport in a district where enforced leisure had created overwhelming demand. There are now good sports facilities, a job centre and a thriving information technology centre, one of the first in the country. We insisted that people from the ethnic communities were found to help manage and staff them. They were. We did make a conscious effort, and I believe that to have been right.

Statutory provision to ensure this is not wise or effective, but for government to act informally and to give leadership by imposing its own conditions on the use of public money can be. In Toxteth, for example, the ethnic community, resident there in large numbers for generations, had not been given enough openings. I think we set employers an example. In another context, the early monitoring of Civil Service employees in Leeds – now extended – was an important government initiative. Again it is a question of balance. Those who reject, as I do, the rigidity and alienating effect of quotas, must recognise that there is a responsibility on employers to see that their employment practices are fair. British banks trade with great success all over the world under non-white managers. Would it not be realistic to see some such promotions here? Nothing would more effectively silence the demands for rigid quotas than the perception that employers within existing regimes, were behaving fairly.

We do not believe in what Americans call positive discrimination. An offer of special help, say with housing, to a black family, if part of a discriminatory programme, will be seen as the conferment of privilege. Among their white neighbours, themselves in comparable need, this will be likely to exacerbate tension, not lower it. In my experience, leaders of minority groups are generally aware of this danger. They do not seek special advantage but the removal of the disadvantage suffered by poor white and poor black alike.

The inner city task forces promoted by the Department of Employment have directed special help with training and employment opportunities to areas where unemployment levels are exceptionally high. The help is not directed specifically at black people, but the great preponderance of blacks in the target areas makes it almost certain that they will benefit the most.

Kenneth Clarke at the Department of Employment has had to be vigilant to see that the targets were hit. He was right, once the task forces were established, to secure agreements with contractors to employ local labour on building projects in Handsworth, Birmingham, where the need for jobs in the local black community was urgent. There was no question of employment quotas specifying the employment of blacks and no need for any such potentially irritant provision. The important thing was to prevent local people standing idle and watching workers from far afield arrive to do the jobs which they themselves so urgently required and were perfectly capable of doing.

There are thousands of ethnic British today on the verge of conspicuous promotion, but much responsibility rests on managers within both the private and public sectors in easing the difficulties of their transition. It is not a question of the promotion of talentless or inexperienced people. There are many capable, intelligent and energetic Britons whose potential is under-used or even untried; but, among these, members of the ethnic minorities are often the most reluctant to put themselves forward to encounter fresh rebuffs. The best employers pay the closest attention to the importance of advancing talented young men and women who are bent on success and who need only reasonable encouragement to attain it. In the interests of their businesses, they ensure proper career-planning and post-recruitment training, to fit their talented but underqualified employees for promotion. From all these good employment practices members of the ethnic minorities stand to gain most. The Civil Service could offer clerical officers and secretarial employees improved opportunities of promotion to executive level, which again would afford valuable openings for members of minorities.

In a number of deprived urban areas public and private agencies now provide practical help of various kinds for those with limited resources to start their own businesses. Members of minority groups have already shown that they can benefit from these. In some areas, however, as a recent study in Bradford has shown, participation has been disappointing. The minorities have particular difficulties, such as a lack of knowledge of English, and services are being successfully and rightly adapted to meet their needs. We do not need new schemes specifically for the ethnic minorities, but greater efforts must be made to ensure that existing schemes are more effective, flexible, and above all, better known. What is inexcusable is to have public schemes available to ethnic minorites about which they do not even know. It would also help if there were people dealing with them who spoke the same language.

The Manpower Services Commission carries a prime responsibility through its youth training schemes in promoting many of those first opportunities to help the ethnic young into jobs. I have seen enough to know of the commitment of those responsible and the constructive atmosphere found in the workplace. Young ethnic applicants should be encouraged to be more ambitious in the pursuit of skills with which they may not be familiar. It is easy to opt for automotive engineering if you have tinkered around with Dad's banger, but there may be limited job opportunities if too many follow this route.

Many Asians have already established very successful businesses throughout the country, from the smallest corner shop to multi-national companies, but the minorities often face artificial impediments when they begin to make their way in business. It is the clearest duty of our insurance and banking services to ensure that racial prejudice is not guiding what should be purely commercial decisions. Banks can make themselves familiar with the particular areas of potential demand that ethnic communities generate. I do not have in mind only Asian businessmen. In recent years we have seen the emergence of an Afro-Caribbean entrepreneurial class which, although relatively small, is breaking through. An encouraging precedent in history can be found in the Jamaican entrepreneurs who in the 1930s settled in parts of New York. So successful did their energy and drive make them that they were dubbed the 'Jamaican Jews' by their envious neighbours.

I have pointed to some encouraging signs, but there are no grounds for complacency. I shall argue in a later chapter that a society which allows it to be assumed that unemployment will stay around three million, or anywhere near it, for the indefinite future takes risks with its stability. Where that unemployment is concentrated, and where that concentration is perceived to be disproportionately black, the dangers become acute. This was something of which I became acutely conscious during my period at the Department of the Environment.

The inner city riots of the early 1980s, serious in themselves, were also warnings of the extra fragility of public order when unemployed and disaffected youths had to be restrained by almost entirely white police. The lesson which they had for government was that the police cannot safely or fairly be expected to treat unaided the symptoms of social ills for which political cures must be found. The Scarman Report was a sober warning of how wide responsibility is spread.

The Tories are fully alive to this responsibility. At the annual Conservative Party conference in Blackpool, in October 1981, a few weeks after the Brixton and Toxteth disturbances, the Party was understandably anxious. As Environment Secretary, I had to reply to the debate on the inner cities. It was clear to me that someone on the platform had to test the party's determination to take up this new challenge to political leadership to do whatever might be done to heal the wounds of the cities and to act against injustice suffered by black or white people.

The Tory Party, like all parties, has its share of bigotry. It was important for the Party and the country that I should secure a generous and not a grudging response, and that my speech and its reception should make plain where the Party stood. The night before the debate I stayed up late, pondering what I should say. When the time came, I reminded the conference of our tradition of compassion and tolerance and recalled the courage and vision of both Benjamin Disraeli and Iain Macleod. Then came the moment to lay the ghost of Enoch Powell: 'We now have large immigrant communities in British cities,' I said. 'Let this Party's position be absolutely clear. They are British. They live here. They vote here.' I added that there were no schemes of significant repatriation which had any moral, social or political credibility. These plain statements of the truth, I am glad to recall, were at once warmly endorsed and applauded by the conference.

Unfortunately we cannot ignore that fact that there are those in our society who would have it otherwise. They seek to divide, and their efforts have some success in widening the rifts to which rapid social change will make any community vulnerable. Sometimes those rifts appear between age groups and within families. Sometimes agitators strike at the very heart of our social stability, for it strikes at the family unit upon which that stability is based. The older values of many ethnic communities seem empty to their children. The second generation, born and brought up in British society, educated here, and looking for work here, have not had an easy time. Some have become alienated not only from British society but also from their own elders. Too many, albeit a small minority, have become frustrated and negative, unemployed and uninvolved. This in turn has made them easy prey for criminal elements and for those who press them into anti-social activities. Such problems can only be cured by accepting these youngsters into the community and giving them a chance to participate fully in our society. The very bleakness of prospect can stimulate an arrogance of attitude which transfers responsibility from the individual to society. The Left will pander to such a view. 'There is no point in you trying because they are against you' is a simple but wicked message. The Left of the Labour Party is today throwing up a black leadership in local government that is alienating the decent white audience whom its language is designed to hurt. It will destroy itself in the end because of the offence which it is also giving to decent, moderate black people. But we must then make sure the moderate voices are heard, and that will present, as always, a particular responsibility for the Conservative Party.

At the other end of the spectrum we have the agitators of the ultra-Right. In the name of Britain and of patriotism they peddle their intellectual filth with the staring bigotry that sent them marching into the Jewish communities of London's East End in the 1930s. They are at one with the yobs on the football terraces who abuse sportsmen for their colour or who harass innocent Asians on the streets. Sadly they are British. They are not patriots. The Tory Party must redouble its efforts to deal with racial attacks and harassment. They stain Britain's reputation and, as the Home Office has acknowledged, blight the lives of many members of our ethnic minority communities.

Racial harassment indicates that prejudice is not a simple phenomenon. The Commons Home Affairs Committee was right in its report last year to urge a change of policy on the police, so that they initiate prosecutions in cases of assault which have racial causes. The police are understandably reluctant to use limited resources in pursuing the vast numbers of cases of common assault, but I hope they will look again at what can be done in cases where racial motives are suspected. As the Home Affairs Committee reported, private prosecution is an unsatisfactory remedy when the victim can have no legal aid but his alleged assailant is given it. It is important to accept the Committee's recommendations in order to preserve good community relations and to increase the confidence of the ethnic minorities.

Police forces in the cities have moved a long way since the riots of 1981 to improve the foundations of mutual trust between them and the rest of the community. Senior officers have admirably increased their awareness of the needs and apprehensions of the districts they police. Many of the home beat officers, especially the more experienced, do remarkable

work. The training in race relations now given to police
cadets is generally agreed to be excellent. It is to expect
superhuman qualities if we fail to remember that early
training can be forgotten in a critical moment, or when
pressure mounts; and it has been suggested, wisely I believe,
that regular refresher courses would be valuable. The police
presence in the deprived areas where many of Britain's black
and brown populations live must be perpetual, and that very
fact multiplies the incidence of contacts between the police
and innocent young people, black and white.

This inescapable circumstance puts the highest premium
on the good behaviour of every policeman on the beat, the
first point of contact which the young person on the street
has with the agencies of law and order. The Government has
rightly diverted significant extra resources to this essential
public service. It is a proper political priority to recruit the
highest quality of applicants for a career that demands
maturity, intelligence, bravery and downright decency in
large measure. To have a police force characterised by
exemplary behaviour, patience, courtesy and, hardest of all,
restraint even in the face of provocation is an ambition which
no one, least of all the police, questions. But the behaviour
of the police is, in some parts of our cities, a staple topic of
conversation wherever members of the ethnic minorities are
gathered. One lapse by one constable under pressure rever-
berates through those communities. A slight, real or
imagined, to one indignant citizen becomes a slight felt by
50 others. The strain on the police is immense. Those of us
who do not share their daily exposure to these problems owe
them our understanding as well as our unswerving support.

Among those who need special understanding are the
slowly growing number of black and Asian police, of whom
there are still less than 900: fewer than 1 per cent of the
total force when this book was written. There is no shortage,
as is sometimes claimed, of well-qualified potential recruits;
the difficulty lies in getting them to come forward because
they know that they may incur the disapproval of their
families and neighbours, who still too seldom see the police
as allies. They are also hesitant to face the sharp retorts that
they might get from some white members of the community.
This is beginning to change. The encouraging local reaction

to police activity in St Paul's, Bristol in 1986 may show a
welcome change of attitudes, but no opportunity should be
lost to identify the ethnic community with proper policing.
The ethnic minorities need safety on our streets as much as
anyone else and in fact often suffer disproportionately from
mugging and street violence. It is in their interest therefore,
as well as that of society at large, that they contribute to
providing a more effective and integrated police force.

The ethnic minorities have to understand that the law
applies to all British citizens, whatever their colour. If a
criminal offence is committed, or the police have reason to
believe that one has been committed, they must have the full
support of the community and the right to carry out their
investigation thoroughly. We cannot accept dual standards;
the law must apply to blacks and whites in an equal manner.
We cannot accept no-go areas. The moderate elements in
the ethnic minority communities, which are after all the
overwhelming majority, must play their part in keeping in
check the criminal and anti-social elements. Without their
co-operation the police cannot easily serve them in their daily
lives.

Schools have an important part to play in helping tomorrow's adults understand the need for racial tolerance and the
need to accept the diversity of cultures that exists in our
society. Education must reflect this diversity, but not by
accentuating the differences nor by giving undue emphasis
to a single minority. On the contrary it is important that
every child, whether Celt, Jamaican, English or Bengali
should have the skills and outlook to enable him to play a
full part in British life.

One of the first signs of a positive development in the
politics of race is the active participation of the ethnic minorities in the democratic processes of this country. Among all
political parties and in many regions, the number of ethnic
minority councillors has increased significantly over the last
twenty years. In the 1982 local government elections, out of
5982 candidates, 246 were identified as being from the ethnic
minorities. Of the two main parties only 3 of the Conservative Party's 40 ethnic minority candidates became councillors. In the Labour Party's case 58 out of the 92 were
successful. In the Conservative Party the presence of members

of the ethnic communities at constituency functions – in London, Halifax, Leeds, Bradford, Huddersfield, and elsewhere – is now commonplace, although there are more brown faces than black. The process which will bring more and more of their representatives into elective office, at all levels, is advancing steadily.

We shall soon see black and brown MPs. They will not be the first to enter the Commons. In the General Election of 1892 Dadabhai Naoroji, originally from Bombay, was elected as the Liberal Member of Parliament for Central Finsbury 1892–5. He was not re-elected, but in 1895 Sir Mancherjee Merwanjee Bhownaggree became the first ethnic Conservative MP, representing Bethnal Green East. Nine years later he was defeated in the Liberal landslide. Shapurji Saklatvala, a communist, represented North Battersea from 1922–3 and again from 1924–9.

It was in Toxteth that a most eloquent black woman, in the aftermath of the 1981 disturbances, explained to me the importance of monuments. Her argument was simple. 'How do you expect members of the young black community', she challenged me, 'to climb the ladders of opportunity which you, as a Tory, so frequently talk about, if there are no monuments at the top of the ladder to encourage them up it?' I understood her well enough. The sooner those young blacks could identify success in society – their society and ours – with their own kind, the sooner their ambitions and hopes would be raised and the dangers of alienation dispelled. If we do not ensure that the ladders of success are in place, people will climb what other ladders they can. If we do not encourage moderate leaders, others more extreme will fill the vacuum.

I have no doubt that this coming generation will produce these monuments.

Our society can and does reap positive benefits from becoming increasingly multi-cultural in its composition. Already there are significant areas in British life where fresh blood, fresh ideas, fresh energy and enthusiasms are all contributing towards a more vibrant and confident community – in industry, commerce, music, the arts, design, craft techniques, sport. Much more can and will follow if we give it the chance, and allow an injection into the traditional culture of this country of the new life and talent of the new communities.

How many gifted blacks are held back because of the ball and chain of those negative stereotypes which our predominantly white society helps to foster? The destructive images of the drug-dealing Rasta or the riotous youngster seem more potent than the solid achievements of a Daley Thompson or a Trevor McDonald.

Once our society has learned to give full play to the talents of our minorities we will be surprised by the contribution they will make. This will not be done by creating special forms of privilege but by allowing all citizens the full freedom of the social, political and economic life of the country to which they belong.

I forebore in my Blackpool speech in October 1981 to quote the famous text which I had in mind from Disraeli's Crystal Palace speech of 24 June 1872. It is perhaps over-quoted but it still seems to me admirably to embrace today not only the Conservative Party's duty to black, brown and all other minorities, but its need to strike roots in all of them and to draw strength from all of them. 'The Tory Party, unless it is a National Party, is nothing,' said Dizzy, and he went on: 'It is a Party formed from all the numerous classes in the realm, classes alike and equal before the Law, but whose different conditions and different aims give vigour and variety to our National life.'

That is what we seek: not conformity from our ethnic minorities, not white people with black faces, but a society in which the variety of our peoples enriches our country.

There are those who never stretch out the hand for fear it will be bitten. But those who never stretch out the hand will never feel it clasped in friendship.

9

Tomorrow's Homes

The Archbishop of Canterbury's Commission on Urban Priority Areas said: 'A home is more than bricks and mortar, more than a roof over one's head. It also means security, privacy, sufficient space; a place where people can grow, make choices, become more whole people.' That was well put. It explains why shelter, together with food and clothing, is one of the most pressing material needs of mankind.

On the previous page of the same report was a more arresting statement, attributed to an unnamed resident of an overspill estate in Kirkby, on Merseyside: 'People here have to live in a mistake.' Of all the mistakes to which government, whether central or local, is prone, those in housing policy can prove the costliest.

It is no surprise that housing is of central political importance. It conditions our whole society. A family that is well housed may not be sure of leading a contented and constructive life: without a home which is dry, warm and in reasonable repair there is little chance of it. People not only want good housing: most want to own their own homes. To purchase a home is usually the largest investment decision which a family will make. The number who have done so ensures that wealth is now spread more widely in society than ever before. We have hardly begun to consider the implications for many of yesterday's children who are now beginning to inherit in middle-life substantial sums from their far-sighted parents.

It has been settled Conservative policy, based on the soundest Conservative instinct, to encourage this commitment to home ownership by stimulating the construction industry and by providing incentives to buyers. Today nearly two out of three families own their homes in Britain. More than one family in four is in the publicly-rented sector. The private rented sector has fallen from 90 per cent in 1914 to only 10 per cent today.

The growth of the property-owning democracy in our time is perhaps the most profound social revolution since the great Reform Act extended the franchise in 1832. Wider home ownership means that more and more people have invested their wealth in social stability. This remarkable change in housing tenure is the result of the continuous application of Tory principles, and would not have been achieved without the commitment of Harold Macmillan and Ernest Marples in the 1950s and the Right to Buy legislation of the present government.

There is more achievement yet to record. The slums have largely gone. The poorest in our society often live in quite unacceptable housing by today's standards, but not by the standards of their parents. Most of the local authority and New Town housing programmes have delivered what was hoped of them. (The conspicuous failures of the overspill estates, the rushed slum-clearance programmes, were born of urgency; and responsibility must be shared by central and local government.)

The Housing Association movement has brought local initiative and experimentation in a flexible alternative to the previous monopoly of public housing. The establishment by a Tory government of the Housing Corporation in 1964, and the revision and extension of its role in 1974, sprang from our deep concern for the quality of public provision and our equally deep suspicion of monopoly.

As a result of all this effort most people in Britain today are well housed. That is not a prelude to complacency, merely a refusal to play the traditional national game of self-denigration. Any objective appraisal of 40 years of housing policy must come out on the positive side. That is not to say that there is nothing more to do.

In this chapter I want to comment on the state of the housing stock. The nature of the problems is not in serious dispute, but there is disagreement about their scale, the urgency with which they can be addressed and the ranking of priorities. The bidding for public support, by the pressure

groups and specialist correspondents who now work so effectively to influence public opinion, will be as active in the
housing lobbies as elsewhere; so the Government will not
automatically accept every new set of statistics which seems
to demonstrate a crisis. Statistics do not always establish
common ground. Often they only provoke debate. Some
argue need on the basis of council waiting lists; but others
recognise that these are notoriously unreliable guides to
genuine need or even genuine demand.

The first problem is the quality of the housing stock. The
English House Condition Survey, and a range of other
evidence, leaves no doubt that, although most of Britain is
well housed, the condition of much of our housing stock is
in need of urgent action.

Although we now have more houses than households, too
many of those houses are unfit. There is still a backlog of
repairs and improvements to council housing, and many of
the 5m council-owned dwellings in England and Wales are
in disrepair or run-down. They comprise over a quarter of
the dwellings in our country, and the Audit Commission
estimates that they are worth over £100b at replacement cost.
The Commission has rightly highlighted this crisis. There are
acute problems, too, in the private sector, where over 2m
dwellings lack one or more of the basic amenities, are in
need of substantial repair or are unfit for habitation. Nearly
half these private houses are owner-occupied, often by the
elderly. 200,000 of them are vacant, together with 110,000
empty properties in the local authority sector.

The weight of evidence points to problems that are massive
and growing. If one has even a layman's acquaintance with
building costs, a few hours on the urban streets, or even in
rural communities where the problem is harder to spot, will
give a fairly clear idea of the scale of investment needed.

It has been estimated that to put all the local authority
stock into acceptable condition would cost perhaps £20b.
This is neither practical nor economic. Some dwellings ought
to be demolished because they have deteriorated to a level
where renewal or replacement is the least cost-effective
option, or because their basic design and layout is inadequate. Many, for example, of the high-rise and deck-access
estates no longer provide acceptable living conditions for

tenants, and never will at justifiable cost. There is no point in throwing good money at hopelessly bad housing.

While we debate the scale of the task, the task grows bigger. In my experience of property, bills deferred are bigger bills when they catch up with you. Today's leaking gutter is tomorrow's rotting wall, and properties left empty are the vandals' playgrounds.

This problem stretches across the country. London and other parts of the South-east face massive repair bills. There are around 500,000 dwellings, mainly flats and maisonettes, built between 1919 and 1970 by their local authority owners which are either vacant, difficult to let or in poor structural condition due to design faults and neglected maintenance.

Not all the fault lies with local government: the initial quality of some of this housing stock was inadequate. I am as critical as the next man when it comes to the poor management or profligate expenditure of local authorities, but we should remember that it was a Labour government that introduced a subsidy system which made it cheaper for a local authority to invest in high-rise and deck-access estates than in conventional housing. Everyone knows what the tenants would have preferred. Conservative ministers in the 1960s advocated system-building, believing that the new stock would better meet people's needs and would safeguard quality.

It surprised me, when I was in the Department of the Environment in the 1980s, to discover how few councillors ever explored the minutiae of control which central government imposed on their councils. The blame was at least shared.

Private sector companies, building for sale to customers who could and did exercise choice, rejected these design solutions. Their contracting arms were building them by the thousand under council contracts, though, on the time-honoured principle that the customer is always right, they cannot carry the whole responsibility for the inherent design weaknesses. The 1960s and 1970s saw the parallel development of large numbers of new private sector homes, and of homes put up by local authorities. By 1979 the huge post-war new-build programme was over. The International Monetary Fund arrived in 1976, and the Labour government abandoned, among much else, its dream of a spreading municipal jungle. The capital housing budgets of local government have not kept up with their total expenditure. In cash terms expenditure on housing went up from £3.3b in 1975–6 to £4.5b in 1981–2, then went down to £2.9b in 1985–6. But as a percentage of total expenditure, the trend has been very much downwards – from 7 per cent in 1975–6 to 4 per cent in 1981–2 and then to only 2 per cent in 1985–6.

In 1979 it seemed both right and economically unavoidable to concentrate on the massive shift into home ownership brought about by the sale of council houses. It made sense to reflect the crude surplus of houses over households by continuing Labour's reduction of public sector building for rent. The agreement I reached with Geoffrey Howe provided that 75 per cent of all housing capital receipts would be freely available for the renovation and rehabilitation of the local authority stock or other capital purposes. Houses that went into private ownership became the responsibility of the new owners, as their improvement soon showed. So we had a coherent approach: satisfy the legitimate demand of council tenants to buy, and encourage local authorities to use these usually privately-financed capital receipts for the benefit of their remaining tenants. It was the only way on offer from which all could have benefited, and I believe we should remove the constraints which the Treasury imposed later when it limited further the proportion of capital receipts which could be spent.

I come now to the future priorities, finance, and balance between tenures, and the land without which demand will not be satisfied.

We must maintain in a cost-effective way the housing which will still have a useful life, and we must make good use of it.

Our primary aim must be to provide proper housing for everyone, within a wide choice of tenure which reflects people's ability and wish to own or rent; to do this, we must provide land on which homes can be built on reclaimed or new sites; we must do what we can to see that there are houses where there are jobs; and we have to do all this within the limits of scarce public resources and of people's ability to afford the private housing which most of them want.

I take land first. My experience as a constituency MP and as a minister has shown me that there is no simple or satisfactory answer to the problems of land release. I represent one of the most attractive of the Home County constituencies, including part of the Thames Valley and the Chiltern Hills. The Town and Country Planning Act, 1948, has prevented an urban sprawl from one end of it to the other, and I strongly support the high restraint and conservationist policies of the local planning authority. On the other hand, complaints about these policies are perhaps my most frequent constituency problem, as individuals seek to pursue legitimate personal interests and are frequently thwarted when they make planning applications to improve or build new homes or offices.

As Secretary of State for the Environment I presided over the process designed to control the release of green land for large-scale building. The builders argued there was never enough, and pointed to the rising land prices to prove it. The civil servants indicated large swathes of available land. The builders said it was in the wrong place. Reconciliation between two such divergent interests founders on the practical reality that the inhabitants of the desired parts of Britain will only take so much and are armed as effectively as the house-builders. Their own interest group, the environmentalists, are in the ascendancy and I am on their side.

The formal process of land release starts with structure planning to indicate in broad terms where development should be encouraged. Prepared by county councils, the plans may be amended by the Department of the Environment.

When I reached the Department of the Environment, only a handful of structure plans had been approved after seven years' work. The opportunities for delay were unending. Assumptions were challenged, the challenges explored and compromises proposed. By that time the assumptions had changed, and it all began again. It seemed quicker for me to approve the plans without further delay rather than to allow the process to go on until we could pass legislation to end it. We pushed the remaining county plans through as rapidly as possible. I never expected that by approving the plans I

would add significantly to human knowledge, but it moved
them out of the way.

They were so vague as to be either obvious or valueless.
They indicated in general terms how many houses should be
allowed for by district planning authorities. Many counties
opted for a lower figure than the house-builders wanted and
the market indicated. Local politicians knew that there
would be no votes in the threat of larger planning
permissions. The Secretary of State in approving the plans
had to accept, amend or reject the county's views.

When I discussed Berkshire's plans, I had to face the arguments from the county about economic growth, spiralling
land prices and the need to house the employees of the hi-
tech industries of Heathrow's sunshine belt. At the same
time, I had to face the hostility of those who already lived
there. I compromised at a level rather above Berkshire targets
and well below the construction industry advice. 'Heseltown'
entered the language of political vituperation, as indignant
protests flooded into the department.

No change in this system is going to prove acceptable to
the conflicting interests. Any move towards a more locally-
controlled policy of planned land release at district level will
lead to more restrictive policies than those in the county
plans. District councillors will encounter and accept demands
to limit and conserve. That is what people want when it is
a question of housing development within their own
community. One family's planning permission is another's
lost view. More local and more restrictive planning would
lead to more appeals and slow the process further.

The alternative would be to put planning control in the
hands of central government. This would mean that land
release would depend on the policy of the Department of the
Environment, as interpreted by the planning inspectorate.
This would make it possible for central government to
impose very specific land release strategies on local authorities and to enforce them through the appeals powers. No
Conservative government could take the strain of large-scale
land release in the southern counties and, if this is true today,
it will be truer tomorrow: both the pressure to build and the
political danger of yielding to that pressure will increase with
the construction of a Channel link. I strongly support such

a link but it will not be without its consequences upon public attitudes to development in the South-east. A proper balance between local interests and the national need for land will depend in the end on the will of central government to achieve it through the appeals procedure.

Given the overwhelming political pressure, this solution is perhaps inevitable, but the more coherently it is used the more trouble it will cause. Trouble enough flows from a site-by-site, field-by-field approach: expand the scale and the trouble expands exponentially, and the opposition parties exploit the position as much as they can.

In an attempt to work through this inherently unsatisfactory situation, the major housebuilders have proposed the creation of privately-financed new country towns. The principal argument for this proposal is that it would concentrate development in defined and limited areas; but that would depend on planning authorities then rejecting all major developments on the fringes of existing communities, and the Secretary of State supporting that rejection.

My fear is that no such cut-and-dried solution would emerge. The outcome would in practice be both marginal development and new towns in the countryside. Local controversy would be inevitable. The idea is not to be dismissed out of hand, but it is bound to be fought wherever it is proposed.

Another route would be a much earlier indication from the Secretary of State as to where his inspectors will uphold appeals and where they will not. In the absence of such guidance, we have today's questionable process in which an appeal is conducted, which can cost thousands of pounds, although the outcome is often easily foreseen.

Part of the answer lies not in changing the planning process but in countering the economic forces which are creating the excess of demand over supply for homes in the prosperous parts of Britain. While house prices rise at 25 per cent a year in Surrey, they may be static or even in decline in Scotland, the North-east, or Merseyside. Formulation of housing policy must take account of the fundamental divide between the two Britains. The economic pressures to invest in the South are too powerful to be thwarted or deflected by restrictive regional policies such as industrial development certificates;

or outweighed by regional development grants. Throughout this book I have stressed my belief that we must remove much of the incentive that lies behind this southward surge, and intensify the efforts to build an environment that will attract people back to the older urban areas.

Any policy of greenfield land release must be against this wider tapestry. If land in the South is the only land to which some new wealth-creating industries will go, then the public sector, in its military, research and administrative activities, should move further north and west.

Every incentive which pulls resources southwards should be examined and continued only if the case is overwhelming. Certainly a less rigidly uniform wage structure is a most desirable objective, and nothing proves this more than the quite different housing costs now prevailing in different regions. The Civil Service, if given a structure of greater autonomy at departmental or regional levels, could lead in the breaking of this mould.

This approach is not about new subsidies. It is one that expects the Government to question itself about the consequences of its policies in establishing the pattern of demand in different parts of the nation.

If all this were done, it would be easier to convince the country that it was necessary to release more green fields. This precondition is essential in the towns and cities, where it must be shown conclusively, before new land is developed, that every plot of already spoilt or under-used land will be fully used. We all know that this is not now the case.

The Government is right to insist on the release of land recorded on the land registers. These registers were created in 1980 to force public bodies to reveal their ownership of land which is unused or insufficiently used. The public bodies include all local authorities, the Post Office, nationalised industries and the public utility companies. At the time, it seemed a proper solution to the problem of despoiled publicly-owned sites which were lying idle because owners either could not afford to remove the long-standing dereliction or had lost sight of their assets. We brought Derelict Land Grant into the cities to deal with this, offering to remove the negative value of idle land at public expense.

No minister ever quite foresees the inertia of British public

administration. The legislation seems watertight, but it takes
two years to prepare and bring to the statute book. By that
time the minister may have moved on, and when his
successor wants to use the power every sort of delay occurs.
The local authority or nationalised industry argues that it
has a plan to use the land. Ministers have so far issued only
a handful of directives, and release of land has taken much
longer than we hoped when we designed the measure.

In retrospect I now see that we should have taken firmer
powers at the outset. I have no criticism of colleagues who
labour under the weight of site-specific detail which present
regimes demand, but I hope that they will learn from my
experience.

There is much merit today in the ideas being pioneered by
Anthony Steen and his colleagues to take a much more positive step. This is the establishment by statute of a development company, a realisation agency, which would take over
Land Register land and be charged with its development.
Machinery would be needed to ensure that eligible land was
registered. The transfer to the company of all unused and
registered sites vacant for two years or more would be automatic. Public authorities from which land was taken would
be compensated in one of several ways. They could be given
equity in the development company or in a specific
subsidiary, or receive loan stock according to the value of
the land. The loan stock would be non-interest-bearing,
redeemable when each site was disposed of. The directors of
the company would be chosen to represent both the legitimate public interest and the property development skills of
the private sector.

The public authority would have a limited time within
which to persuade the development company to hand back
a site, if it could satisfy the company that it had both a use
for it and the necessary cash. Disputes could be resolved by
ministers. The company would be eligible for government
grants as at present – derelict land grant, urban development
grant or urban reclamation grant – but would otherwise
raise its money from the private market using its property
portfolio as security.

If we are to rebuild our cities to make them attractive
places in which to live or invest, we should not allow old

industrial sites, long abandoned or run down, to hinder the
overriding public interest in comprehensive redevelopment.
New housing, however, cannot be limited to recycled land
within the urban areas. In a demand-led market economy, if
we are to make these urban areas an acceptable alternative
to suburbia, we must build an environment which is competitive with suburbs and green fields. This leads to a second
and controversial conclusion. We will not make much of the
older inner cities attractive if we continue to concentrate
public resources only on improving and repairing the existing
housing stock. There are limits to the role of housing action
areas, general improvement areas, improvement grants and
enveloping schemes. We need balance. Compulsory acquisition for improvement or demolition has been largely abandoned. To create an attractive environment, sites of sufficient
size are needed to allow architects and developers – both
private and public – to build new communities and not just
new housing in declining areas. This will require some further
comprehensive redevelopment. At the present rate of demolition this is not a serious possibility: demolition has fallen
from a peak of over 80,000 houses a year in the late 1960s
to fewer than 20,000 a year today. The total housing stock
is 22m, which means that at the present rate we will renew
the stock every 1100 years. This makes no sense.

The bulldozer conjures up an era of wanton destruction
of comfortable communities and their exile to the concrete
jungles; but we must not forget that there was a need to
clear appalling housing. A glance at the fading sepia photographs of pre-war Britain's urban communities should
remove any doubt that the clearance was necessary.

There are now 1m houses that are classified as unfit for
habitation on standards laid down more than 25 years ago;
and a further 1m which, while not classified as unfit by these
outdated standards, are lacking in one or more of the basic
amenities, or need substantial repair. It is arguable that we
should increase the demolition rate to perhaps somewhere
in the region of 50,000 a year, thus creating new sites. This
could be done without making unrealistic demands on the
capacity of the building industry.

Of course we have to remember the people whom clearance schemes would affect. My memory of compulsory

purchases for road-building brings back two thoughts. First, generous compensation is the cheapest policy because schemes go ahead faster. Second, there were examples of hardship which I found particularly difficult to take. Sometimes the value of a property to be acquired is low, and the owner of a poor but precious home cannot afford to buy another, and has to rent from the council or a private landlord. The State should not turn owners into tenants in the name of public interest. A fair and attractive way to overcome the problem would be to establish an entitlement to compensation adequate to secure ownership. If the compensation did not allow a reasonable purchase, the acquiring authority would provide an interest-free mortgage to bridge the gap.

I have advocated changes in our policies towards land. Next I consider ways in which money can be made available or used more flexibly. The problems which I have described cannot be solved within the existing pattern of expenditure. To begin with, too many local authorities do not maintain their stock to a decent standard. The private sector, on present rents and with present tenure restrictions, will not do so either. New building for letting on any scale cannot be financed at existing rents. Many of the most acute needs are felt by people already living wholly on public provision.

Some local authorities pursue housing policies which fail to address the strategic objectives which I have outlined, and to which I believe a Conservative government is committed, with continued damaging consequences to their cities. Even if allowed to spend more money they would be unlikely to change direction. On the other hand, the market in private housing for sale is, by and large, buoyant. Rising prices reflect rising demand, higher earnings and expanding credit.

The privately-owned sector should be the easiest with which to deal. The building societies and banks are more than able to provide the finance needed, and market interest rates appear to overcome the lurching consequence of feast and famine that used to upset the market so often. Building societies are about to embark on an exciting new phase of their history as the restraints that prevented them from owning land, or from building for rent or sale, have gone. But the inability of the elderly and relatively poor owner-occupiers to maintain their homes presents a problem which is growing as the length of retirement increases in an ageing population. Building on experiments advanced by this Government, the concept of 'care and repair' has developed. A local housing association, for example, can offer a service that brings together builders, improvement grants and interest-only building society loans to take the anxiety off the shoulders of the elderly while helping to maintain the fabric of their buildings. This is a concept which needs expansion.

Attitudes had begun to shift by the late 1970s. The activities of the building societies, which have served society well for 100 years, are changing fundamentally in response to their wider opportunity. They played a significant role in the Financial Institutions Group and pioneered shared ownership with the housing associations. Today they not only earmark special funds for problem areas, but seek the comprehensive upgrading of these areas to protect their investment and to help local people.

The Building Societies Act of 1986 opens up a new world of experimentation and competitiveness. A new generation of chief executives is taking over. The signs are that they will put 'building' back into building societies. They will certainly make possible our intention to meet much of our future housing needs.

It is only a decade since Peter Shore rightly confronted the societies over the unwritten practice of 'red-lining' declining areas and refusing mortgage finance for houses within them. Nothing was so certain to tip the area finally over the edge. The pioneers in the building societies remembered their social purpose and felt a genuine concern at the deprivation they saw.

Clive Thornton, the chief executive of the Abbey National, and now the chairman of Thamesmead, came from the North-east. Lawrie Barratt, who is a builder, led housebuilders into the inner cities, and showed what could be done. He comes from Newcastle. They took risks, and there were others like them who showed a most attractive face of modern capitalism. Thornton took risks in persuading his society to invest in perhaps the most remarkable experiment of all – the revitalisation of Cantril Farm, now Stockbridge Village – one of the most deprived and squalid estates in

England. Barratt bought a half-destroyed block of walk-up flats in Toxteth, converted them and sold them – with building society backing – often to local people.

In seeking funds for local government housing we should build on the success of the Right to Buy legislation. The Treasury's restrictions on the spending of the local authorities' receipts have thwarted part of our objective. With lower receipts now likely as the sales rate declines, I would give local authorities freedom to spend all new capital receipts on the repair and improvement of their own housing. This change of policy would encourage them to maximise their sales of houses and land. The present policy provides little incentive to realise assets. Accumulated receipts, which amount to £6b, should be released for investment at a rate which would not fuel domestic inflation. If necessary, this could be done on a regionally varied basis to reflect differing levels of economic activity. They should be released only to authorities which could show proper standards of management on their estates, in order to ensure that new money is not being thrown after bad.

Another leap in housing finance could be possible if we did for public housing what we have done for publicly-owned industry. Government could accept responsibility for outstanding debt charges if complete estates were sold at their market value to housing trusts, housing associations or such approved private sector landlords as building societies. Market value would take into account the returns from rents, and a calculation of outstanding capital sums required for necessary repairs.

There is a precedent for this. We have recognised that, in coal, steel, airways and elsewhere in publicly-owned companies, there has been indifferent or bad investment, and we have written off the capital debts. In other words, they were transferred from the industry to the taxpayer, and the industry was given the chance to start again with a realistic balance sheet.

If we were to introduce the same realism in municipal housing, there need be no time limit. On the other hand, as Geoffrey Finsberg showed with the GLC housing estates, if government wished to speed the process, it could divest authorities of all or part of their housing empires. This might be necessary where obduracy, as opposed to practical argument, was the cause of resistance. It could be the biggest phased privatisation operation of all, involving the sale of up to 5m homes and producing anything up to £20b or £30b, over a period. There is no point in transferring without a plan to rehabilitate the stock. To invigorate and release an explosion of new resources and opportunity throughout urban Britain is an exciting prospect. It implies new standards of management, new authority for tenants and, perhaps for the first time, control by the occupants over the standards of housing maintenance.

The fewer homes the local authority owned, the more it would be able to concentrate on the strategic responsibilities which it possessed. It could concern itself more with the quality and provision of service, rather than its detail and execution. In pursuing their strategic role, the authorities would need nomination rights over a significant proportion of the homes that moved out of their ownership.

I now show the relevant public expenditure figures spanning the past ten years, and I have put together several lines of figures which are not usually grouped in this way:

| | (£ billion – current values) | | |
	1975–6	1981–2	1985–6
Total public expenditure	£48.9	£92.7	£133.6
DOE housing expenditure	4.111	4.674	4.246
Housing benefit (rent allowances and rebate)	0.292	0.557	3.16
Mortgage interest relief	0.895	2.050	4.75
TOTAL:	5.298	7.281	12.156

The Government controls each of those figures. They represent the totality of the central government's financial support for housing.

The table shows the extent to which mortgage tax relief is now the largest element of support. It has served a huge purpose in establishing the property-owning democracy. But does this profile of public support now conform to the nation's housing priorities? The politics of the situation are obvious. No political party can expect support from six million owner-occupiers asked to agree to give up £4.75b of tax relief. The Labour Party threatens to deprive top-rate taxpayers of higher-rate relief. They deserve no credit; it reflects their conviction that there are few votes for them in such circles. But the climate is moving. Since Britain has one of the highest levels of owner-occupation in Europe, with a growing demand for cash to restore the housing stock and rebuild our towns and cities, all within a constrained economic climate, it is important for those arguing for change to say how it should be paid for.

There is another more practical argument which undermines the case that mortgage interest relief (MIR) is an essential feature of the housing market. When this government was elected the average house price was about £20,000 and the ceiling for MIR was £25,000. Seven years later the average price has increased by 50 per cent to £30,000 while the ceiling for MIR has increased by only 20 per cent to £30,000.

The further south one comes, the more striking are the figures. We have to ask ourselves if MIR is really essential to the home-buying process. How have house prices doubled in the South-east when MIR has risen by only 20 per cent? In practice, pay increases and extra credit have financed the house-price explosion; prices would not have exploded if people could not pay them. To raise the MIR limit now will only enable more people to offer higher prices than they can today. That will further push up demand and therefore prices, as the supply cannot be increased sufficiently within existing land and planning policies. Just as I argue that it is desirable to end the rigidities which keep southern wages lower than they should be in relation to provincial wages, so it must follow that it is better to pay more in the congested areas to reflect demand there rather than to subsidise home buyers at ever-rising costs.

In America, lower income tax rates have been accompanied by fewer tax allowances. Nigel Lawson spelt out the case when he did the same for our companies, reducing corporation tax and abolishing capital allowances. Is there any way to square the political circle? I think that with courage, and on the basis of three conditions, there is a way forward. First, it would be wrong to withdraw MIR from those who enjoy it. Anyone with an existing mortgage will have to be allowed to keep the concession for the life of the mortgage. Second, we should recognise the difference between those on the ladder of ownership and those anxious to take the first step. For the latter we could leave MIR in place, or find an alternative which would give first-time buyers an incentive to buy without promising its continuance for twenty years. Third, we must present the change as part of a long-term proposal that balances this phasing-out with lower income tax rates and a higher capital investment programme, together with the basis for a new universal housing allowance. Such a policy would slow the increase in house prices, attract those who want lower taxes, meet the concern of first-time buyers and release resources to rebuild our towns and cities.

Some are worried that the value of their house would fall. The evidence in the South and London does not support such a view. As the value of MIR has declined relatively more in these areas, it has coincided with an above-average increase in house prices.

The concept of a universal housing allowance is now well documented as a result of the Duke of Edinburgh's report and other studies. This proposal is to switch subsidy for the less well-off from the house to the person. There is no realistic way to tackle the appalling condition of the private rented sector, or to encourage new build for rent, which does not recognise the need for higher rents; but, since much of the demand for rented stock comes from people with low incomes, it must be better to reflect their inability to pay by helping them directly rather than to inflict long-term and prohibitively expensive damage on our housing stock by a low-rent regime.

I come finally to the sort of homes people want: to the choice of tenure.

We have a housing stock that is two-thirds owner-occupied. There is still some scope to increase this proportion, and the Conservatives will push hard to achieve it. The Opposition still underestimates the strength of public feeling on this, as we saw in the demand by council tenants to own their own homes. It was as if we had flung open a window for them on the first day of Spring. Many tenants suffered from municipal indifference, remoteness and poor service. But it was a deeper emotion – a fulfilment of a dream previously offered only to others. Tenants wanted to control their own lives. It had often been members of their own families who had bought and moved to a greener suburban world. In some cases the urge to move was simply a response to mismanagement and poor environment.

John Stanley, the Housing Minister, who had an insatiable capacity for work and the imagination to explore and expand the housing market, was largely responsible for other ideas designed to bridge the gap between owners and renters. To help those on the margin of ownership, low-cost starter housing and shared ownership were introduced. The starter homes enabled those who would otherwise have joined the list for council housing to buy instead. John persuaded local authorities to sell land at cost to builders who guaranteed to sell homes at low prices and to offer them first to families on the waiting list or in other priority categories. Many were built on cleared sites in built-up areas.

Shared ownership offered part-purchase of a home, with rent paid on the rest of it until that too could be bought. Buyers raised up to 75 per cent of the cost from the building society, so that the element of public investment was limited – an early example of 'leverage', the fruitful use of public funds to enable a larger private investment to be made.

Housebuilders responded with other ideas which increased their market. They pioneered sales in the inner cities and in the London docklands, and promoted housing for sale in New Towns to a level which enabled us to stop building for rent. Two thousand new houses a year are now built for sale in London's East End, where a few years ago 98 per cent of householders were council tenants. Local authorities claimed that electors wanted more homes for rent, but their tenants have bought the new houses. In some towns rehabilitated council stock was saved for a new generation of owners. Bad council estates, classified as 'difficult to let', were sold to private developers who improved them and found new buyers.

Over the same period, local authority housing performance has been patchy. In rural districts particularly, and in the authorities where human scale has been preserved, it has often been excellent. Much that is good was built before 1939, and areas with mainly pre-war stock do not have to bear the debt charges which burden those larger authorities which had to pay for post-war slum clearance. In Liverpool, which has some of the worst and worst-managed housing in England, rents were among the highest in the country. An effective market should produce the opposite result. The worst local authority housing has been, and in some cases still is, a disgrace – whether judged by its management, its physical design or the social imbalance which it creates.

The appalling condition of some local authority stock is often linked with incompetent, over-protected and over-paid direct labour departments. In Liverpool, where I saw how bad the worst housing was, the low standard achieved by the direct labour department, which employed more than 1,600 men and had a turnover of 24m, convinced me of the need for competition and new accounting methods. Well-managed urban housing authorities offer an efficient and commendable public service. Others have tried hard to make good past defects. In Liverpool, I could scarcely believe the indifference which the union leaders whom I met displayed. Repair programmes were planned to suit the workload and practices of the council works department. Costs were inadequately controlled and estimates regularly exceeded. The workforce had extracted bonus schemes which were inadequately monitored and frequently manipulated.

Much local authority housing has been badly built, and central government must share responsibility. After the 1979 election we changed the relationship so as to get better value for money. We changed the approval system for new subsidised housing: instead of requiring positive clearance from regional offices for every design detail, we asked authorities to attach with their drawings and applications an estimate of value. We took into account for the first time the interest payments which would be incurred from the time of site acquisition to completion of the finished houses. If a council did not hear from us within two weeks, they were free to proceed. Instead of crawling over every local authority scheme, we investigated only 5 per cent in detail. We abolished the Parker-Morris standards which required councils to build houses with larger rooms than the private sector offered. It meant that private buyers sometimes subsidised council tenants who were not only better off than they but enjoyed more living space.

I have said that I would give greater freedom to local authorities to use their capital receipts, but would impose conditions. Restoration of sensible funding levels must require in return a new approach to management, giving a real sense of involvement and responsibility to council tenants.

Home ownership can be a family's most tangible evidence of wealth and independence. It should not be assumed that council tenants do not want to enjoy that same sense of independence. A householder who chooses to take a tenancy has chosen to leave responsibility with the landlord; but for most local authority tenants there is no choice. I am convinced that, the more tenants become involved, the more they will exert influence over the management of the estates; and in time this helps to build the spirit which makes for stable communities.

The success of the Right to Buy policies naturally reduced the number of publicly-owned homes, and it was equally natural that houses sold more readily than flats. Our housing policy must ensure that the remaining tenants do not feel abandoned to the worst-designed or worst-managed public housing. Many tower-blocks or deck-access maisonettes need substantial expenditure to transform their forbidding environment. Others will have to be demolished. The key to effective management of the remaining estates must be the fullest involvement of their tenancy, and we would betray a crucial part of the Tenants' Charter, which bestowed the right to buy, if we were content to let those who could not buy remain in deteriorating ghettos.

There is now a new perception of how local authority housing should be run: an acceptance that people should come first, that management should serve the customer and that decisions should be local and immediate. Managers should be seen and questioned. It is a simple philosophy and it works. In the housing trust developments, first at Stockbridge and then at Thamesmead, the involvement of tenants is central to the concept of a trust. There are tenants' co-operatives in Liverpool, and in 1986 the pattern of community-based housing authorities was extended to three local authority estates in Glasgow.

Municipal estates are now commonly divided into local management units, with separate direct labour or private sector maintenance contracts. A tower-block on the Wood-church Housing Estate in the Wirral, that was 'no-go' in 1981, is now properly secured and portered, and has its own community committee, run largely by the elderly. It is a joy to visit. A similar transformation can be seen at York House on the Thorpe Edge Estate, a direct-access block in Geoff Lawler's Bradford constituency where a dynamic woman, who chaired the tenants' committee, persuaded the local authority to give them a role in management. On Merseyside we set up community refurbishment schemes in which we took building workers off the unemployment register and employed them, under the community programme, in repairing their own estates.

The Tenants' Charter is best known for the right to buy, but it was much more than that. It offered a better deal for those who remained tenants as well: legal rights to be consulted and to become involved in the management of their estates, to compel their landlords to carry out necessary repairs or to have them done and reclaim the cost. This part of the Charter attracted less attention and is taking longer to make effective, but is of equal importance. The Government must be ready to develop it further.

A high standard of management must now become the norm, not the exception. That is why I would make the release of capital conditional on each local authority introducing a management plan which put tenants' needs first. There is no need for uniformity. Estates can be taken over and controlled by their tenants, on the lines of the community-based housing associations, but that is not easy: it requires training, organisation and professionalism. It will lead to a growth in management services offered by building societies or housing associations. It implies that the professionals in local government will take on a more strategic role. The prospect is of an improvement in council housing which will stand comparison with the effects of the right to buy.

There is a stark contrast in the growth of the public sector and the decline of the private rented sector, which has come close to being written off as a significant contributor to our housing needs. With the new approach that I would advocate for the public stock, we need a new regime for the private rented sector also.

Rent levels that fail to reflect capital values, and sometimes even to cover the cost of adequate maintenance, have had their effect. As always the minority – probably the tiny minority – of landlords has chilled the climate. In all walks of life that minority is present, and any changes we make will therefore need to be tested carefully for the use that the unscrupulous may make of them.

Once, by chance, I overheard a conversation between Rachman and one of his managers in Bayswater in 1956. It was brief and unforgettable:

Manager: 'A young girl has fallen off the balcony of one of our houses and died.' Rachman: 'Are we insured?' He drove away content: they were. I do not want to see a future Tory government visited by such ghosts of the past.

New lets in the private sector could be freed from control. This will lead to higher rents and strengthen the case for a needs-related allowance, without which another door would close on the poor who depend, disproportionately to their numbers, on the private rented sector. It would be wise to impose conditions on these lettings, to ensure that there is a written contract with a minimum term of notice. This change will not of itself, however, solve the problems of the private rented sector, and it will attract the same political hostility from the Labour Party which destroyed that sector. The shorthold provisions were intended to increase private sector lettings, but because of Labour's threats only a few such agreements have been made.

Few will invest money in long-term housing to rent in a field so subject to the swing of the political pendulum, and most investors can secure higher and safer returns elsewhere. Shorthold will bring some existing properties into the rental market, but not many.

The basis of a new system is another scheme which we introduced in 1980 and which has attracted no Labour veto: the assured tenancy scheme. The scheme, which approached the difficulty from another direction, was based on the provisions of the Landlord and Tenant Act of 1956, which governs commercial lettings and has stood the test of time. The tenant enjoys security but pays a market rent. The good landlord gets his return; he is not seeking short-term capital realisation. A fair deal is struck and, so long as the terms of the lease are observed, the tenant enjoys security and the landlord enjoys a fair return.

The assured tenancy was designed with the institutional investor in mind. To ensure that it was not abused, we restricted it to approved landlords. We applied to the business of letting housing for rent exactly the same regulatory climate as we now rightly apply to transport operators, providers of commercial credit, employment agencies, betting shops or licensed premises, and for the same reason: to protect the legitimate majority of those who provide services, while denying territory to the cowboy and the spiv.

The most urgent area for reform is the rent-controlled private sector. The combination of assured tenancy regulation and a needs-related rent allowance could bring controlled property back to an economically sane regime. The choice now before us is to trust the market place or to watch the housing stock rot: there must be a middle way.

I would back the concept of the approved landlord such as the building society. The landlord would be entitled to a reasonable return on capital, the tenant would pay an 'affordable rent', defined as a proportion of his total income. If the permitted rent was less than the affordable rent, it would be paid by the tenant and he could claim no public subsidy. If it were more, the balance would be met by the new personal housing allowance.

Existing private landlords would be able to apply, as now, to become approved landlords and to agree the terms on which their controlled estates would move to the more sensible regime which I have outlined. If they were prepared to improve their homes and manage them properly, then the opportunity of approved status would be very attractive both to them and to their tenants.

Housing associations, some set up by building societies, but many registered with and under the control of the Housing Corporation, are beginning to break into this area. At St Mellons, in Cardiff, several hundred new homes are

being built with a subsidy of around 30 per cent. Rents are
set at the market level, which is not much higher than the
old fair rents, with assured tenancies. The rest of the investment is to be provided by low-start building society finance.
The Housing Corporation itself is using £30 million of grant
in 1987–8, again restricted to 30 per cent of capital costs,
to support registered housing associations in providing up to
£100m of new housing, much of it for homeless families and
job movers, on assured tenancies throughout England and
Wales, with the backing of the private sector. North Housing
Association – Britain's largest – has announced a £100m
scheme of its own for assured tenancies.

Here is a first step to reviving the private rented sector. If,
as well as implementing the Tenants' Charter, the Government could stop and reverse the decline of the private sector,
it would have achieved much.

It is worth experimenting with tax concessions to private
landlords. It is unlikely that freedom from the fair rent regime
for approved landlords will result in market rents that offer
returns of more than 4 per cent in many parts of the country.
Those who wish to rent rather than buy are often those who
cannot afford to buy. A return of 4 per cent or less will not
compensate an investor, who would otherwise be content to
wait for capital appreciation, for the loss in value when a
house with vacant possession becomes tenanted. Building
societies, who have to compete for their funds in the open
market, are unlikely to invest more than a small proportion
in rented housing at these low rates of return.

It is possible by fiscal relief to reduce the cost of the
original investment in a new vacant-possession house to its
value as a tenanted house. The effect would be to increase
the return on the net investment to an acceptable level. There
are two ways to achieve this. The Business Enterprise Scheme
could be extended to allow an investor in newly-built rented
housing to write off his entire investment against his income
tax. His net investment would be reduced by anything from
29 per cent to 60 per cent, and his present 'fair rent' return
of 3 per cent on the gross investment would become a return
of between 4.5 per cent and 7.5 per cent. This tax incentive
would be clawed back if the house did not remain rented for
a minimum period of, say, twenty years. If it were sold,

capital gains tax would be payable only on any excess over the original gross cost. Alternatively, tax exempt bonds could be permitted for this purpose.

Of course, there is a cost to the public purse in all this, but the public purse already pays for housing the poor, often at a higher cost. Incentives, as I have suggested, could bring private investment back into the provision of new rented housing. The tax foregone in attracting the private sector would be between 29 per cent and 60 per cent of the cost, which compares with current capital grants to housing associations which may reach 85–90 per cent of the cost.

One question remains. How many houses do we need? As Secretary of State for the Environment I was sceptical of all the precise calculations of housing need and the impossible expectations which they stimulated. I remain a sceptic.

No country or company can argue responsibly for programmes that are beyond its means. That is not to say that all the calculations are invalid; but they are based on assumptions each of which is arguable.

The policies which I have discussed attempt to realign priorities and release resources in a way most likely to meet growing and acute demand. Some require only administrative decisions; others will encounter the fiercest political opposition.

The major assumption underlying my proposals is that local authorities will continue to be responsible for housing strategy. Many of my arguments are for changes in the way these authorities conduct their business. Tenants' Charters, the right to buy, the sales of estates, the enlarged role of housing associations, the Land Realisation Agency, the enhanced opportunity for the building societies, banks and private housebuilders – all could be seen to diminish that role. This is the wrong interpretation: the right one is to see local authorities standing back from the detail to ensure better provision all round.

The authorities must recognise, and central government through its funding policies is right to insist that they recognise, that they must take a wider view, concern themselves with the quality and not just the quantity of housing, and allow both owners and renters the fullest possible scope for determining how they are to be housed. The State cannot finance more than a fraction of our housing needs: the private sector must be welcomed as a partner, and our purpose must be to ensure a balanced community, with the widest choice of tenure, in the continuing effort to meet the nation's housing needs.

10

Education: Investing In The Future

Of all the elements on which Britain's prosperity depends and which governments can control, none is more important than education. Education is the mainspring of our future success, and a society of opportunity starts first with opportunity in education. It was in Scotland that an understanding of the value of a national education service first led, in 1691, to the passing of a law to provide parish schools and secondary schools in every town. There was then an interval of nearly 200 years before Parliament enacted a similar law for England.

Government's role has been indirect and often weak, and the evidence of this weakness in recent years has made education a matter of the most acute public concern. The Conservative Government has been wise to respond to this concern by asserting its national responsibility. It has taken a number of steps to improve the education system for future generations, which, taken together, constitute the most important reforms since the 1944 Education Act.

A decade ago Shirley Williams focused our attention in a 'great debate' about education. I do not object to debate on any scale, except where it is a substitute for action. That is largely what it was.

The debate has been converted by this Government into a series of initiatives on standards, the curriculum, examinations, vocational education, parental rights, the management of schools, the needs of minorities and the structure of the teaching profession. The broad range of this activity is in marked contrast to the Labour Party's concern not with the quality of education but with its egalitarian and ideological aspects. Our purpose must be to establish a proper framework within which the talents of our young people can be fully developed.

I have stressed elsewhere in this book the need to secure better management, better performance assessment and higher standards in many aspects of our life. We need to apply these criteria to our education policies.

I see no need to change the basic structure of our education system. Much is good and some excellent. It requires, rather, a change in emphasis and direction, and it is on this basis that I have framed my thoughts. Most of the country's teachers, in both schools and higher education, prove themselves every year to be a competent cadre of professionals. They work hard, although the best have not, until recently, been rewarded well for it. The drab assumptions of unionised mass membership, with its emphasis on low differentials and conformity instead of wider differentials and recognition of responsibilities, have exacted a price in this occupation, as in so many others. The management systems within which teachers have to work are often defective, and the excesses of some local authorities have made the tasks of teachers and the lives of their pupils harder and, in extreme cases, intolerable.

It cannot be over-emphasised that teachers are at the receiving end of such powerful social changes as diminishing family cohesion, growing urban deprivation and high unemployment. They do not create the problems. They have to try to cope with them.

That does not mean that we should rest content with the way in which our schools are run. We have to look at the management of schools and the organisation of the school system. But since we cannot run the schools without the current stock of teachers, it is essential to conduct a dialogue with them which recognises the value of their contribution. We need to determine what framework will help them do their job most effectively and obtain the best possible results. No solution will commend itself to all teachers. Most education ministers over the last few decades would have liked to abolish the Burnham Committee, the teachers' cumbersome pay-negotiating machinery. The Audit Commission added its voice. The Government was right to act, so that now the bizarre practice that enabled pay to be negotiated in one forum and conditions of service in another has been ended.

The first duty of education must be to ensure that people develop their personal, social, practical and intellectual skills to the utmost. It should leave them with a lifelong curiosity and thirst for learning. It should also instil the confidence to compete and succeed. Children are different: given the same opportunities, some will advance farther and faster than others. Clearly, opportunities are not equal across the country. The Labour Party, however, still celebrates a false dawn in its belief, twenty years into the comprehensive school revolution, that comprehensives can be effective instruments in creating social equality. The doctrinal campaign to abolish grammar schools robbed many gifted but poor urban children of opportunity. The wish to restore what Socialism took away, as well as recognition of the inevitable disparities in facilities, aptitude and inclination, persuaded me – as I explain later in this chapter – of the importance of widening opportunities for adults to return to education.

The quality of Britain's primary education is good almost everywhere. There are faults, but the schools have come well through the extensive re-organisation forced by the collapse in the number of children seeking places by a third over ten years. School closures, both in rural areas and in inner city areas of declining population, have been largely completed at the primary level. There can never be enough good teachers: quality in every field is limited. But those in the primary system have provided a good start for children and it is unjust to criticise primary schools in general for not 'getting back to the basics'. I believe, however, that many teachers would appreciate a clear statement of the standards their pupils should reach by the time they are ready to transfer to secondary schools. Strict guidelines are, I believe part of other countries' success.

The most acute difficulties in British education lie in the 11 to 16 age-range and in the nature of post-16 provision for those who do not opt for higher education. Higher education itself is in a state of flux. Financial pressures have forced some rethinking about priorities, but other countries, as recent events in France demonstrated, have had to face equally awkward changes.

In secondary schooling, as in so much of our society, Britain is a land of sharp contrasts. Secondary schools in most middle-class counties and suburbs work relatively well. Many consistently yield impressive overall results, and have been a force for good in their communities. We cannot say that about many schools in the inner cities. Inspectors have issued report after report on their disheartening state. Inner London has been a prominent target for their criticism, which proves again that pouring out resources with more liberality than intelligence does not solve problems; but performance across the country is uneven. Several urban authorities have better records than the Inner London Education Authority, but there is no automatic link between high spending and good results. As a matter of fact, Japan spends proportionately less than we do.

The concept of the comprehensive school resolves nothing in itself. Indeed, it can simply make life an obstacle course for the able, while failing to teach basic and practical skills to the less able and therefore more vulnerable. Even if we ignore the worst schools, there is a pervasive drift to mediocrity which is deeply disturbing. Those on the receiving end – the employers and university staff – tell of appalling writing standards and no breadth of reading. Neither literacy nor numeracy matches the standards expected by working society today. The average results of British 16-year-olds, despite many high achievers, fall persistently below those in other advanced nations, the gap in maths being particularly acute.

Often it is the less able and less motivated inner city youngsters, precisely those for whom Labour's social engineering was designed, who have lost most from the comprehensive system. Neither their inclinations nor their needs have been recognised. In our deprived inner cities, high unemployment and social tensions can combine to make a local comprehensive school a source of anti-social behaviour. In these areas the voice of reason in the schools themselves can often be drowned. As the quality of the school declines, the more ambitious and more mobile families move out, so hastening the deterioration of both school and neighbourhood.

As in other areas of inner city life where I have tried to describe the forces at work, a pattern of low expectations and poor results is established. There is little challenge or excitement. Pupils sense little of relevance between their activities and the world of work outside. At home there may be no books and little encouragement from parents, who may both go out to work or be on the dole. It is a wretched downward spiral; falling rolls, declining teacher quality and morale, an ever-decreasing range of subjects, poorer and poorer results.

Kenneth Baker's scheme for city technology colleges is a sensible experiment. The curriculum, laid down by the Secretary of State, will have a technical and scientific emphasis. Trustees will control the spending of the private money which they raise and of the grant aid which they receive from government. They will circumvent traditional local authority control. They will establish high standards to provide a competitive spur to others, and boost the technical education so urgently needed. The Left argues that these schools will be élitist concentrations of hand-picked teachers and carefully-chosen children supported by a comfortable level of resources. This is false and the attitude is the one that destroyed the grammar schools in the first place. It must by now be clear to all that removing or frustrating high standards is not a formula for levelling up but for levelling down. The victim is the talented child of poor parents. For bright children, white or black, these schools could provide the first step to a better life. If successful, they may also help to revive one part of the life of the run-down areas in which they are sited.

There is a stiff challenge in the teaching of those pupils whose home background, personal qualities and talents place them in what the world of education calls 'permanently under-achieving' groups. They are not by nature drawn to the virtues of competition; but the rewards in satisfaction to teacher, pupil and employer alike are there to be had.

The need to improve education from 11 to 16 is not just pedagogical theorising. The path into the world of work is increasingly rocky. Schools have a responsibility, forgotten by some, to guard against a mismatch between what they are teaching and the rapidly changing skills needed to pursue a livelihood. Teachers have a profound effect on young people's perceptions, and schools can help to change the climate of enterprise by raising the status of business in the eyes of able pupils. A striking success of Industry Year 1986 was the increased rapport it brought about between schools and the world of business, with an increase from 25 per cent to 75 per cent in the proportion of secondary schools linked with local employers. There were successful secondments of pupils into business to 'shadow' executives as they worked. It is of vital importance that, with the end of Industry Year, these contacts should be maintained and strengthened.

There is an impatience today that we have allowed so wide a gap to open between those who teach young people and those in a position to employ them. The more young people understand and appreciate the role of industry and commerce, the more schools can help to implant the realis- ation that a first-class technician is likely to be both happier and more useful than, say, an incompetent sociologist. Neither academic nor personal values need be sacrificed in giving schooling this stronger vocational thrust. It is clear from the results achieved at the best of our secondary schools that the most effective antidote to adolescent boredom in the final years of school is a well-taught and balanced injection of personal and vocational skills.

However much 1986 may have stimulated a renewed interest in a closer relationship between school and employer, the relationship in its infancy remains fragile. Both sides of the present divide must work to close it. Here the chambers of commerce might raise their profile, and help to promote fruitful collaboration between industrialists and teachers on the curriculum. Help by local companies with maths and physics teaching might be arranged. More advanced pupils might be attached for some of their classes to local firms, to work in laboratories or on computers. Industry Year estab- lished that the ignorance in many schools about business was matched by the ignorance of most employers about what went on in schools. There would be clear mutual advantage if more representatives of local business and commerce sat on school governing boards.

Among the cultural components of our society has been a natural antipathy between those in schools and those in industry. It is not new. In the last century, and between the wars in particular, both independent and government reports expressed concern at this country's poor performance in the invention and design of manufacturing goods and the gross disparity between the numbers of skilled young people produced in other countries and the mere 'labourers' produced in our schools. Our rivals have long been putting down firmer roots for industrial supremacy.

The Second World War brought home forcibly our shortage of qualified manpower, but the hopes of establishing a technical secondary school in every town foundered on local authority priorities. A Conservative minister, David Eccles, secured in the 1950s a nationwide expansion of Technical Colleges. As a result, night school at 'the Tech' came to Britain 70 years after a Royal Commission on Technical Instruction in 1884 drew attention to its significance in Germany. 'Techs' are now Further Education Colleges, with wider scope. We must draw them closer to the job creators – a task in which the inspectorate can help. The inspectorate in turn would be helped if its assumptions were tested by cross-posting with industry.

Our system of education is heavily decentralised, with local authorities free to adopt any ideas, imaginative or harebrained, that may attract them; but ultimate responsibility rests with central government. Kenneth Baker and his colleagues have asserted this responsibility. The Department of Education and Science has returned to the pursuit of standards where, until recently, the more flexible budgets of the Department of Employment had been making the running. National standards, implying central control of the curriculum, should head the agenda.

Reform is not designed to make the life of teachers more difficult, nor to add another layer of bureaucracy to the running of schools. Indeed we seek to free schools from the extremes, constraints, and vagaries of local government and at the same time to reward better performance. We have to safeguard not only annual expenditures of £9b but our only permanent national asset – the capacities of our people.

When this Government was elected, standards were largely determined by the syllabuses laid down for GCE. These were influenced by the academic requirements of our universities.

School was a path designed to lead to university. But it was a narrow path which encouraged early specialisation, too often involving the dropping of maths and science subjects. The curriculum was often largely irrelevant to the needs of society as well as to those of the individual. In 1938 the Spens Report criticised the domination of the school curriculum by university entry requirements when more than 85 per cent of pupils left school as soon as they reached the minimum leaving age. Nothing much changed in the next 30 years.

One of Sir Keith Joseph's undervalued achievements has been the reform of school-leaving examinations, including the introduction of new vocational qualifications for those not aiming at higher education. Using money from the Manpower Services Commission he also supported the Technical and Vocational Educational Initiative (TVEI), which has provided less academic 14-year-olds with a more practical education. After a three-year pilot scheme, TVEI was extended in 1986 and the money to pay for it was offered to all local education authorities. Its value is now proven and the time has come when all local authorities should be required to adopt it.

It is an example of the long tradition in English education that makes it difficult for the Department of Education and Science to act decisively. The tradition is to grant permissive and discretionary powers to LEAs, so that the country is dependent on the initiative – or inertia – of scores of council committees. Some local authorities on the Left are interfering increasingly and dangerously with the curriculum. We have also given teachers a unique degree of discretion over what is taught. This delegation is out of line with practice in most other countries.

The Germans, French and Japanese insist on a national interest beyond that of the individual, the company or, for that matter, the school or the teacher. In Britain, until the 1902 Education Act, the Board of Education did exercise direct authority over the schools; the government then devolved its authority to the counties. Eighty years of experience suggest that, as far as standards are concerned, this decision was wrong and should be changed.

In the pursuit of change, Sir Keith Joseph secured from Parliament an important enhancement of ministerial power.

The Secretary of State now has a budget which he can spend. In 1984, it amounted to only 0.5 per cent of the educational budget (about £30m). Two years later, that percentage increased to 1.0 per cent, and is bound to increase further now that the principle of total financial delegation through local government has been breached. A window of exciting opportunity has been opened. The Secretary of State could now bring to life a wealth of innovative teaching ideas by enabling individual schools to tender for extra resources to be allocated to particular objectives, such as closer industrial links, special careers teaching or language teaching.

The British system of local delegation has thrown up further problems. Local education authorities have not made the financial savings expected after the dramatic collapse of the birth rate, the effect of which on the demand for secondary school places was clearly foreseeable a decade ahead. Continued failure to match lower numbers with a more realistic provision of facilities entails much wasteful expenditure and curtails the range of subjects available in many schools – particularly in the inner cities. The continued maintenance, cleaning and heating of surplus buildings drains off money urgently needed elsewhere.

Good practice is not spread widely enough. The potential scope for savings which could be invested is shown, for example, by the disparity between the various London boroughs on annual cleaning costs of between £105 and £38 per pupil.

The Audit Commission has identified potential savings available to local education authorities' from falling school rolls of between £500m and £700m a year by the 1990s. To realise anything like these savings will require school closures to be made at more than twice the current rate. All closures are unpopular, but they would be made more acceptable if the resources which they released were available for use on improvements in other schools. We could start by increasing the 30 per cent of local authorities' capital receipts which they are permitted to use each year.

Again, we could experiment with more specialisation in secondary schools, not by returning to selection at 11-plus but by encouraging our city schools to develop centres of excellence. Schools with strong departments in, say, maths, music, computers or languages could build on them and draw in from other schools pupils of identifiable potential in those subjects, stretching their ability to the full. It would promote both choice and achievement.

It is not the role of schools to provide specialist training for those going into industry, though they cannot properly ignore the job needs of their pupils. But we have fallen behind France and Germany in involving industry in the training of apprentices and the teaching of technical skills. In America they do not have such formal structures as the Germans, but the commercial ethos there means that successful companies run very effective training programmes to meet their requirements.

In Britain we have neither. Our apprenticeship system does not compare with that of France or Germany, and too many British companies offer little training. The average company in Britain spends only one-sixth of the sum which its foreign competitors devote to training their workforces. Fewer young people in Britain continue in full-time education after the age of 16 than in most other advanced industrial countries. In Germany, 700,000 young people complete apprenticeships each year – ten times the British figure. German employers see training as a responsibility and an essential investment; too many British employers see it as an expensive optional overhead.

The Victorian self-help, pick-it-up on the job attitude, coupled with the restrictive attitudes of many crafts, is still too common in British industry. So is the stand-off attitude of shareholders in our large companies, with the consequent pressure to keep profits high and expenditure on research and training low. Neither industrial managers nor shareholders can afford to ignore the danger. Not all do. But Mr Bryan Nicholson, chairman of the Manpower Services Commission, was reported in March 1986 to have told Nottingham businessmen that, compared with that of competitor countries, the British workforce was 'a bunch of thickies'. He recalled that a survey of 45 comparable companies in Britain and West Germany, which all produced similar products using simple equipment and technology, had found that productivity was 63 per cent higher in the German than in the British firms.

The taking of greater responsibility for standards by central government should be balanced by putting more authority into the hands of the schools themselves. Schools could be controlled much more by their governors, the executive responsibility vested in headteachers. This is not a revolutionary idea: it is how the public schools are run.

The largest single group on a governing body should be parents, whose representatives should be elected by a ballot of all parents. The other governors would be appointed by the local authority which should be under an obligation to select half of them from among those who represent the experience of local employers, in consultation with the local chamber of commerce. Central government would reserve the right to appoint governors as a last resort if it appeared that the proper provision of education was at risk. Sadly, the Leftward lurch of some councils indicates that such powers would prove necessary in some areas to restore and preserve public confidence in education. The governors of each school would appoint the headteacher on contract for, say, five years, and he or she would in turn appoint the staff. The head would have the power to terminate appointments, within the present framework of employment legislation, but there would be a right of appeal to the governors. The head's own appointment would be reviewed at the end of his or her contract, and if it were not renewed there would be an appeal to the LEA. At least for the interregnum, severance pay, which should be generous, should be met by the LEA.

As chief executive, the headteacher would have responsibility for the expenditure of the school budget – covering teaching and administrative costs as well as equipment and maintenance – and for the standards of the school. The principles of executive responsibility are as appropriate for schools as for government officials. Any funds raised from industrial or commercial companies, from the hiring of premises or from any other source, would remain at the disposal of the school. Examination results would be published, as would reports from local or national inspectors.

The LEA would be responsible for laying down minimal staffing standards, and for providing the management training which heads would need to handle their new responsibilities. The LEA would also be responsible for the in-service training of the teachers. Executive responsibility would, however, free heads from any obligation to use local authority services, including direct labour organisations.

We have to make the whole of education much more aware of the importance of assessing performance. Teachers, pupils and schools must demonstrate, on the basis of agreed criteria, that the system as a whole, and its separate components, produces the best possible results. There is in the world of education a reflex response that educational standards cannot be measured. But good schools are known to be good schools because of their results, and good teachers never fail to acquire good reputations, even in difficult schools and tough districts where it is a hard struggle to obtain good results. The universities, which at first resisted the idea put forward in Alex Jarratt's report that the quality of performance can be measured, have accepted the concept, and argument is now directed to the best means of measurement. In schools, the basis of performance assessment already exists; it has to be improved and codified. The schools inspectorate, local and national, must play a central role in this, with more regular and frequent school inspections by HM Inspectorate.

These changes should be welcomed by the vast majority of teachers, pupils, parents and society as a whole. Certainly they would draw the schools closer to their communities and to those who will offer jobs to pupils when they leave. I believe they will lead to better schools with more successful pupils, and will allow heads and teachers a far bigger role in determining how to give to the best of their ability.

As the expansion of higher education gathered pace over this century it was only to be expected that the emphasis and pattern would be based on the traditions and attitudes of our older universities. As centres of excellence and intellectual power houses of world status, it was Oxford and Cambridge which produced most of the people who took the decisions. Even today half of Britain's university vice-chancellors are products of Oxford and Cambridge, as were a third of all staff in British universities in the late 1970s. They were steeped in the experience of an intimate relationship between tutor and taught, the belief in close collegiate living and a commitment to academic freedom of choice. The main stream was a liberal education in the humanities.

This century has seen a growth in the number of educational establishments, but all too slow a shift in emphasis towards business and technology.

Governments assumed the lead in both these key objectives, and rightly so. Decade after decade, they have sought to tip the balance in higher education towards the interests of business and industrial development. Between the wars it was government which proposed to the universities the desirability of establishing our PhD degree system, in the general belief that Britain was falling behind Germany and the United States. Government decided in the 1950s to improve the low-status university colleges of the 1930s; it created nine new universities and upgraded the colleges of advanced technology in the 1960s; it established a parallel public sector range of institutions in the form of the 30 polytechnics. The universities themselves, however, moved slowly.

In the early decades of the century the so-called 'red-brick' universities were pitched firmly in the world of commerce. Based on urban colleges, they received their backing from the local business world – in Birmingham, Manchester, Leeds, Sheffield, Bristol and Nottingham. By contrast, in the 1960s, while the Colleges of Advanced Technology in urban areas were converted into universities, it was the county towns rather than the industrial centres of Britain which were chosen for new green field campuses: York, Lancaster, Canterbury and Colchester, for example. Imperial College was launched in London at the turn of the century, but has been one of the few to stay outside the general trend by remaining a specialist institution.

Superb engineering and other applied departments grew and prospered: some professors developed links with companies. But these were the pacemakers. The pace itself remained too slow. With distinctly different traditions, higher education in continental Europe, America and Japan placed far greater emphasis on the application of knowledge. They achieved a different balance between the scholarly and those who manage and market – those who 'do'.

Their systems are also much bigger than ours (Germany

producing nearly twice the number of graduates each year that we do), so that the number of engineers available to their industries is commensurately much larger. We produce less than a quarter of the number of engineers graduating in Japan and only half as many as the French.

The Save British Science campaign in 1986 highlighted the gravity of the situation in scientific research, including a dramatic drift of British scientists to American universities and companies. But as the Finniston enquiry pointed out in 1980, the real national failure has been our inability to recognise that science alone is not enough: its economic value depends largely on the quality of engineering brought to bear on science-based products.

The hand of central government, in higher as in secondary education, held few implements and in the use of its principal implement – finance – it was encumbered by a system designed to limit its influence.

Each university was autonomous, and they were freely funded. During the phenomenal decade of expansion after the publication of the Robbins Report in 1964, the Treasury met the requests of the University Grants Committee. The students poured in. The cash followed. Many of the Oxbridge assumptions remained dominant in high staff-to-student ratios, the trappings of collegiate life, costly residences.

Student choice determined the direction of growth, and students preferred arts subjects and the new social science courses. Between 1965 and 1970 there was an increase of 35 per cent in the number of university students taking social science courses, of 49 per cent in arts subjects, but of only 16 per cent in engineering. In the non-university sector there was the same preference: an increase of 173 per cent in social sciences and 146 per cent in arts courses, but only 66 per cent in engineering. For the period 1967–72 the universities were set the target of a science to arts ratio of 53:47. Science students did not come forward, and higher proportions of arts and social science students were recruited for more than a decade. Only by 1984–5 did the balance turn in favour of science (including medicine and dentistry) as revealed by a ratio of 52:48.

Looking back, one can see the familiar pattern. Cash was

the concern, with too little regard for output. The indiscriminate outlay of public money creates problems instead of solving them. Shirley Williams' advance in 1969 of thirteen 13 points for reform remained no more than advocacy. The crunch was bound to come and the pain was as great in higher education as in the rest of our society because there, as elsewhere, people believed change was about someone else.

To reduce scale is to enforce priorities. A world of safe assumptions came to an end. Staff were bought out; sometimes the better, more entrepreneurial people saw the positive opportunity which severance terms provided and were the first to go. Academic tenure will soon be a thing of the past, and conditions of service in polytechnics and public sector colleges will have to become as flexible as in other occupations.

In many ways it is harder to co-ordinate retreat than advance, but the more selective approach to funding adopted by this Government makes sense. We must build on quality.

Co-ordination is lacking between universities and polytechnics. The great cities of Britain have both polytechnics and universities alongside each other; their buildings are put up and their courses developed independently of each other. This artificial line is wasteful of resources. The so-called binary divide in higher education between universities and polytechnics should be scrapped.

The polytechnics are not second-class institutions. There is no easy distinction any more between a more heterogeneous university system and the polytechnics, although the essence of the polytechnics is a concentration on the practical application of knowledge, but not merely in the engineering or technical areas. They cover all applied areas, including the social sciences. They provide the bulk of part-time education. They have an important opportunity to build up middle-management skills, by developing more short courses and diploma work. The army recognises the sergeant-major as the key figure in the discipline and management of the company or battalion. Would it be too much to hope that the battle for Britain's industrial survival will be fought on the campuses of the polytechnics? It would counterbalance the notion that the Battle of Waterloo was won on the playing fields of Eton.

Polytechnics have passed through their period of apprenticeship. We should reconsider their ownership by local authorities. The equivalent institutions in Scotland, the Central Institutions, are funded directly by central government, and are just as responsive to the needs of their local communities. If the polytechnics were allowed their freedom from local authority control they would draw closer, become even more responsive to the market place, and be free to re-invest in their own success.

The logic of our policies is to transfer power to the polytechnics themselves, with government funding arrangements merging with those of the University Grants Committee. A government that rightly proposes to transfer council estates to their tenants can hardly claim that the principals of polytechnics and their governors would be unable to shoulder the responsibility.

I would argue for centres of excellence. In distributing public money the University Grants Committee is seeking this same objective. At the same time it treads a tightrope in seeking to ensure general provision to an adequate standard, and opportunities for new centres of excellence to emerge. Competition has a role here, as in so many fields. The danger is that selectivity becomes self-perpetuating if the criteria are too narrow.

Increasing flexibility in higher education opens up the opportunity for attracting private as well as public resources. Public money will lead, but the extension of higher education does not need to be imprisoned in past funding arrangements. Professor John Ashworth of Salford University has been conspicuous in drawing more than 40 per cent of his university's income from outside and private funding. Vice-chancellors and principals no longer expect to sit back and wait for government cheques. But who can or should? We have moved into an incentive society. As I have pointed out in the field of urban policy and housing, the attraction of private funds by the promise of public cash has increased opportunity and injected discipline by driving the public sector closer to the market. Education can be no exception. Institutions should be encouraged to display greater ingenuity in fund-raising. Oxford has one professional fund-raiser; Princeton has 57.

To expand opportunities in higher and further education for the population at large will require the system to run at lower unit costs than in the past.

The Audit Commission in 1985 discovered wide variations in average class sizes and unhealthy fall-out rates in public sector further education.

Classes of five or six were not uncommon and, tragically, classes were particularly small in those cities with the highest unemployment. Sheffield was an exception, and seems to prove that an emphasis on marketing courses, after establishing the views of those who might benefit from them, has been much undervalued throughout the system.

It cannot be right that Britain, almost alone in the Western world, is planning to produce fewer graduates at the end of the century than now, but tens of thousands of extra places could be provided if staff/student ratios approached the standard of 1 to 12 set by the National Advisory Body for Local Authority Higher Education. Only 48 per cent of polytechnics and 25 per cent of further education colleges currently have a ratio that is greater than 1 to 11.

The present student grant system also imposes restraint on the growth of higher education, while failing to meet student requirements. If we want more students, and we want those students to reflect on what jobs the market will offer them, we need to look afresh at loan schemes to help self-supporting students.

Britain is moving through a period of great change. Much of that change we share with similar societies, but much of it takes a more drastic form here because we avoided or fought it long after others embraced it. We have also lacked within government the appropriate machinery for the timely and joint consideration of the respective needs of industry and education, as I have argued in Chapter 5.

A much more flexible work and leisure pattern, with knowledge continuously updated, will both increase the demand for education and impose change in the pattern of it. For example, we face an acute shortage of computer specialists. The Department of Industry's IT Skills Shortage

Committee in 1984 argued that we would need to double the number of people with computer skills. The only way such a goal can even be approached is by retraining programmes. Our higher education system has inhibited 'broken study' and the late entry of mature people from work to education. In future we will need to offer people more opportunities to put together an amalgam of studies leading to a recognised award. Flexibility is the essential principle. The transferability of qualifications, and the recognition of work already completed towards a qualification, is now facilitated by the establishment at last of a computerised database. Information on courses, regularly updated, will be available through PRESTEL to would-be adult students so that they can 'build' their own degrees.

Ultimately there is a logic in making learning a much more personal activity. New technologies will dramatically extend the horizons. The Open University has demonstrated what can be done. Directed private study, involving correspondence courses with some face-to-face tuition, offers many possibilities. Teachers may have to be more peripatetic, and take instruction in future to the work-place or to the laboratory where the right equipment is to be found. Higher education will have to reach out to many more people. By definition, it has to be seen as a much more comprehensive source of provision than merely 'the university'.

If we are to offer working adults the chance to improve their career prospects by intermittently taking higher education courses – from traditional academic study to more specific vocational skills – then it is only reasonable that they should make some financial contribution towards it. There are powerful arguments for providing incentives for this. Educational mortgages, the interest on which could be set against tax, or simply educational loans with generous repayment conditions, would make as much sense as would tax benefits or other inducements to companies to offer scholarships through college.

Education is going through its most significant change for decades. The need for change is both desired and important. The changes which I favour lie at the heart of our philosophy. They fit the Conservative determination to improve the country's industrial and commercial prospects, as well as our belief in setting the people free. To educate is to liberate. Our pursuit of liberty here is as ambitious as it is overdue.

11

The Unemployed: Will They Work Again?

The consequences of large-scale unemployment raise the most pressing questions of the day and the hardest for the Government to answer. Since March 1983 nearly a million new jobs have been created, but the number of those seeking work has increased faster as the bulge of those born in the 1960s has reached the labour market and greater numbers of women wish to work. Since 1951, the labour force has grown by well over 4m, with a quarter of the increase taking place in the last ten years. Ministers justifiably take credit for the growth in jobs, and have no trouble disclaiming responsibility for the growth in the work force.

In truth the Government has done much better than the crude statistics of the numbers unemployed suggest. It has shown ingenuity and persistence in starting new training schemes, new enterprise schemes, new initiatives to help the unemployed; but such is the scale of the problem that these devices have not made much impression on the total number out of work.

As the number of jobless has climbed to well above 3m and remained at that level, the electorate has shown remarkable forbearance. Opinion polls show that most of the unemployed do not blame the Government for their misfortunes. The Labour Party's main theme during its general election campaign in 1983 was to fight mass unemployment – a phrase which fell hourly from Michael Foot's lips; but Labour failed to persuade the country that this pestilence had been spread by the Conservatives' mismanagement or neglect. The Conservatives recognised the electorate's maturity and reminded them that this was not uniquely a British disease. In country after country, under governments of every political colour, unemployment has risen persistently since the early 1970s. Over the past five years unemployment has risen by 81 per cent in West Germany, 49 per cent in Italy, and roughly 35 per cent in Britain and France.

Perhaps when the Labour Party talks of creating a million new jobs people remember how, under the last Labour Government, the number of unemployed more than doubled, from less than 600,000 to 1.3m, and ask themselves whether Labour is really likely to have acquired a new and special insight or skill that it was denied in the 1970s.

But of course any opposition party will attack when it senses vulnerability in its opponents. I do not remember complaining when Saatchi's brilliant poster, 'Labour isn't working', adorned Conservative billboards during the 1979 campaign; and I was not too indignant when James Callaghan in February 1974 produced the slogan 'Back to work with Labour'. The game of mutual recrimination is inevitable. But party politics must not divert us from the truth: governments can only do so much about unemployment. The electorate recognises this and political parties cannot pretend otherwise.

I doubt if many people are impressed by Labour's recipe for buying new jobs with extravagant public spending; and there must be many Labour supporters who know that their party's new commitment to a national minimum wage would tend, if implemented, only to put even more people out of work. Prices would rise, bringing an immediate loss of competitiveness and markets. More capital investment would substitute more machines for people. Job creation would be better served by a freeing of wage rates than by imposing a more rigid and expensive conformity. At present the difficulties of the regions are increased because of national pay structures which take no account of the real economy of southern overheating and provincial under-employment.

Before we consider remedies, it is worth noting again the extent of the affliction. There is argument about measurements and about the soundness of monthly figures based on claims for benefit. Some do not claim, although entitled: some who claim are not really seeking work. But no one denies that at the end of 1986 there were more than 3m people out of work in Britain of whom most wanted work but did not find it; and there is no ground for believing, whatever we may hope, that it will soon fall to levels that are substantially different. Beside these 3m are one third of a million young people on Youth Training schemes, at a cost of over £1b per annum, and a third of a million more who are being helped by special employment schemes such as the community programme. The present two-year YTS, with the prospect of 20 days off-the-job training and a qualification at the end, is a significant improvement on the initial programme. All these forms of help are of immeasurable value to the spirit and the prospects of the beneficiaries; they also tend to conceal the real fragility of the labour market.

Even if we split the difference between the Government's old and new bases of calculation, the average figures for all regions of the United Kingdom showed that during the winter of 1986/7 one worker in eight was without a job. That is daunting enough, but of all average figures this is the most misleading in its picture of where casualties are found in greatest numbers. A quick look at the map showed that the North/South divide was no cliché; unemployment in South-east England was 8.5 per cent, in the North 16 per cent, in Northern Ireland over 19 per cent. Unpack those packages and there were cells of hopelessness unimagined by the hundreds of thousands living in communities where work was plentiful. In Merseyside average unemployment was over 20 per cent but in some travel-to-work areas and parishes there were local levels of 40 or 60 per cent.

As I write, the prosperous South-east is itself very far from being uniform: in certain areas and among certain groups unemployment is distressingly high. Among the white population it is 7.5 per cent on average, but as high as 12.8 per cent among Asians and 17.2 per cent among Afro-Caribbeans. In the Parliamentary constituencies of Hackney and Peckham – which include some of the poorest parts of East and South London – unemployment is of the order of 25 per cent. In prosperous Twickenham it is only 5 per cent, less than half the national average.

Within all these figures there are important variations of age and skill. There are districts in North and North-west England, Scotland and Wales, where even the skilled and relatively young have given up hope of finding work again after too many wasted visits to job centres.

Objective examination of the trend during the past winter does suggest, as ministers have claimed, that the darkness grows slightly less dark; but let us suppose, with unjustified optimism, that in three years' time the queue will be shorter by as much as half a million. The mountain still to be climbed will seem as massive as ever, and there will still be millions of people and scores of communities for whom hope will again be deferred for an eternity.

There is no convincing evidence to suggest that ten years hence unemployment will be less than 2m, or that the most vulnerable groups and regions will be less vulnerable. If so, the level of unemployment will be as unacceptable in 1997 as it is today, with the sense of injustice and anger much greater and possibly explosive. I simply cannot think it right for politicians to go on making speeches about how things are going to improve, if by that they mean that we shall gradually move from levels of 3m to 2m out of work. If so, we deceive great numbers of people who at present can only expect to remain for many years as deprived, as under-privileged and as firmly enmeshed in an environment of hopelessness as they are today.

We know that the market will not find jobs on the scale which the crisis demands. It will find some, and there is much that the Government can do and is doing to increase the size and efficiency of the market and to train people in the skills which it requires. It must also be true that the number of people seeking employment will decline as the birth-rate bulge works through. I take some comfort, too, from those economists who argue that, as living standards rise, so a demand for leisure which people will increasingly be able to afford will further reduce the numbers of people seeking work.

I believe that the growth over the last two decades of local employment initiatives, with business, local government and voluntary groups helping new enterprise to germinate and grow, has immeasurable potential and is one of the more reliable grounds for hope of recovery. Certainly no Treasury caution or apprehension of abuse must prevent as free a climate as possible for the self-employed.

Despite this, a return to full employment as we have understood it in the thirty years that followed the Second World war is out of sight.

The waste and the hopelessness of unemployment both defy measurement, although we know that both are very great. As to the cost in cash, the Government does not accept calculations which assume so many billions of tax revenue lost, which would have been collected had the unemployed been earning. Nor can any sensible estimate be made of the extra demand which extra workers with extra money in their pockets would create. But these are great losses and even if they cannot be accurately calculated their message should not be ignored. The measurable cost of benefit paid to the unemployed, according to Government calculations, is in itself likely to amount to £5.6b in 1986/7. It has to be paid for and it is an overhead which by its necessity denies the use of those resources for other priorities.

If the physical cost is great and undiminishing year on year, the human cost is also great and being paid on a constantly rising tariff as children follow parents into unemployment. Conservatives who extol the values of the family and its central position in a stable society cannot ignore the harm done to the cohesion of families when unemployment and impoverishment descends to the second and sometimes the third generation. Those of us who see individual responsibility and enterprise as the foundation of prosperous communities know how much is destroyed when the individual is forced into dependence on State benefits.

Where unemployment is long-established and deep-seated, its corrosive effect goes equally deep. The rising generation is made vulnerable to the friend or brother, the teacher or political activist, who says: 'This is a rotten society, which offers neither you nor your parents a fair deal. Why cling to its phoney values? Join us on the streets.' It is not only political protest that is to be found on the streets. The world faces growing levels of crime. It is not a phenomenon of British society, it is a phenomenon that stretches across most advanced societies of whatever political persuasion. Against a background of high unemployment the invitation to crime becomes more appealing. Idleness becomes a resentment that gives crime an indefensible normality. Drug peddlers may accept that what they are doing is wrong but see no other way to earn a living. Macho kids take to copy-cat street offences because one more force in society pushes them in that direction.

So long, then, as we fail to make visible advances in the campaign against persistent high unemployment, so long will we encourage this challenge to our society; so long will our failure promote anarchy in the family, in urban politics and also, and not to our comfort, on the Leftward fringe of the Labour Party. The lack of purpose and the absence of hope for worthwhile activity that are consequent upon unemployment generate their own reactions.

Here as elsewhere I would distinguish two communities: side by side with those whom we must strive to help back into employment, there are those in work from whom society asks great effort for little gain. Society is providing a choice which seems increasingly unjust. It asks large numbers of people to go through the discipline of rising early, travelling to work, carrying out what is often a routine task and returning home five days a week to find themselves materially very little better off, if at all, than an unemployed neighbour who has gone through indignity but none of the discomfort and toil.

There is a hidden heroism among the thousands who commit themselves without complaint to tedious jobs for pay of less than £80 a week; but the gap between the after-tax sum in many a worker's wage packet and the income he could claim in benefit is sometimes so narrow as to offend the most selfless citizen's sense of justice.

A society where people think it an affront to be denied work is healthy; a society where those who are in work begin to feel affronted may be in some danger.

Most people want to work, find self-respect in work and will do all they can to maintain that self-respect. It is the few who begin to question the rules and who set the first examples. Snowballs begin small but can grow rapidly, and I think that is happening in the calculation about the benefit of working or of claiming.

The rich have been known in effect to rewrite fiscal laws which they find too burdensome: they should hardly be surprised if the poor share their approach. In the 1970s when Labour raised the top rate of income tax, including investment income surcharge, to 98 per cent, there were many who were not prepared to pay an impost which they considered punitive. It became worth their while to buy advice and to order their affairs so as to avoid, and sometimes no doubt to evade, what they considered to be inadmissible demands by the State.

Neither the rich nor the poor man is willing to accept instructions from anyone to work for an infinitesimal margin. The man who draws his benefit and works for cash part-time makes much the same judgement as those at the other extreme who a few years ago would have banked in the Cayman Islands. Excessive taxes weakened the moral standards of much of middle-class Britain. The marginal division between the material rewards of work and of public provision is spreading these lower standards more widely in society.

For the lowest paid, there may be no cash advantage in earning a living rather than drawing benefit. A married man with two small children will be about £13 better off in work if he earns less than about £80 a week. At £140 a week he is only about £12 better off than he would be if out of work. Even at £165 a week he is only about £25 in pocket.

Here again is a threat to the stable society. There is a rough but effective justice in military law which punishes the thief and also his victim whose carelessness puts temptation in his way. If civil laws were the same, then shopkeepers and shoplifters would presumably find themselves picked up in equal numbers and the courts would soon have less work on their hands. In all seriousness, we cannot go on for many more years with a benefits system which provides every incentive for honest men and women, whose wages scarcely feed and house a family, to drop out of regular paid employment, draw benefit and join the black economy.

It is difficult to estimate the size of the black economy with any accuracy. The most widely accepted figure suggests that this amounts to between 6 per cent and 8 per cent of GDP, or about £15b on which the tax loss may be some £4b.

The reality of the income and employment traps disposes of the argument, which is still sometimes heard on the Right, that there is a sizeable class of the shiftless whom nothing will induce to do an honest week's work. Yes, there are a few who should be so described. There are many others who have the choice and for whom the level of wages offers little incentive to work: some of these are content not to work; but the more significant fact is that the very great majority unhesitatingly choose, from strength of either character or habit, to earn their incomes.

There is a third group whose will to work has not withstood the long years of repeated rejection and disappointment. The Government's experimental Job Clubs, which are now spreading throughout the country, have shown how often the morale of the long-term unemployed can be lifted and their confidence restored by practical help with hunting and applying for jobs. Distaste for work is not part of the British disease. Unemployment never fell below a million between the wars, and some baffled politicians found it convenient to assume that many men must have been unemployed from choice; but the level of assistance paid first by the local committees and later by the National Board made the accusation unconvincing. During the Second World War and for thirty years after it, the same men who had stood in the dole queues in the thirties showed themselves more than willing to take regular work when work was available. There are no grounds for assuming that those of the present generation who are now denied work would not behave like their parents.

In more prosperous parts of the country conditions are very different. In some areas there are mismatches between skills available and skills required. In a survey conducted by the Manpower Services Commission in October 1985, a third of the jobs that were assessed as 'hard to fill' were thought to have been unfilled because of skill shortages. Others are not in work because the level of remuneration offered is below their estimates of their worth; or because there are sources of family income which match or exceed what the jobs offered by the job centre would pay.

Where there are vacancies but too few takers, the narrowness of the gap between benefit and wage levels is most likely to distort the market and encourage abuse. It is not easy to reduce this gap from either side. On the wages side it is open to government to swell the pay packet by raising the tax threshold or introducing a lower rate band. The Government's Job Start scheme looks promising: this pays an extra £20 a week for six months to anyone who has been out of work for a year or more and is willing to take one of a million jobs which at present offer gross earnings of £80 a week or less.

There can be no question of reducing any family's income below the level which social security is designed to maintain. I do not think it can be seriously argued that the present level is over-generous. The adequacy or inadequacy of provision has to be judged not only by conditions in those parts of the United Kingdom where jobs can be found but against the background of urban deprivation and very high unemployment levels where jobs are not available and not remotely in prospect for many genuine job-seekers who are unlucky enough to have relatively low attainments and skills.

What can be done? The Left promises to create a million jobs but that is a cruel deceit. The money is not there and Labour would do incalculable economic damage if it were ever allowed the opportunity of trying to prove the contrary. There remains only one practical alternative.

We must change the assumption that underlies all support for the unemployed, which is that even those who are able to work and available for work are entitled to draw benefit without giving some part of their time in return.

One point which the Government's critics delight in making has been that it is wasteful to pay people to be idle. From the Labour Party the point is usually made with a sneer: it goes with their infamous accusation that the Conservative Government has had a policy of unemployment, that we have deliberately fostered unemployment to weaken trade unions. That accusation deserves no reply; but the accusation that we are paying people to be idle is one that I do not believe the Conservative party can leave unchallenged. Let us in future pay the unemployed, wherever we can, not to be idle but to work, for themselves and for their communities.

The time has come, I believe, to experiment seriously with what the Americans have called 'workfare', or working for welfare. The principle is that anyone who is capable of working should be prepared to earn his or her welfare benefit.

The concept has been tried and tested in different ways in some 25 states in the United States. Schemes vary to fit the requirements of each state, with some concentrating on able-bodied males and mothers of school-age children, others including all unemployed persons.

The common element is that all schemes require recipients of benefits to actively seek jobs. If they cannot find employment they are required to perform some public service for part of each week, without additional pay, in return for their welfare benefit. Many states provide coaching in job-hunting skills which, like the Job Clubs here, have helped many people regain their confidence and cope successfully with job interviews. The Americans have found in practice that workfare promotes financial independence by giving people greater incentives to seek unsubsidised employment. Most recipients say that they have benefited, and that the regular work has boosted their morale. They have done jobs which were required in their communities, but for which funds could not be found to recruit full-time workers: they have worked as firemen, truck drivers, library and police assistants; they have helped to keep the cities clean and to look after children of mothers at work. It requires little imagination to identify an almost endless list of things that need doing in our society.

Britain led the way in the post-war years in creating one of the most comprehensive welfare systems in the world. Unemployment benefit, and later supplementary benefit, ensured that the small numbers of people who became unemployed in the 1950s and 1960s were tided over with the short-term help which was usually all that was needed. The Labour Government framed their National Insurance Act of 1946 to limit the period for which unemployment benefit would be paid, so sure were they that unemployment would never be more than short-term. The structure proved adequate in those years of relatively full and stable employment; but today's world is a different one, and none of the assumptions of the 1940s can be above challenge.

Until now the assumption in Britain has been that if someone is unemployed he has the right to a cash benefit. In the long-term this is of limited value: it rescues but does not rehabilitate. Rather than prepare a worker to reach for a higher standard of living, the State benefit as time passes tends to foster increasing dependency on the State. In that sense it is bad for the recipient and for the country. The State's help may even lower the recipient's living standards by discouraging him from re-entering the labour market; and in the longer term the habit of withdrawal from the market, as many studies have shown, makes more and more difficult a vigorous search for a suitable job.

I believe we should experiment with a modified system of workfare in this country. I would, wherever possible, pay the unemployed a 'community benefit'. To be recipients they would be expected to take useful jobs in the community which otherwise would not be done. For many it will maintain their work skills and, perhaps more important, their dignity and pride as participating members of society. In itself, community benefit would not restore prosperity; but it would help to ease the pain of unemployment by giving the unemployed and their families some new hope.

It is depressing to realise with absolute certainty that the Left of the Labour Party will be hostile to community benefit. To some Labour politicians any change in the benefit system is like cow slaughter to a Hindu; any hint that a benefit should be earned, let alone withheld, is robbery. I hope that some at least in the Labour Party will not share that contempt for the British people which assumes that unemployment will have stripped them of self-respect and that they will grudge an opportunity to give some service to their neighbours. I believe, on the contrary, that most will welcome a chance of useful work and that the difficulty may lie elsewhere.

The trade unions will be instinctively hostile to any scheme which allows people to do even part-time jobs which they see as the preserve of their members. It is regrettable that the Government's excellent community programme to help the long-term unemployed has been limited and made much costlier by the unions' insistence, out of fear for their members' jobs, that participants should be paid at the going rate. That simply means that there are fewer places than we need and could afford. In hard times it is not surprising to find the unions fiercely protective of their members' interests.

They are entitled to expect that a community benefit scheme would not be used to hurt their members, either by challenging their jobs or by undermining their wage rates.

Americans recognised this difficulty and assured the unions that employers would complement and not replace existing union members. The purist will argue that the unions should recognise that they have simply over-priced their members and that the market must prevail. I would acknowledge the unions' interest, but offer no compromise over our right to introduce such proposals. The unions serve their members often at the expense of consumer, company and national interest. They must have no veto over a genuine attempt to help the unemployed.

I should like to see not only acquiescence but active support from the trade unions, who have not always shown practical sympathy for the unemployed once they drop out of the ranks of union membership. Community work for many unemployed may, after all, be the start of a journey back to regular work, to a prouder place in the community and, in time, to full-time active union membership.

If trade union leaders at either national or local levels decide, after all reasonable assurances, to be obstructive then their objections will have to be set aside. The Government needs to do all it can to make any lifeline available and it should not allow shortsightedness or selfishness on the part of trade unions or any other body to snatch it away.

Let me again distinguish not two but several nations. The 3m unemployed in the United Kingdom do not share one predicament, as we have seen. From region to region there are innumerable variants in the proportions of skilled to unskilled, long-term to short-term unemployed, young to old, black to white, and the many groupings experience every gradation of difficulty.

The supply of acceptable and appropriate work which could be undertaken in return for a community benefit payment will also vary greatly from one district to another; as will the willingness, no doubt, between one community and another to respond to the offer and the challenge.

The Government has objected, when something on the lines of community benefit has been suggested in the past, that it would not be possible to find 3m productive jobs.

Perhaps not, but I believe that useful work could be found for a significant proportion of the unemployed. Where there is no suitable work clearly no work will be done, and we are no worse off.

The existing schemes to help the unemployed would continue, but where worthwhile tasks could be found they should be carried out.

For the younger and more flexible of any age, training and education should be the first consideration among the options; but there is an almost unending list of worthwhile things that need doing in Britain that could be done by those now paid to do nothing.

If education is at one end of the spectrum, the litter in the towns and cities is at the other. Are we going to accept this for ever with standards of cleanliness that are now conspicuously lower than other European countries? Is it sensible on refuse-strewn council estates to have unemployed building workers sitting indoors watching TV at public expense? The introduction of community benefit will require the solution of a number of practical problems, but the objections of principle which have already been raised against similar proposals are unconvincing. Many are based on a spurious morality.

When every year the old die of hypothermia, is there some moral superiority about a society that pays the unemployed in a community to stay at home rather than to drop in with a cup of tea?

Children are often left to roam the streets while parents work. At the same time society pays prematurely retired neighbours to do nothing rather than getting them to organise recreation, sport and leisure. The unemployed could even be usefully trained to do such mundane but useful tasks as looking after community homes and gardens.

A recent poll showed that 44 per cent of young people favoured military conscription. The Ministry of Defence does not, but there is no sign here that unemployed young people would resent some home-based, part-time, quasi-military training or more formal commitment as one option in a range of choices under a workfare programme.

If a national policy to provide opportunity for young people were adopted the Ministry of Defence should be expected to play a part. Without doubt the calibre of recruits would not equal that now available to the professional armed services, but if as a nation we faced not peace but war the value of such people would not be questioned. To offer voluntarily to unemployed youth an experience of military discipline and training, as an alternative to idleness, cannot be wrong.

The Government says it fears that workfare would exert an upward pressure on wages. I doubt this, and so do the unions, who might take a more favourable view if they believed it to be true. There would be no such pressure since the only extra payment that would be made would be compensation for travelling costs to get the unemployed to their place of work. It says that there would be problems of supervision, which seems to me an entirely groundless fear; but if there were occasional failures here, what could the country possibly have to lose, since at present nothing at all is gained by requiring the unemployed to be idle?

Here, too, I think the Government needs to study one of its own successes. The urban development grant, the urban programme and the derelict land grant have all been used to lever funds from the private sector. Already the community programme employs specialists who then in their turn train YTS trainees. The thrust that is needed is to use the community programme to recruit key staff, and to recruit staff in the fields where groups of unemployed can then be organised.

The Government has over 300,000 community programme places. It is easy to see the potential inroads that gearing could make in the numbers of registered unemployed if places in this programme were specifically designed for this purpose.

An extra social worker could lead a team of the unemployed in support for the elderly. An extra sports instructor would train a team of young unemployed. An extra foreman would lead a gang of building workers.

I recognise that the South also contains the most concentrated pockets of the long-term unemployed and areas of poverty, but in many places there are opportunities for work which are not taken because of disinclination or disincentive. The unexpectedly high number of benefit claimants who have dropped off the register when called for interviews in recent months under the Restart scheme suggests strongly that the introduction of a little daylight has unsettled one or two corners of the black economy. A degree of discipline or even the promise of a slightly more attentive management may help claimants to decide how seriously they are looking for work.

In northern cities where jobs have been scarce for years it would be unjust and unwise to apply pressure; nor do I think it would be necessary. Those who live amid dereliction do not need to have it pointed out that there is plentiful scope for useful work to be organised in their communities from which all would gain. If the Government commits itself, as I have urged, to greatly increased expenditure on urban renewal there will be a response. If devastated sites are cleared and homes made habitable and gardens planted, I believe the able-bodied unemployed, if wisely led, will join in and make their contribution with pride.

12

Our European Destiny

Early in 1973, I happened to be the first British minister to visit the United States after Britain became a member of the European Economic Community. To my American audience I argued from conviction that our decision was on every practical consideration the right one – that the greater unity of Europe, and its greater economic strength in combination, could only benefit our peoples.

My belief in Europe had always been strong. My experience as Minister for Aerospace had made it stronger. What I have learned since, both in and out of office, has fortified my conviction that, unless the British government and people play the fullest part in the continuing construction of the European Community, we will not prosper.

I doubt if the Little Englander's voice, though sometimes strident, has ever represented England, let alone the rest of Britain. When Harold Macmillan in 1963 announced in Parliament the Conservative Government's decision to apply to enter the Community, one of his own backbenchers shouted 'traitor'. It showed that he had done violence to some deep feelings and that he faced a hard political fight. Indeed, the certainty of that sort of response from some in his party, and from the Opposition benches, was a measure of his courage at a historic moment. But the Conservatives under Macmillan, and ten years later under Ted Heath, were drawing on a long tradition. 'Britain in Europe' was a slogan in the 1970s, but it was the best of slogans because it was a simple statement of an unchallengeable truth.

The sense of British separateness seems to have grown with Empire. It was not a feeling confined to the British people; it was a favourite theme of Charles de Gaulle. If the

English Channel was a state of mind, as some have said, it was one which possessed the French and the Dutch no less than the English. The notion of separation is illusory. The Channel has proved the most permeable of barriers: it has kept out Spanish, French and German invaders, but it has never kept the English, Scots, Welsh or Irish, whether as soldiers of the Crown or adventurers, out of any European war in which they had a mind to join. To the precious common elements of our European culture, physical separation has fortunately offered no barrier at all.

The real barriers to trade, movement and civilised living which still divide and stunt Europe in the late 1980s are not to be blamed on any supposed aloofness or lack of European spirit on the part of the British, whose present Government is now pressing and working for their removal. They are the creation and the curse of us all. It is some comfort to recall that they are also historically an aberration. Six hundred years ago an English traveller with the French tongue at his command and gold coins in his pouch could travel freely through continental Europe and transact whatever business he pleased, without passport or licence or quota. A merchant of Chaucer's time reborn today would never understand how we Europeans could have destroyed such an inheritance.

I speak of commercial Europe, and the restoring of this ancient, lost commonality is an important prize which will soon, I believe, be won. The political construction of Europe since 1945 is a story of triumphant success.

Thirty years on from the signing of the Treaty of Rome, both the creation and the continuance of the European Community seem miraculous. The first was a triumph of good over evil, of neighbourliness over a thousand years and more of belligerence. The second depends on the daily containment of the strong national spirit which still possesses the member states, and its subordination to the common goal of political stability and economic betterment.

It is sad but true that both Labour and the Conservative Party after the war lacked the imagination to join in the early stages of building a new united Europe. It is fortunate that Jean Monnet, Paul-Henri Spaak and their friends in the Six had the vision, the persistence and the practical statesmanship to make the miracle happen.

After the war, Britain wanted to see the emergence of a stable, united Europe to maintain the peace, but our leaders did not then see the union as one which would include Britain. We took steps to stabilise Europe, but without a wholehearted commitment to participate as equal partners. Indeed at one stage we took the lead in the creation of the European Free Trade Area, as a defence against the growing strength of the EEC. It offered no substitute for the substance of the real Europe. The French were more single-minded and clear-sighted, and Britain allowed them to mould a Community on lines that were then to France's advantage.

Ted Heath achieved the fulfilment of Macmillan's ambition and secured his place in our history. The Conservative Party was slow to change but, when change became essential, it was a Conservative government which had the courage and determination to spell it out and carry it through. Labour, as always, was split. Harold Wilson resorted to the device of a referendum to camouflage his party's inability to put forward an agreed policy, but the British people's response settled the question of membership once and for all, with a two-to-one vote in favour. It was an expression of practical common sense, if not of enthusiasm.

By the time a Conservative administration was returned in 1979, not the principle of membership but the terms of our budget contribution were in question. History will debate whether the conduct of the subsequent negotiations was as constructive as it might have been. Certainly it will be strongly argued that, without the toughness and single-mindedness that was shown, there would never have been a settlement which took proper account of British interests. The previous Labour government had failed to secure anything that approached the results concluded in July 1984 at Fontainebleau.

It serves no purpose to reopen the controversy here, but it is almost certainly true that any renegotiation would have soured relations. It is not in the nature of politicians to concede what they hold when the glare of national publicity attends their every move. The adjustment had to be made, to prevent the imbalance assuming a scale that would have thrown into doubt our membership itself. The doing of it may have encouraged doubts about Britain's commitment, and it may also have given the Community yet another excuse to avoid decisions.

Europe is moving forward in a direction that is certain but at a pace which is not. We are wasting opportunities by sharing too reluctantly and slowly our European resources. We tend to relive old rivalries in a modern commercial conflict.

Progress is never easy. Christopher Tugendhat, for eight years a Commissioner, said that life at the top of the Community resembled the labours of Sisyphus. The boulder has been moving upwards every year since 1950, but the movement has been slow. In a generation the Community has achieved much; but an immense amount remains to be done to fulfil the aims of the original treaties. Until we build a more coherent political, economic and social Europe, the member states will place an unnecessary brake on their own future. We have taken only the first few steps. I want Europe to complete its journey.

Europe's greatest potential strength, but still its weakness, is its market. With 320m people it is in value terms the most important in the world. As a trading bloc it is one and a half times as big as the USA and almost three times the size of Japan, providing about a fifth of the world's trade.

In reality the twelve member States largely remain twelve separate markets, ranging in size from 366,000 people in Luxembourg to 60m in Germany. The hundreds of barriers that divide the members constitute a hidden cost in nearly every single aspect of economic activity. It has been estimated, for example, that frontier formalities alone cost 1.2b ECU – some £0.85b a year. Similarly, it has been estimated in a study by the consultancy firm McKinsey's that the cost of not developing a Community-wide information technology industry will be the loss of 4m jobs in Europe by 1990. These figures are indicative only, but it is clear that the cost of 'non-Europe' to everyone – consumer, taxpayer, government, businessman – is enormous.

Europe behaves as though it has hardly woken up to the opportunity that a larger market offers or to the challenge posed by the vast and efficient economies of Japan and the USA. It is not a case of ignorance: every European minister to whom I have ever spoken knows the urgency of the problem. But inertia, and the inbuilt resistance of every national pressure group, limits our progress to the speed of the most sluggardly. I would love to say 'it can't go on.' The awful truth is that, unless the politicians of Europe decide otherwise, it will.

Unless we rouse ourselves, the industrial strength of Europe will remain fragmented. We have infant organisations born of an acceptance of this case, but no European companies and too few Europe-wide standards. Half a century from now these weaknesses will have been made good, but every year lost exacts a price. These are surmountable problems, but there is a lack of will. It must not be a lack of British will.

One of Britain's two Commissioners, Arthur Cockfield, has put forward a detailed plan for making a reality of Europe's internal market. The idea of creating a European market in which goods, services, people and capital can move without hindrance is not a new one. It was the core of the Rome Treaty. But this plan is by far the most ambitious attempt to make it a reality.

The Cockfield Plan seeks systematically to remove within seven years all the physical, technical and fiscal barriers that divide the Community. Three hundred legislative proposals have been put forward to create this great market.

To encourage trade flows and reduce unacceptable administrative costs – ultimately paid for by the consumer – the physical barriers have to go. Technical barriers frustrate the creation of a common market for industrial goods. As a result, manufacturers in Europe are forced to focus on their own national rather than European markets, with consequent increases in costs. Everyday consumer goods have to be adapted to different national standards. More than 80 different types of television sets are made to meet different national standards; 16 types of electric shavers are made; air fares in Europe are held artificially high by national regulations and cosy monopolies.

Fiscal barriers have also to be taken down if goods and services are to move as freely from one member State to another as between England and Scotland. Unless we move to a much smaller variation in tax rates, we will continue to have unnecessary distortions of trade.

This is, at last, the first concrete plan for a proper internal market. The key to its completion is a commitment in all the national capitals for it to succeed. Progress on any front will require progress on all fronts, so there must be agreement on all subjects in all the capitals.

Some proposals to remove barriers will be greatly in our favour, and others which we will dislike will seem crucial to other countries; but we cannot pick and choose.

In Britain the service industries have grown up in a liberal framework. In France and Germany they have been rigidly regulated. If we want deregulation – whether of air fares, road transport, financial services or telecommunications – the trade-off will be tighter environmental laws, statutory involvement of employees at work, or what have you: it would be cheap at the price. Europe moves forward only when all its members know that they have a common interest.

Creating an internal market will not be enough. I have argued for a British industrial strategy, and no such strategy is conceivable except in the context of Europe with its potential for transnational partnership. In improving our industrial base in the Community the old truth about the right products at the right price remains. Each of the twelve countries, attempting to re-invent the wheel with its taxpayers' research budgets, holds the totality of Europe back by wasteful overlap, and each suffers for it.

Europe collectively must devote more of its resources to the industries of the future – biotechnology, information technology, communications – to keep up with what is happening across the Atlantic and the Pacific.

A number of Community-wide programmes have been set up to co-ordinate the new technologies, but they are only the first step if we are to match the Americans and Japanese. The SDI programme amounts to $36b over five years. That will take America's capitalist companies to the frontiers of tomorrow's civil and military technologies, which are interwoven. But increased funding is not the whole answer: the aim of existing European programmes such as ESPRIT and EUREKA is to select winners, and the money is being used where it appears most likely to show a pay-off. Europe cannot abandon such initiatives; the scale is under constant debate, but in the face of growing world competition it will increase. We must ensure our share of it.

The need for co-ordination is nowhere more obvious than in the field of defence procurement, which is a large component of public expenditure in each of the twelve countries of the Community. It generates constant demand for costly new products, primarily for the defence industries but ultimately spinning off into products for the civil market. The obstacles which frustrate fruitful co-operation in defence procurement, and the potential gains from their removal, became clear to me early in my political life, when I was appointed Minister for Aerospace and Shipping in 1972.

It is rare in politics for a minister to launch an idea and to see it through to practical effect before the Prime Minister or the electors move him on or out of office. If it is rare in domestic politics, it must be almost unheard of in European politics.

Here the story of the European Space Agency (ESA) is instructive, because it is the story of all European endeavour today. It began for me when a file landed on my desk, seeking approval for the commitment of some £6m of taxpayers' money to help a British high-technology company to keep ahead, in one field of space development, of the French and the Germans. On this occasion the three countries were engaged in battle on the classic European pattern. No winner was likely to emerge. It seemed to me as ludicrous as it had become typical. At the time the Americans were spending many millions of dollars a year on programmes which had already taken them to the moon. How could another trivial competition between French, German and British companies do anything to help Europe in the real competition in space technology with the United States or the Soviet Union?

A British minister's natural instinct is to support a British company. The submission received from officials was eloquent in explaining the substantial sums of money that the French and German governments were putting into their companies, rivals in the same field.

I asked for figures to show the total European and American expenditure on space technology, and I discovered that the budgets of the European nations put together, although not approaching the American effort, were not insignificant in comparison. If I remember correctly, Europe's pool of funds, if added together, would have been about one-sixth of the size of America's; but since there was no European pool the scene was like toy-town. Each European country was serving what it believed to be its own national interest; each was researching many of the same problems and pushing back the same frontiers.

A closer look at Britain's expenditure showed an even more depressing picture: the Post Office had a space budget, and the Ministry of Defence, and the Department of Trade and Industry. The Department of Education and Science was sponsoring the space research of the Science Research Council. There was no co-ordination of this British national effort, let alone European co-ordination.

I decided that an attempt at co-operation must be made, although the prospect was not encouraging. Britain had withdrawn a few years earlier from the European Launcher Development Organisation (ELDO) after years of complaint about its rising costs. This had harmed our standing as potential partners in a new co-operative venture. It also left France with the only launcher capability in Europe. The Americans had invited Europe to join them in the post-Apollo programme to put a laboratory into space, but the British Government had shown no interest.

Britain had, however, just joined the Common Market and discovered a more positive attitude to European matters. I went to my colleagues with little optimism but considerable determination. The obvious proposal was that we should first rationalise Britain's space programme and then approach our fellow Europeans and try to persuade them of the advantages of combining our national programmes into a European programme that would have some weight.

If there was to be a ghost of a chance of success we would have to rejoin the French-led launcher programme and also support the Germans who were anxious to participate in the post-Apollo programme. Our interest, as outlined in that submission to me, was in communication satellites. The offer we made was that if the Europeans agreed to merge ELDO and the European Space Research Organisation (ESRO) into a single European Space Agency, Britain would wish to be a member, rejoin the launcher programme, take part in the post-Apollo programme and take a leading role in the development of the new communications satellites.

From my British colleagues I got less than I wanted but more than I expected. None was prepared to give up his department's budget, but most agreed that if I wanted to try my unlikely ideas on the Europeans I should be indulged, and allowed, if I wished, to trade in my own budget as part of a bargain.

My European colleagues accepted the plan. The European Space Agency was born. Britain rejoined the launcher programme, took on some of the post-Apollo work and secured the lead in communications satellites. The ESA quickly proved its value. Now four-fifths of British government investment in space is made through the agency, and British Aerospace, Marconi and other British companies play prominent parts in building satellites for the agency's customers. In January 1987, British Aerospace won a £100m contract to provide a communications satellite for NATO, the first European contract of its sort.

The experience taught me what every minister who does business in Europe learns. Even where there is agreement in principle to go forward, the planting of each step requires the most determined exercise of will. Although it was clearly right to establish the ESA, there was no certainty at the crucial meeting that the right thing would be done.

A dozen delegations gathered in the early afternoon in a large Brussels conference hall to approve a draft agreement, only to separate almost at once into rotating clusters of bi-lateral or tri-lateral meetings. We bargained over the sharing of costs, the leadership of design teams, the location of establishments, until about three o'clock in the morning. (Some politicians feel the need to prove their virility by sitting late to persuade an audience of national onlookers that they have fought the good fight. There was one French minister who understood the essence of the process: he did not turn up until everyone else had exhausted themselves in the early skirmishes.) We then tumbled out triumphant and exhausted into the Belgian night and the Press gathered round the distinguished figure of James Hamilton, the senior British official, to hear the news. Looking every inch the minister, James amused himself briefly before directing them to me.

I have never doubted that the effort of European co-operation must be sustained and that the prizes are great. Nor have I doubted that the national solution, the non-European option, even when it is wrong, will always seem seductively easy by comparison.

I tried hard at that time to achieve a degree of co-ordination between the airline procurement activities of European countries. Huge sums of money were at stake and enormous manufacturing opportunities, but the rivalries were intense and a common solution hard to see. I tried for two years to arrange a joint meeting with the German and French ministers who shared with me sponsorship of their national airlines. I then had to cancel the meeting because of the approaching general election.

Ten years later, as Secretary of State for Defence, I found myself once again immersed in the dialogue about European co-operation. As soon as I arrived Geoffrey Pattie, as a very experienced minister responsible for procurement policy, brought me the sequel to the story of the European Space Agency. We needed to decide on the new generation of fighter aircraft for the RAF. I was not in the least surprised to learn that Britain had its proposals and so did France. British Aerospace, with the success of its partnership with Germany and Italy in the Tornado programme, was energetic and persuasive. In France, Dassault naturally saw the solution through different eyes.

Powerful arguments were advanced to me in favour of Britain going it alone. The British aircraft was better; it suited the RAF; it would do everything required of it; and all the work would be under British control. I do not read French well, but I would have needed no translation to tell me the content of my French colleague's brief. Another reason was put to me for Britain to build its own aircraft: the French and Germans were going to combine their efforts anyway without us, and there was nothing we could do about it.

I had been round the course before: there are few new arguments in politics. I was appalled at this proposed dissipation of European strength and so reckless a rejection of the co-operation which had built Tornado. I asked to see the German and French defence ministers and we met in Paris.

I proposed to Manfred Woerner and Charles Hernu, the ministers of the Federal Republic and France, that we should create a project that would enable Europe to work together, pooling its skills to provide a fighter which would meet our needs. As we face a single threat, it seemed within the grasp of reasonable men to devise a common response; and moreover it would provide Europe with an aircraft which European governments would buy in huge numbers and which we would be able to sell to a world only too willing to avoid a commitment to one or other of the superpowers.

Rather more than two years later, the original Panavia Tornado partnership – with the most welcome addition of Spain, whose defence minister played a growing and important role in drawing his country into European defence co-operation – signed an agreement to proceed with a feasibility study for a single aircraft.

It would not have happened without the steadfastness of my German, Italian and Spanish colleagues, who shared my determination. We gave long hours to the search for effective co-operation, and the four of us could have concluded an agreement much earlier than we did if we had not explored every chance of bringing France also into the deal.

It was not to be. As I sat in my office into the small hours of a summer morning in 1985, approving by telephone the final details of the agreement which was being negotiated in Turin by the national armaments directors of the four countries, I heard the news of success with mixed feelings. The agreement saves the defence budget £1000m; it is the largest industrial contract into which this country has ever entered, and the most ambitious co-operative venture Europe has achieved. My regret is that France decided to go it alone.

I had done my best. I asked Charles Hernu if I might visit Dassault to urge them to participate: and he readily agreed. It was an unusual scene. I sat in the Dassault headquarters on the outskirts of Paris while their senior people explained the incomparable qualities of their own prototype. I had to tell them that there could be a European deal, but that it could not be a French deal. Dassault, like so many companies founded by brilliant entrepreneurs, do not find co-operative ventures easy. They see only one role for themselves.

My visit had one important result. I believe that my efforts to win round the French were taken in other European countries as proof that I was genuine in seeking a fully collaborative European project.

It would be difficult to overstate the pressures which such collaboration has to overcome, and the number of political, military and industrial arguments – all powerful and persuasive – which are ranged in every European country against any collaborative project of any consequence.

The first resistance begins, perhaps, with the gleam in an Italian scientist's eye, or the anxious look at tomorrow's order book by a British defence contractor. It may start with the first murmurings of discontent in the regiment or warship, where someone says: 'This kit is out of date'; or with a telephone call from a company anxious to explain its latest breakthrough. Within each national entity new solutions then begin to emerge which are necessarily British, French or German solutions; in each country the participants become more excited and committed, they begin to base plans on certain equipment specifications, and, before you know where you are, that first indication of interest has become a working drawing, then a development project, and the taxpayers' money has begun to flow. It is flowing in lire, marks, francs and pounds, and in a great many directions. By the time someone questions the overlapping and suggests joint procurement, each country is half committed to building what it is convinced is better than anything that any other country can offer.

Then comes a powerful diversion. The Americans will invariably have developed an excellent weapons system at their own taxpayers' expense. American companies will arrive with licence agreements, offering offset work on equipment which is guaranteed because it is already in service with the American forces. A European company is offered a deal which it cannot refuse, and next day and for weeks to come its representatives are inside the ministries in Rome or Bonn or Whitehall, arguing the supremacy of the American system. They have predictable allies in the finance ministries of Europe.

European ministers have no illusions about the pressures and forces at work. Among the most interesting conversations I remember took place between the Euro-ministers –

the European NATO ministers – informally over dinner. There was total accord about the waste and inefficiency of this internal taxpayer-financed competition. But ministers dining on the best of European fare are far from the front-line trenches of the research laboratories, the factory floors and the military planning units; and the arguments which flow next day across their departmental desks are very different.

To a minister in his national capital the easy and traditional way forward is to wrap a project in the eloquence of the Union Jack or the Tricolour – in Washington the expression is to 'bald-eagle' it – and to avoid the stress of conjuring co-operative effort from foreigners who (everyone will tell you) are out to cheat you and steal your technology. That is, if the foreigner is accorded credit for any technology in the first place. For every Frenchman whom the British suspect of cheating, you can be sure there are two in Britain whom the French wholly distrust. In every field of technology where a British company believes itself to be ahead there will be a German company convinced that the British have hardly begun. In every country, government and firm, and in the breasts of countless officials, the old rivalries and suspicions thrive, and only ministerial will can overcome them.

There are many ways of testing that will and that devotion. Exactly the same test is applied to ministers in other countries as in Britain. It is natural for the leading companies in each country to push continually for supremacy, and natural for officials to join industrialists in putting to the minister what appears to be the national, the patriotic case. The industrialists in every country have access to the member of parliament whose constituents they employ, and to the journalist hungry for stories of ministers who are about to sell the national interest short.

In Europe progress on specific high-profile projects, where the savings are obvious and big and the arguments clear, is hard enough to achieve. Ministerial effort is well worth spending to secure agreement for such large projects as the space agency or the fighter aircraft. The potential saving from joint procurement of less costly equipment would seldom justify the ministerial time which would have to be spent in reaching agreement. But the defence ministries of the European alliance are spending many billions annually on a bewildering range of equipment. Together, the separate potential savings are enormous and, if achieved, would make Europe's present defence budgets stretch much further. Co-ordination throughout the equipment range, so that the savings through efficiency were spread across Europe's whole industrial base, would yield an enormous cash prize; but getting that co-ordination would be a task of a different order of magnitude.

It can only be achieved at the behest of ministers, but the detailed complexity demands not ministerial initiatives but systems to achieve results. Large numbers of people in ministries and drawing offices and boardrooms have to get the habit of working consistently over many years with people of other nationalities; and they have to work to common specifications within a competitive environment that is Europe-wide. This co-ordination is required at every stage of research, development and production. The present duplication and triplication diminishes the value of our budgets for research and development. America and Japan, in competition with Europe and with their highly sophisticated national co-ordinating machinery and genuine internal markets, are much better placed to get value for money. America has the Pentagon and NASA; Japan has its Ministry of International Trade and Industry.

It is invariably sensible for a minister who wants progress to adapt or revive an existing body rather than spend time creating a new one. At the MoD we found that there was a tool lying largely unused – the Independent European Programme Group (IEPG). Someone pointed out to me that the IEPG, with thirteen member countries, had been put together in 1976 and in seven years had never met at ministerial level. Its impact had been predictable.

How best to breathe life into it? We had first to agree to meet at ministerial level, to set agendas and, critically important, to meet again. There was a fascinating struggle to get agreement that we should continue to meet regularly. Pressure was applied to reduce the frequency of meetings, from six months to nine months, then no doubt to eighteen months. The reasons were always plausible. One government had a budget statement, another had to fight an election. I resisted the pressure. Ministerial meetings bring results, because a meeting without results is a humiliation. The more frequently ministers meet, therefore, the more urgently the machine will deliver results for them to endorse and to parade.

I was determined that the IEPG would go on meeting, and at Secretary of State level. After I had woodenly refused to be denied my half-yearly rendezvous it was suggested that junior ministers should take over. Again I resisted. Junior ministers would have been asked to delegate further, and we would soon have been back to meeting at official level. Progress would have stopped.

In fact, we made significant progress and the IEPG is beginning the long process of trying to secure co-ordination from the early stages of research and development to procurement of finished weapons systems. Already it has become the main forum for European defence collaboration. It is, incidentally, unusual, if not unique, as a creation within NATO in that it enjoys the full support of the French. There is little difficulty in getting the support of the French where their commercial interests are involved.

When we first assembled, the research directors of the laboratories involved in European defence technologies had never met as a body. Yet often it was the gleam in the eye of one of these men, a German or an English gleam, that began the divisive movement. No one had ever thought of bringing them together, until we arranged a conference, the first of its kind, in London in 1986.

The European spirit, I believe, grows slowly stronger, but in every country and every parliament it still has to accommodate itself daily to national sentiments which grow no weaker and which national institutions, old and immutable, sustain. We need to develop practical arrangements which make collaboration more natural and straightforward. Sometimes a major national company will take the lead but that often provokes the suspicion that others will be cut out. For large projects we need to develop the science of managing collaboration in companies based on a European model. It has to be a single management team, not a committee, if efficient conduct of the enterprise is to result. A chairman of one nationality is balanced against a chief executive of another, a technical director against a managing director, in a kaleidoscope of power-sharing which will rein in the national instincts of the participants to the point where they concentrate on the success of the project for the benefit of all. There is no point in ignoring the suspicions that exist. Either they will keep us apart or we will neutralise them in a framework that, by being balanced, ensures fairness. Panavia, the European company that manages the Tornado programme, is one such model and is now operated efficiently.

Efficiency is essential, and a primary purpose of drawing Europe together is to get a market place that can sustain within itself large-scale competition. But national procurement budgets will not be committed to international co-operation if the principle of *juste retour* is ignored. This requires that each member country receives a share of work proportionate to its ultimate purchase of the product. I have seen enough to know that it is compatible with efficiency, and that the combination is both feasible and necessary. Once the main contract is placed, the distribution of work on the sub-systems is put to competition and any re-allocation of work amongst nations to reflect the *juste retour* principle can also reflect the best prevailing price. In practice, where public money flows, an appropriate sharing of work has to be part of the bargain.

As time passes, we will achieve a European market that will encourage the Europeanisation of our industry and the merging of our companies. It is unrealistic to believe that governments will stand back from either process. The strategic interests are too important and the politics too sensitive. But the full integration which will be needed if Europe is to possess world-class companies in key industries will be easier if the Euro-companies of tomorrow evolve in partnership and in shared experience along the way.

In this chapter I have set out my commitment to the opportunity of Europe and my experiences in pursuing some part of it. If I am impatient it is not from dismay at lack of progress but from awareness of the prize yet to be won.

We have a democratically elected European Parliament, although its powers are limited. We have now passed, with minimal controversy, the Single Act to permit progress by majority voting in the Council of Ministers, although admittedly in a limited range of fields.

Visionaries will say that this is not enough, but then visionaries are not destined to die content. Opponents will remain unreconciled in their trenches. I suspect that most people in Britain, if shown such a balance sheet in the 1950s, would not have believed it possible for Britain in Europe to have moved so far, with so little pain.

The rate at which the making of Europe continues lies in its leaders' hands. The motive power will continue to be a mixture of imagination and collective self-interest. Once the Common Market is completed and working, the area of common interest will gradually enlarge, fusing perceptions of national interest to a point at which a common foreign policy will emerge. Not until a common view of Europe's global interests is held with conviction will Europe be ready to combine to defend them.

Today there is only a rudimentary common foreign policy among the Community's twelve member states. Divergent interests threaten every common position. Historic and former imperial ties are strengthened by trade and aid, so that sentiment and commerce coincide in the calculations of each capital, where different questions are posed and different answers found. Ten of the twelve, having few important commercial interests in South Africa, may be more prepared to urge tough action against Pretoria than Britain and Germany, who have much to lose. Libyan involvement in Italian industry, the French engagement in Chad, and the close relations between Greece and the Arab world, give each of these countries different perceptions about how the Community should respond to the Libyan problem.

At present there are no interests outside its own territory that Europe could be relied upon to defend. We have not begun to contemplate the opportunities which would open up if we could put together our knowledge and experience, so that South America, Africa, Asia and the Pacific could hear the voice not of yesterday's imperial past but of tomorrow's Europe.

Only where our commercial interests merge are European enthusiasms beginning to grow. We have seen this, for example, in the Tornado and Airbus programmes. This commercial, self-interested Europeanism will steadily develop with the aggressive conquests of new markets by European companies. It will grow stronger as events elsewhere provoke a response. EUREKA – the pan-European programme of civil research – was the European response to the challenge of the SDI research programme and the prospect of the Americans gaining greater technological advantage.

A common resolve to resist the western expansion of the Soviet Union gave Europe the most dramatic impetus towards unity in its history, as well as strengthening its links with North America. The strength of NATO is that it is American-led. Its weakness is that France is no longer a member of its integrated military structure, so that Europe lacks co-ordination even in the face of the clearest case for it.

While I was at the Ministry of Defence, and heavily involved in trying to draw together Europe's industrial efforts through the IEPG, the French proposed the resurrection of the Western European Union. I felt little enthusiasm, but having been persuaded that we should respond I attended the meetings in Rome and made positive proposals to try to make it work. I discovered that that was not what was wanted. The WEU is a talking shop. Politically it does not represent the whole of Europe, and as a group which does not include Europe's principal ally it could not meet our defence needs.

For these reasons I believe more than ever that the WEU is an impediment to the advance of Europe. We have a European Parliament. We have an administrative machine. We do not need two of each. The WEU is a diversion, nowhere near as valuable as the Euro-group of NATO ministers and incapable of mounting a serious defence strategy. If the WEU's continued existence is necessary for reasons of French domestic politics then it will continue; but the pretence that it has any value should be dropped.

Recently there have been most welcome signs of a more open French approach and, in responding to this, Britain – as the only other nuclear power in Europe – could play a critical role. Our aim should be to persuade France to take her proper place among the leaders of the European group of NATO ministers, for IEPG to become an instrument of the European Community and for the WEU to be given an honourable funeral.

The urgency of driving forward the work of completing the European market is such that I believe there should be a second cabinet minister in the Foreign Office. No one doubts the commitment of that department, nor of recent British foreign secretaries, to the European cause. It is a question of the workload of ministers. If the Treasury never sleeps, the Foreign Secretary never stops. He lives on a conveyor-belt which takes him from conference to conference, country to country. We recognised the special need for a minister in the Cabinet who had no other responsibility than our relations with the Community when we were negotiating access. The need to complete the market warrants again the extra vigilance and determination which a second senior minister would be able to add.

Anyone who looks to Europe for painless solutions to Britain's industrial decline deludes himself. Europe is an opportunity. We need to come to terms with its competitive thrust and win our place within an enlarged market. Outside the market we could face that same competition, and would have to watch it bestow ever greater benefits upon the Community's members which would be denied to us. If we look beyond Europe to the competition of America, Japan and the Pacific basin, we can see the challenge which, if we were alone and outside the Community, would overwhelm our relatively poor national economy. On our own we could expect a diminishing influence in world affairs, both in trade and foreign policy: as part of the Community we speak as the largest economic unit in the world. This should never be underrated. The Japanese, for example, are unlikely to take threats of trade retaliation by Britain alone very seriously; but when the Community decides to get tough with the Japanese that is a different story.

Inside Europe we are part of what will be a world power. The national sovereignty which we lose is more than made good by a share of the much larger sovereignty which we get from participation in Europe. Our imperial days are over, and while we cannot rule Europe in place of our Empire we should be an influential senior partner. A strong Community offers the best prospect for a strong Britain.

The movement towards a Europe whose citizens are free to exercise their professional skills and to sell their wares from Antrim to Athens without seeking officialdom's leave will recover for Britain a sense of partnership in a shared destiny.

The final proof of Europe's maturity will be when, after difficult meetings of the Council, the London and Paris newspapers, briefed by ministerial sources to print only the unimproved truth, carry if not identical, at least mutually corroborative accounts of the previous night's work, with no winning or losing countries, no heroes or villains.

If that is too fanciful, let me put forward another vision. The European Community will have settled to serious work and will earn its peoples' regard when its ministers can meet in the early afternoon to tackle a five-hour agenda in the knowledge that they will have a full night's sleep; and when they can be certain that they will earn no credit, but only Europe-wide contempt, if they sit through the night to prove their obstinacy. The clocks in Europe have been stopped too often, and for too long.

13
The Superpowers

Since victory was achieved in Europe in 1945, the wisest Europeans have understood that their continent's security depends on the continuing commitment of the United States, the power which twice within a generation has spent its citizens' lives and treasure in helping to end wars which were not of their making.

Most happily for Europeans, the wisest Americans have understood equally that their continuing commitment to Europe in time of peace was the surest safeguard against yet another European conflict igniting the whole world.

The speed and thoroughness with which America acted, before the 1940s ended, still looks remarkable forty years later. The institution by the United States of the Marshall Plan and the formation of the North Atlantic Treaty Organisation were based on self-interest, as are all great alliances for peace or war; but never has the self-interest of any nation been pursued with such generosity to others. Europe acquired a material debt which can never be paid and of which payment is not sought. As for the debt of gratitude, such debts are never paid by nations and seldom even acknowledged.

The Atlantic Alliance endures, and our peace still depends on America's commitment. That in turn will depend on where America in future believes her interests to lie. It may also depend on Europe's reciprocal goodwill and good sense which, I am afraid, flow less strongly than they once did. I am concerned that the Alliance may be weakened or imperilled by European shortsightedness or carelessness. Some Europeans these days seem to show increasing ignorance of and insensitivity towards America's needs and feelings; too much goodwill is assumed and too little given; most damagingly for Britain, confusion, silliness and outright mischievousness have increased their hold on the British Labour Party which still sees itself as a serious contender for office.

I want to examine the state of the Atlantic Alliance, and in particular the relationship of Britain with the United States, because only the fullest understanding will ward off the danger of fatal mistakes being made through ignorance. I will then examine the threat from the Soviet Union which the alliance was called into being to counter.

Europe is entitled to nothing from America. The long years of dependency after 1945, and the continuing and necessary reliance on American protection within the mutuality of NATO, have sometimes engendered, especially I think among the British, an assumption that we are entitled to America's general support and goodwill which, in spite of such ruptures as Suez, has become almost habitual. The truth is that Europe can rely on American support, staunch though it has been, only so long as we continue to earn it. There are ties of sentiment, of course, but the basis of all government-to-government relationships, in defence or trade or diplomacy, is the deal struck between friendly and well-acquainted allies who seek mutual advantage.

The United States is not about to desert Europe. In spite of the recurrent and understandable pressure from Congress for a reduction in America's share of the cost of European defence, and the attempts of Senator Sam Nunn and others to cut the number of American troops in Europe, I believe that future administrations will continue to keep hundreds of thousands of American servicemen on European soil so long as Europe welcomes them. It is important to remember that Senator Nunn acts as he does not from hostility to Europe but from a desire to preserve a proper balance of contribution, and thus respect, upon which the alliance depends.

There are strong reasons why American troops in Europe serve America's interests. The first is the one which first brought them here: the undiminished threat of Soviet expansion. The Americans may not need to defend their homeland on the soil of Europe or over its skies, but by leave of the

Europeans they will do what they can to deny to the Soviet Union the territory, the economic strength and the industrial capability of Western Europe.

America's second concern is to protect its own increasing penetration of Europe's industry and commerce, which for us in Britain is most tellingly measured by the fact that American investment sustains one in eight manufacturing jobs. America has doubled its export trade in the past decade, and the drive to increase it further creates a significant additional pressure.

Third, and by no means least, is the American perception of the shared values of freedom which her every instinct would be to defend. There is no need to separate this more sentimental link from the other two. Without them it might not be enough, but with them it is a powerful reinforcement of America's more practical commitment.

There are counter-pressures of which Europe should take heed. America is changing. The growing economic strength of the countries of the Pacific basin, and their increasing importance as trading partners, draws the American gaze westward. With the south and westward movement of the population and the rapid growth in economic and political importance of California, the centre of gravity of the American nation moves steadily away from the Eastern seaboard and from Europe. Asian Americans – of Chinese, Japanese and Filipino stock – and American citizens of Hispanic and African descent, with no European roots or links, are increasingly numerous and influential. Even on the Eastern seaboard, in New York City today, the proportion of the population of Anglo-Saxon origin is surprisingly small.

On both sides of the Atlantic the lapse of time since 1945 has had its effect on the popular mind. Twenty years after the Soviet invasion of Czechoslovakia, the threat of Soviet military adventure in Europe has become less real in the eyes of younger Europeans. Middle-aged Americans have unfading memories of the Vietnam war; of those who fought in a European war the numbers dwindle. It has always been foolish, and would be more foolish than ever today, for Europe to take it for granted that American electors are fully alert to the Soviet military threat and are resolute to confront it in Europe.

If the British people still possess that much discussed special relationship with America, as I think we do, we have also a special responsibility to keep relations between the European and American allies in good repair. I believe that we could do better. Perhaps some such thought was in the mind of Helmut Kohl when he is said to have mused: 'I know the British have a special relationship with the Americans, but the question is have the Americans a special relationship with the British?'

The British people have no more right than other Europeans to presume on American support and friendship, which we are prone to do. At our worst, we expect uncritical support, as during the Falklands campaign, while reserving the right to be severely critical, for instance of the American bombing of the Libyan capital.

As a people we are, I fear, less generous than they. We admire America's technological feats, such as their astonishing achievements in space, and we acknowledge the managerial brilliance which brings them to fruition; but we are disdainful of many aspects of American life, of the ruthlessness of their corporate rivalry or the seaminess of much American politicking, and we easily persuade ourselves that British ways are better. At best we are smug; at worst, envious.

By contrast, there is much evidence of warm American feelings towards and interest in Britain. More American visitors come to Britain each year than go to France, Germany and Italy put together. It may be simple curiosity that brings them, or something more profound; it should not be undervalued, any more than we undervalue the commerce which they bring, or dissemble the distress of Britons employed in the travel trade when Americans feel unwelcome or unsafe, and stay away.

Britain has often benefited substantially from the good nature shown us by Americans. At the start of the Falklands dispute, with the notable exception of the United States Defense Department under Caspar Weinberger, the Administration was reluctant for understandable reasons to take Britain's side. The view in the State Department was that Argentina and Britain were both valued allies and that Washington's proper role would be that of an active but neutral intermediary. The ordinary people of America, on the other hand, took Britain's side from the first and made their feelings plain, first to Congress and then, through Congress, to the Administration, and great was our gain from what seems to have been a spontaneous upsurge of pro-British sentiment. I do not think that America, if similarly placed, could count on similar pro-American sentiment making itself felt here. That is a pity. It has always struck me as odd that British politicians who side openly with the Americans when there is good reason to do so are criticised by the Left as America's poodles. Meanwhile politicians of the Left do double somersaults to find grounds for praising the Soviet Union: for example for making tentative steps towards standards of civilisation that we have long since taken for granted.

Between governments, the Anglo-American relationship is, I believe, better understood. It needs vigilance on either side and constant repair, but it is well founded and tested and likely to endure most foreseeable pressures. I do not see, however, how this relationship would withstand the election in Britain of a Labour government led by Neil Kinnock and resolved to put into practice the anti-nuclear and anti-American defence policies which the Labour Party has embraced.

The basis of the Anglo-American relationship since 1940 has been the community of military interest between our two countries. Our common language, our shared inheritance of law and democracy, our many personal, professional and family links with the white Anglo-Saxon protestants who spoke for most of America a generation ago, even the closeness of Franklin Roosevelt's friendship with Winston Churchill, all helped to make the initial wartime bond both firm and enduring; but military necessity, and a common view of how world peace must be kept, has preserved and strengthened that bond.

The Second World War was a task shared and a victory jointly achieved; neither Britain nor America could have conquered without the other. If Britain had not held out in 1940 America would never have crossed the Atlantic, but if the Americans had not then come we could never have mustered the force to restore liberty to continental Europe.

After the war America might have withdrawn its strength

if the Soviet Union had not moved its tanks into Eastern Europe and, in 1948, confronted the Western powers over Berlin. When they did, the then – Labour Government was quick to join in urging the Americans to remain in Europe and establish NATO. The benefits of that alliance for Britain need no restating. The stabilisation of Europe under America's leadership has been a triumph of that country's diplomacy and resolve.

The emergence of the Soviet threat to replace that of Hitler's Germany established a unique closeness in military co-operation between Britain and America. No other European power plays so comprehensive a role as Britain in the alliance. Britain has its own nuclear capability, makes a significant contribution to all three military arms of NATO and is convinced of the need to contribute to peace-keeping activities beyond the NATO area. Although planning is on a smaller scale, much the same analysis of policy requirements exists in the British Ministry of Defence as in the Pentagon.

I do not make light of the role of other European members of NATO, but each of them contributes, for different reasons, within narrower constraints. The French have an independent nuclear capability, but they inflicted upon the Americans the humiliation of the instructions in 1966 to close the NATO headquarters in Paris and to remove troops from France. The Germans have no nuclear capability and, although they provide an immensely impressive conventional force, backed by American nuclear capability, they have a near-prohibition on out-of-area activities. The Italians, with their NATO bases, have played a conspicuous part in the maintenance of the American nuclear umbrella but have no nuclear capability of their own.

The most potent symbols and proofs of the closeness of the Anglo-American relationship are again military. The Polaris treaty was made possible by the confidence between John Kennedy and Harold Macmillan, and was sufficient evidence of Britain's incurable Atlanticism to serve at least as a pretext for De Gaulle to break off the first negotiations for our entry to the European Community. The agreement on Trident was similarly based on the mutual trust between Jimmy Carter and Margaret Thatcher. Where such trust exists, and self-interest allows, then the most fruitful working arrangements are possible between British leaders and American Presidents.

The latest significant instance was the agreement reached at Camp David between the American President and the British Prime Minister setting out the basis upon which Britain would take part in the research necessary for the Strategic Defence Initiative, to be conducted within the Anti-Ballistic Missile treaty of 1972.

The Americans are tough but splendidly reliable dealers, and generous in the help they will afford to a willing partner. Our contribution to the nuclear arm of NATO gives us a special place in America's eyes. Our contribution to joint intelligence gathering world-wide is greatly valued by America, and in sharing its fruits we receive far more than we are able to give.

They expect loyalty but they respect strength. Their industries will compete, as we have seen, to sell Europe what Europe would do better to make for itself; but where Europe's industries and governments combine to compete better, and to increase European strength to keep American technology at bay, America's leaders do not see this as hostile to their interest. Once Europe had proved its determination last year to build the European fighter aircraft, Caspar Weinberger sent a letter offering America's full co-operation.

In 1962, during the first negotiations to enlarge and so strengthen the European Community, President Kennedy, in a notably generous speech in Philadelphia, welcomed the prospect of America's European friends forming a closer union; and he hoped one day for a mutually beneficial Atlantic partnership between that European Union and the old American Union founded in that city one and three-quarter centuries earlier.

I wonder if the leaders of the Labour Party have any idea of what they are putting at risk, when they prepare to ask British electors to give them leave to dismiss all American nuclear weapons from Britain. It is just possible that Neil Kinnock and Denis Healey may be right – if it can be assumed that they agree on this – in their belief that the Americans will continue to underpin the defence of Europe with the weapons which Labour thinks suitable and without those which they themselves believe to be essential. It is presumptuous folly to rely on such a belief.

To do what Labour proposes would be to risk incalculable danger to European stability and peace and to the unity of the Atlantic Alliance. Labour's policy is irresponsible and self-indulgent. In taking decisions about an unpredictable future it is necessary to assume the worst. There are no grounds for assuming that the Soviet menace has abated, that American Atlanticism is immune to rebuffs, or that a unilateral gesture by Britain would achieve anything but the incredulous contempt of the Soviet Union. We made such a gesture when we abandoned our chemical warfare capability. It encouraged no response.

Sober politicians act on calculations not of what they wish to happen but on what, in different circumstances, may happen. Only the unity of North America and Europe in NATO offers the scale of deterrence that makes unacceptable to the Soviet Union the risk of launching an attack in Europe. For deterrence to be adequate it must deter nuclear and chemical attack, not just conventional. To be credible it must be based on America's presence here in Europe. Britain's independent deterrent adds another dimension, by complicating the Soviet Union's judgement. A future Soviet leadership, in contemplating action against Western Europe's democracies, may be tempted to rely on a belief that the United States would be unwilling to risk its territory or its people in defending its allies. The possession by Britain of its own deterrent means that any Soviet aggression would entail the taking by Moscow of a literally incalculable risk. This element of confusion is welcomed by our allies.

It is not possible, as Labour suggests, to weigh such deterrent strength against any conceivable conventional weaponry. As George Younger has said, the saving from cancelling Trident would pay at most for two more tank divisions: that would allow the deployment on the central front in Germany, where the Warsaw Pact has a supremacy of 30,000 tanks, of 300 more British tanks. The cost of Trident is high but manageable. The bills will be paid over a 20-year period, and will absorb on average 3 per cent of the defence budget or 6 per cent of the equipment programme. The Tornado programme is much more expensive, and is similarly being absorbed. It is a case of priorities, and no programme has higher priority than Trident. There were cheaper alternatives, but no system so much cheaper that the loss in credibility would have been justified.

The political stability of Europe and the defence strategy of the NATO alliance are a seamless robe. Begin to unravel one thread and all the fabric may be lost. The process of unravelling might take a number of forms and its pace cannot be predicted precisely; but the danger areas are clear.

There must be a great risk that America would respond to an order to remove her nuclear weapons from Britain by running down her entire military presence in the UK. American public opinion and Congress could overwhelm any administration that tried to do otherwise. In any event, Washington would know that any other response would be an invitation to other European nations to follow Britain in repudiating their commitments. NATO strategy for the defence of Europe depends on rapid reinforcement through Britain from America. As America lost confidence in Britain as an ally, so the credibility of this strategy would also seep away.

Germany, though anxious to keep 50,000 British troops on her soil, would come under internal political pressure to follow Britain's example and exclude US nuclear weapons, thus destroying the key component of American nuclear credibility in Europe. No American government could continue to base substantial ground and air forces in Europe unbacked by a credible nuclear component. As US forces withdrew, European countries would be left to come to terms as best they could with overwhelming Soviet military superiority. Whether the response was towards neutralisation or heightened nationalism, the stability which has kept the peace in an area which has spawned two world wars would be lost.

Perhaps France, as the only remaining European nuclear power, would gain an ascendancy in Europe that would fit with De Gaulle's vision of holding a pivotal position between the two Superpowers. But the problem would remain of accommodating superior German economic strength within a stable strategic framework – of meeting German needs and interests and those of her neighbours both to the west and to the east. No one with experience of government would lightly discard the arrangements which have brought Western Europe together in partnership with the United States.

The collapse and disarray might be even swifter. The closer the friendship the crueller the blow. The Americans would have every justification for interpreting their treatment at the hands of a British government, acting in the name of a people whose welfare they have cherished and for whom they have made great sacrifices, as the blackest treachery. It would hardly be surprising if ordinary Americans in their tens of millions responded with outrage and forced Washington to recall American troops from Europe. If so, we in Britain would have betrayed not only America but our fellow Europeans and ourselves.

I do not believe the British people will contemplate taking this route. I do think it vital that Conservatives continue to take seriously the need to teach a new generation, untouched by war, how much of our freedom and safety we owe to the friendship and protection of the United States. We must counter the hard Left's assiduity in representing every American action as base or foolish; and we must expose the feeble Left's weak-minded pretence that the two Superpowers – the open democracy and the closed oligarchy – are equal threats to the peace and freedom of the world.

In Britain, friendship with America must be fostered and the alliance worked at. America's leadership of the West, freely offered and accepted, imposes disciplines on her allies which Labour politicians have neither the patience nor the skill to acquire. America is engaged on our behalf and her own in a power struggle with the Soviet Union in which each side seeks to extend its influence and exploit any weakness of the other. Leadership is a lonely occupation, and in the end grave decisions have to be taken alone. Not every scruple of every ally can be fully allowed for, nor is it feasible for an American President or Secretary of State to prepare a negotiating brief in open consultation with his allies, however intense their interest. That said, the extent to which the Americans are open to influence and seek to involve their allies in decision shaping is demonstrated after every round of substantive discussion in every security conference as the

Americans sound out and weigh the views of their fifteen fellow-members of NATO and their many concerned friends in other theatres.

By contrast, the unique openness of American society offers her allies a bonus, if they are willing to exert themselves, in the opportunity to bring their views to bear in scores of ways, by winning to their cause senators, congressmen or officials who through one channel or another may shape or represent US opinion or policy.

Here again, steadfastness both of effort and of friendship brings rewards. At the Ministry of Defence I saw how tough it can be to sell to America. Selling to the Administration is only the first fence, and that is high enough. The contract must then pass the scrutiny of six committees, three in each of the two Houses of Congress, their members all alert to strike out any line to which their various constituents may object. An American salesman in Britain needs to persuade only the Ministry of Defence. One signature and the deal is done.

The American market, thus heavily protected, demands persistence. Sometimes the Administration can help, but no Administration has unlimited credit in Congress, and no President or cabinet member will want to help an unreliable or carping ally.

Criticism in Britain of America's intervention in Grenada delayed for a year the sale of Hawk fighters to the United States Navy. The criticism was justified, not because the American action was wrong – it was not – but because the handling of it fell far short of what the British Government was entitled to expect, and put Geoffrey Howe in an impossible position. All the same, although the Defense Department wanted the Hawks, Congress was affronted and no member of the Administration was going to waste his time in pleading for the sale to be ratified.

Britain does well to remember that her special relationship with America is not exclusive: on the contrary, it is one of several special relationships. In spite of the exasperation with its European allies which Washington often shows, links remain strong with all the countries of the old world which the ancestors of many of today's Americans were so happy to leave behind. Italian-American and Greek-American pressure groups and their counterparts abound. Jewish-Americans have a veto over policy in the Middle-East. Irish-Americans can at times make British arguments inaudible.

Nonetheless, I believe that the British people know well, even if they do not often care to say, that they are lucky in this dangerous world to possess so powerful and so reliable an ally. They are not likely to trust this possession to the care of a party whose leaders show no comprehension of our dependence on America, and little affection for that country.

I warned at the start of this chapter that ignorance of the United States and neglect on this side of the Atlantic of the roots of the American relationship with Britain and Europe might lead to fatal mistakes – fatal because I see the alliance with America as an indispensable guarantee that the lives of the free peoples on either side of the Atlantic will continue to be free.

'Fatal' is perhaps too strong a word. When the alliance is unsettled our danger is certainly increased, but the community of interest within the alliance, and the long habit of friendship, entitles us to hope that even grave mistakes in our dealings with America will sooner or later be open to correction. We should not expect our future relationship to be more trouble-free than it has been in the past.

In our dealings with the Soviet Union one serious mistake or misjudgement might well prove impossible to retrieve. For all the potential goodwill between the Soviet peoples and ours, there is a settled, ideologically driven hostility on the part of Moscow towards the institutions and the States of Western Europe. That is an unhappy truth which must never be forgotten or obscured. It has been demonstrated repeatedly to us for 70 years. It is established anew every day and every hour in by far the greater part of the many utterances made about the West by the Soviet State.

A neighbour who declares himself your enemy is harder to study than one who proves himself a friend, and in the case of the Soviet Union the difficulty is greatly increased by the secrecy of the workings of its political system. Sometimes the Soviets seem perverse in their failure to understand the Western mind in spite of its openness, while we in the West suffer the handicap of having to comprehend the narrowness and immobility of the official Soviet mind. We suffer from having few shared traditions of thought or behaviour or social organisation. We have too few opportunities for face-to-face contact. The barriers to mutual understanding can seem formidable, and all efforts to penetrate them pitifully weak; but persistence is vital and no effort of thought or imagination can be too great.

One of the many unfortunate consequences of the Soviet invasion of Afghanistan was that it led Western governments to reduce to a minimum official contacts with the Soviet government and Soviet institutions. This was a perfectly understandable and proper reaction on our part at that moment. But our longer-term interest – to which we must work particularly – is to develop a dialogue which goes wider and deeper than that at the level of heads of state, foreign ministers and professional diplomats. The focus of interest of the Ministry of Defence is overwhelmingly and necessarily on the military policies of the Soviet Union. It is therefore important for it to have its own independent source of advice on the course of disarmament negotiations, and for that reason I created a disarmament unit in the ministry. I regretted that there was not more contact between our military staffs and their Soviet opposite numbers, not only to help avoid misunderstanding but for the broader reason that it can only be to the good to have a deeper understanding of one's potential enemy.

I was struck by how limited was the effort made within government to understand the underlying basis of Soviet behaviour. Enormous resources were invested in intelligence on Soviet military capabilities. But the discussion of underlying Soviet intentions and interests was often in the form of the simplest stereotypes. I believe a more sophisticated approach is needed if we are to find the basis for mutual security at lower levels of armaments on both sides. An effort of comprehension is needed to see the world through Russian eyes, the better to calculate how practical bargains may be reached. Anyone who seeks such an understanding should be under no illusion about the importance of consistency of purpose and underlying strength in negotiating with the Russians; that is what they appreciate and can respond to.

One of the least useful exercises is the frequent discussion of whether Russian history or Marxist-Leninist ideology is the more powerful influence on the behaviour of the Soviet State. I doubt if the question has an answer. It is clear that both are worth studying and, whereas the effects of the ideology are sometimes opaque, much of the history is both clear and instructive, and unquestionably important.

If Britain's freedom from foreign invasion for 900 years makes us one of Europe's most fortunate countries, Russia is the least fortunate. No country, not even Poland, has experienced both the devastating reverses and the incalculable human cost borne by the Russian people over this same period. Certainly their rise to superpower status is the product of policy and not of fortune. Most people, I think, accept that the actions of the Soviet Union are totally dominated by the Soviet experience, but I believe that the roots of what we take to be typical Soviet behaviour reach down to fears and hopes which have been a feature of the Russians' experience for many centuries.

The search for secure frontiers, and the expansion of Russian domination, are two views of the same activity – the first a Russian description, the second that of their neighbours. This growth has been seen by historians as a continuum with a life so far of some 700 years. It began with the principality of Muscovy, which at the end of the thirteenth century covered perhaps 10,000 square miles, and it may or may not have ended with the seizure in 1979 of Afghanistan.

The successive thrusts to the Barents Sea in the fifteenth century, then to the Baltic, the Black Sea and, in the nineteenth century, the Sea of Japan, can no more be attributed to accident than can the acquisition of the British Empire. But at every step the lack of defensible frontiers encouraged the Tsars and their generals to take more steps, and they stopped only where their power encountered greater power. The Tsars' successors exhibit the symptoms of this historic craving for security, which may be obsessive but is real enough. It would be an ignorant man who discounted it, and a foolish one who forgot this centuries-old determination to extend first Russian and later Soviet domination, and to do so by military means.

The Bolsheviks inherited a huge multinational empire, stretching across a continent. It was an empire disintegrating in the face of attack from the German Empire and this disintegration gave the heirs their opportunity.

With the collapse of the defeated Russian army and State, there followed the civil war with its catastrophic loss of life and economic cost. The part played by the Western powers in support of the anti-Bolshevik forces, for all its political and strategic logic at the time, is now part of the Russian mythology of the fledgeling revolution and its struggle against the forces of reaction.

The victory of the Red Army in the Second World War gave the Soviet Union the opportunity to win back the territory lost at the end of the First World War. With the exception of the bulk of Finland and of central Poland, Stalin regained the whole Imperial inheritance of the Romanoffs, and went on to achieve effective control of most of Eastern Europe. If Peter the Great's defeat of Sweden at Poltava in 1709 made Russia a European power, the victory at Stalingrad in 1942 gave the Soviet Union a claim to world power status. Since then we have seen a relentless growth in Soviet military capability in search of parity of status with the United States.

What lessons might be drawn from this bent for expansion? By the nineteenth century, as the largest of the European peoples in population and territory, the Russians under the Tsars included many who believed that they had some kind of right to exercise authority over the whole of Europe. Their Orthodox Christianity taught them, in particular, that Catholic Europe, the 'rotten West', was decadent and evil.

Traces of this thinking remain. The concept of 'Holy Russia' has been replaced by an atheistic ideology, but the sense of unique potential lives on, and owes much to the fact that Russia was the birthplace of the first Communist revolution; and the international nature of Communism provides a convenient political justification for expansion when the imperial mission of the Tsars, like that of the European colonial powers, has long since ceased to be a defensible basis for policy.

The problem is to judge whether this drive for expansion has any natural limits. Living in a post-Imperial world, we have to guard against seeing the Soviet Empire as a unique case: Russia is not the only country to have spread across a continent.

Russian history has another recurring and strident theme. From the time of Genghis Khan to the wars with Sweden, Napoleonic France and Hitler's Germany, it is a history of conflict and invasion. Repeated Russian attempts to accommodate the dominant power of the day, so as to be free to expand their influence elsewhere, have seldom proved successful. For both the Russian and the Soviet states a dominant and real problem has been the combination of huge territory and a lack of natural frontiers, most notably perhaps with Poland. For the Soviet leader, as for his Tsarist predecessors, the easiest answer to the question of which frontier is secure may present itself as: 'one where we are on both sides'.

Concern over the lack of natural frontiers has been heightened by experience of the domestic consequences of military defeat. In the history of Russia defeat has stimulated change. Defeat in the Crimean War led directly to the emancipation of the serfs, and the other extensive reforms of the Tsarist state; that by the Japanese in 1905 led to the effort to create a viable constitutional monarchy; that by the Germans in 1917 led to the Bolshevik revolution.

Stalin's slogan of 'socialism in one country', as opposed to Trotsky's doctrine of permanent revolution, epitomised the defence of a Communist fortress, and his economic planning was geared in part to creating an effective defence-industrial capability. In the event, Stalin was deceived by Hitler, and the Soviet Union was unprepared for the German attack in 1941. Moscow was again threatened, and twenty million Soviet citizens died. It is not hard to understand the determination of today's Soviet leaders never to be caught unprepared again.

Stalin's actions, in seeking to restore the Tsarist frontiers in the post-war settlement and in establishing an East European cordon of satellites, must be seen partly as establishing protection in the area from which nearly all attacks on Russia and the Soviet Union had come in the period after the Mongols. The same concern may be seen today in the Soviet response to any danger of destabilisation on their borders. Of course, a different danger is felt by those beyond the borders to whom it is very plain that to advance a frontier in the name of stabilisation is to prepare for a further advance.

We have, then, one part of the rationale for the phenomenon with which we find it so difficult to come to terms: an historically expansionist power obsessed with the threat it faces and apparently unconcerned about the threats which it poses.

The primacy which the Soviets give to military power may not derive only from this imperative of security. There is a further intriguing continuity in Russian and Soviet history in the effort made to keep pace with the leading powers of the West. In spite of the reforms of several Tsars, Russia always lagged behind the most modern European states in economic and political development. What always guaranteed Russia's international status was the scale of the army which the Tsar could put into the field. After 1945, power based on conventional arms, even on the Soviet scale, no longer seemed enough to the Kremlin. Parity with the United States in strategic nuclear systems was necessary not only for military reasons but also because it conferred superpower status. Now the constant ambition is not merely to keep level but, such is the sense of insecurity in the Soviet Union, to establish a margin of advantage. With little else to offer if the attempt to reach equality or superiority in the military field fails, military goals take on an extra importance.

In one more area the very size of the Russian Empire has helped to determine the structure of the Soviet State: in the organisation of government and the place of the military. It was Peter the Great who took steps to reduce the vulnerability of Russia, of which the huge size and sparsity of population made government hard. He made service to the state, civil or military, compulsory for the nobility and gentry, taking strict control over their social life and dividing them into a system of fourteen ranks which survived for 200 years until 1917.

The need to secure service and the latent fear of subversion promoted rapid expansion of officialdom which, in turn, devised ever more elaborate controls over expression and movement. There was tight control over both foreign and internal travel, and Russians were not free to move at will. The control over its citizens which the Soviet Union exercises today is of a different order, but its people have a tradition of subordination to authority which is not known in the West.

The need for a strong centralised autocracy was as strongly borne in on Lenin as it was on Peter the Great. The nature of Marxism-Leninism advanced the centralising process, and techniques which were in their infancy in 1917 have now been dramatically extended by ideology and technology. Today in the Soviet Union civil and military service is the dominant factor in the lives of most men. The universal logic of a firmly established bureaucracy has added its own momentum: the ever-increasing regulation of daily life and the association of rank with privilege.

I am not searching here for an all-embracing explanation – let alone justification – of Soviet behaviour, but there are traditions which may well bear on the present. Practices established over time helped to shape both how governments believed it is legitimate to act and the acceptance by the population of conditions which we, raised in a different political culture, would find intolerable. Russia experienced neither a Reformation nor a Renaissance, and some aspects of its culture have scarcely been disturbed for 500 years.

There is a further dimension of the inter-relationship between the State leadership and the Armed Forces which is of direct relevance to this day. Under the Tsars, at least until 1900, the closest relationship was established between the two, in part reflecting a shared aristocracy of birth as well as a shared interest. Under the Soviet system the relationship of the leadership of the Party to the Army would appear to be more complex. Since Stalin's time the needs of the Armed Forces have been regarded as paramount and they have been given priority in resources and status. But there may also be a fear of latent Bonapartism, as seen in Stalin's era in the purges of the 1930s.

Perhaps because of this fear, the formal weight given to the military interest in Soviet policy-making is small, and the Politburo has no professional serving officer among its full or candidate members. But in a bureaucratic society the five million members of the Armed Forces, organised in a centralised hierarchical structure, must command weight;

and in a society in which military goals are so important those who articulate them must have powerful influence.

The interesting question, particularly in relation to arms control, is how much room for manoeuvre the Kremlin has if it wishes to pursue agreements which cut across high-priority military programmes. While the Party is clearly in control, the problem of ordering civil and military priorities becomes progressively more difficult as the rate of growth of the economy declines.

We have, then, a country with an historical record of expansion, and an obsession over its own security; a closed, often isolated, society run by a highly bureaucratic government in which military interests play a strong role. This is not a picture of a country driven solely by the ambition of world revolution; but neither can it be seen as a peace-loving state with no ambition to spread its interests.

The Soviet Union brings together the ancient Russian concept of its right to extend its country's power with a modern mission to bring the world to Communism. It is not a question of extending Russian power or of spreading Communism: it is both, and the evidence suggests that messianic goals will still be pursued, though pursued with discretion. Opportunities will certainly be grasped, but only if the price is limited and acceptable. The 'inevitable march of history' can be helped along on Leninist principles, but not at a pace which puts everything at risk.

Is 'history', then, on the Soviet side? For the Marxist-Leninist an affirmative is central to his faith. The rest of us are entitled to ask the question, and we may wonder whether Mr Mikhail Gorbachev ever has doubts about the answer. How can he explain developments at home and abroad in terms which fit the precepts of the Party?

Fortunately, he should have rather more on his mind than plotting our destruction. At home and abroad there are daunting difficulties. He must maintain economic growth within an ossifying political and administrative system. There is the persistent inadequacy of Soviet agriculture. The incongruity between resources and results in the economy seems bound to grow worse as effective competition with the West requires more and more innovation. Centralised planning and state privileges sit uneasily with rapid technological progress. Information technology and modern management systems are alien to a nineteenth century ideology.

Between the Soviet Union and its satellites there are tensions. The leadership must be concerned at the changing relationships between European and non-European republics, and at the European republics' resentment of the share of investment flowing to Central Asia with its burgeoning populations. Nationalist sentiment in some republics has shown itself in restlessness, and the growth of Islamic fundamentalism on the Soviet borders must give Moscow further concern. China looks increasingly to itself and even to the West. Soviet influence along its southern and eastern borders depends less and less on shared ideology.

The leadership faces the classic problem in all empires of how to handle minorities. Up to now the Soviet Union has kept non-Europeans out of key posts in the Armed Forces and the Ministry of Foreign Affairs. It has maintained control by entrusting to European hands the vital Party posts in the capitals of the republics which carry responsibility for defence and security, and Gorbachev is still having to dismiss non-European Party secretaries.

The relationship with the Eastern European satellites is not only a problem of economic support and of avoiding uncontrollable political liberalisation. At the military level, the leadership cannot be confident of the response to the increased deployment of shorter-range nuclear weapons, nor of how the satellites would respond if hostilities should break out in Western Europe. The Soviet policy of controlling Eastern Europe to stabilise its western frontier is not a proven success. The non-conformity of self-willed, talented and would-be independent peoples remains a headache for Moscow.

On the wider stage there is no evidence of global advance. Forty years ago, with the spread of Communism across Europe in the wake of the Red Army, and with the Chinese Revolution, there was a spectre of monolithic Communism on the march. Decolonisation in Africa and Asia enabled the Soviet Union to pose as an anti-colonialist power and a natural ally of newly independent countries. The domino theory held sway.

The outcome has been very different. Tito first showed in

Europe that Communism was no monolith. The Sino-Soviet split showed that the Soviet difficulty in living with neighbours had nothing to do with capitalism.

Communism has had successes elsewhere, in South-east Asia and Cuba, and the struggle goes on, with Soviet and Cuban backing, in Central America and elsewhere. We cannot for one moment ignore the danger, but over these 40 years the record of Communist achievement looks limited.

The Soviet record on economic aid to the Third World has not been of a scale or consistency to fuel the revolutionary flames. When coupled with the political strings and the style and outlook of the archetypal Soviet adviser, it does not offer an attractive deal for the nationalist leaders of the Third World.

The record of success is hardly better in those areas closer to home to which the Soviet Union attaches importance. Leninism is finished in Iberia, Italy, France, Germany and Scandinavia. In the Middle East, Soviet influence is limited to Syria, Iraq and South Yemen. For Moscow, there must be a strong sense of lost opportunity, above all in the complete reversal a decade ago of the former Soviet position in Egypt.

In South-west Asia, the record is more difficult to judge since it hinges on the assessment of Soviet aims in Afghanistan. Was the invasion a considered move forward, or a defensive response to the fear of a reversal of socialism in a bordering country and perhaps of something worse, a Muslim fundamentalist state on the Soviet border? Or was it simply the wish to replace a disobedient with a compliant satellite? Probably there was a mixture of motives, but the consequences were damaging. The invasion brought an end to detente with the West and earned the condemnation of non-aligned countries.

Above all, the Soviet leadership has found that the great effort put into achieving military strength approaching that of the United States has not brought advantage. They now face yet higher expenditure on weapons systems of a level of technological sophistication which they may find it very difficult to maintain.

The Soviet Union's lack of success does not allow the West to be less vigilant. We must continue to deploy sufficient military strength and economic and political effort to ensure that there are no risk-free opportunities for it to exploit in areas of our own vital interest.

Beyond this there is a choice. Each side can stare uncomprehendingly at the other across the trenches, bayonets fixed, or seek greater mutual understanding on which better relations can be built and through which arms reductions may one day be agrred. My own clear preference is for this second choice.

We have little to fear from a comparison of Western values with Soviet ideology. Indeed it is bound to favour us. The comparative record on human rights alone gives the West a great advantage, and the gestures late in 1986 to Sakharov, Orlov and Irina Ratushinskaya have shown that Moscow knows it. I believe that we can afford to speak softly about the merits of our own system and the drawbacks of the Soviet one, and that strident rhetoric is self-defeating.

Without neglecting our own security, we must guard against any approach which heightens the insecurity of the Soviet Union and its sense of isolation. It is, of course, easy to remember the boasting claims by Khrushchev that Russia would overtake America by 1980 or his threats to bury the West. But Soviet leaders know the reality as well as we do, and the more they visit or consider the Western world, the more apparent the success of the enterprise economies must be.

To them that is a threat. They manage a rigidly centralist system and are all too aware that there is no such thing as a little freedom. Solidarity was infectious and therefore dangerous. It is not possible for them simply to draw a line beyond which freedom may not go to prevent it from penetrating the very essence of the social order in which they believe. If we are to bring them to a more sympathetic understanding of its virtues and expose the fallacy of its threat, a policy of defence and deterrent should, with caution, go hand in hand with a willingness to restrain and hopefully reduce the weapons of war deployed by both sides. Our interest rather must be to encourage an increased sense of security in the hope that the Soviet leaders will direct more resources to the genuine interests of their people. It is not impossible that increased Soviet prosperity, and prosperity in Eastern Europe, might develop from inside a structure which felt confident to experiment with a more liberal and decentralised economic system, one which was open to thoughts and developments in the West.

To encourage that, the need for dialogue and an increasing range of contacts, cultural, social and economic, become self-evident. There are, I am told, some grounds for believing that the situation may be less frozen.

Throughout Central Europe, there seems to be a bubbling up of change, of economic experiment, the growth of consumer interests and the increasing importance of religion. There may also be a build-up of pressure within the Soviet Union from a better-educated and more ambitious younger generation against the restrictive nature of the present system. Mr Gorbachev himself seems to be encouraging – within limits – economic change and a less repressive society. Of course a more economically advanced, better-led Soviet Union is in a sense a more formidable adversary; but we need not fear the capability of our own societies in such a competition.

We must not overestimate the benefits of dialogue. We have to remember Mr Brezhnev's description of détente, that it is 'just another aspect of continuing confrontation and struggle which may well have to be intensified'.

If the Soviet system is over-extended, either militarily or economically or both, the Soviet State is no less dangerous for that. There must be no less realism in our approach to both arms control and dialogue. Nothing in Soviet history indicates that we should look for sudden change or improvement in East-West relations. Indeed we must guard against sudden shifts in the Western position related to short term electoral considerations. We must play a consistent, well-prepared hand over a long period. Equally, the Soviets are not likely, in spite of Afghanistan, to rush into risky adventures or to seek to upset a careful balance of power.

Any progress to a better relationship will be gradual and, unless we keep a credible defence commitment, impossible. The evidence, nonetheless, is that the Soviet Union, while incapable of anything approaching warmth for the Western democracies, may need a period of equable relations with

them, at least for the next several years, and may be
conscious of that need. It must be the duty of Western statesmanship to be alive to every opportunity to make a mutually
beneficial response.

14

The Tory Vision

I explained at the outset that I would not attempt in this book to cover the whole political spectrum or to deal with any part of it exhaustively, nor have I. The mixture is part conviction, part proposal, part discussion.

In reading over what I had written I looked for a theme. I found several recurrent themes, but only one that is common to every chapter; the conviction that only in the philosophy and practice of the Conservative Party is there any promise of a safe and better future for the people of Britain. I did not ask myself if all my ideas were consistent with some grand structure of belief. Sometimes there are things to be done that are right, that everyone knows to be right, and that the practical Tory will never postpone while the search for theoretical justification goes on. Principles are guiding lights, not chains.

That said, there are themes. One is a pride in the past, when extraordinary men and women did extraordinary things in Britain's name. If the Elizabethans, Georgians, Victorians could win against the best, so can we; but we will not match their deeds without their confidence. Members of the younger generation will carve their own way, as they must, but they will note what their seniors do and say. If we believe in ourselves, they too will believe in us. Where there is no conviction there is no inspiration. They deserve also an unimpaired material inheritance. They will have to find the means to pay the pensions of an ageing population, and we must not through negligence impose on them also the burden of having to rebuild the homes and cities and industries of Britain.

The future which we shall leave with that younger gener-

ation lies in Europe, where the British people and their continental neighbours have an opportunity never given to earlier
generations to build a common strength and enjoy an undivided peace.

There is a sophistication needed to maintain across a continent and an ocean an alliance in peace which far exceeds the
all-too-easy recourse to arms of earlier times. We have to
learn to work and stick together because our lives depend
on it. The horror of humanity's power to destroy itself
imposes the strictest disciplines, but the balance of deterrence
is a balance for peace.

Most modern governments play a bewildering role in the
lives of those they serve. Even in the most open societies free
peoples look for leadership, and expect their governments to
make full use of the powers entrusted to them. Without
leadership, we will not rebuild our cities or our industry, nor
draw together those groups and strengths which in Britain
are so often needlessly opposed.

In our Civil Service, the armed services, police, teachers
and many other public servants, government has the sinews
of a civilised society at its disposal and also in its care. Here,
too, is a responsibility of leadership, which need not be
assertive to be strong. Without firmness in government,
exhortation is vain. Hectoring abuse turns the best away.
Leaders need not be loved; they must be respected.

The Conservative Party, by its leadership in two successive
Parliaments, has implanted a new confidence in the British
people and put before them new opportunities to use their
natural ingenuity and enterprise in shaping their future.
These two prizes will be lost if any other party is elected to
power. There is now, I believe, a growing demand for a more
humane as well as effective capitalist system – for a caring
capitalism – and the satisfaction of that demand is the
Conservatives' opportunity.

Limited though its powers are, the indispensable agent of
national recovery is government, and it is within the Party's
ability, as its record proclaims, to give our people liberating
government. We know what to do.

For any democratic government, the challenge is to take
people a little farther than they can go by themselves; to

offer hope a little brighter than their daily lives provide; and when need be, to show that compassion for which the market makes no allowance. Where there's a will, there's a way.

February 1987

Three months after this book appeared, the challenge described in the last paragraph was offered again to a Conservative government. The general election of June 1987 had a remarkable outcome in the return of the Conservative Party for a third successive term and in scarcely diminished strength. I was surprised by the size of the Conservatives' overall majority of 102, but never doubted that we would win.

There was the daily exchange of gunfire from the head-quarters fortresses of the political parties, and the campaign fought by and through the press and broadcasting media with their fascination for opinion polls. But there was no evidence that the battle had any effect on the decision of the people.

It became clearer day by day that most minds had been made up before Parliament was dissolved, and there was little change between the start of the campaign and the finish. This strong impression was confirmed in a survey of 4,600 voters by ITN and Harris Research, conducted on election day, which found that three in five had decided how to vote before the campaign opened. On the streets, in the housing estates and shopping centres, there was a sense of certainty about the outcome and every sign that voters were losing interest in the political arguments as the days passed. A BBC employee told me that during the campaign their audience for their main 9 o'clock television news dropped from 9m to 4m. The smiling faces of the proprietors of video shops, whose businesses boomed as the British public sought to escape the nightly repetition on their television screens, told a similar story.

For four weeks I lived the life of a nomad, denied as I drove through the night the chance to see the television screen. When we all try so hard for the plum television spots, it is frustrating to realise that the public has a choice and that the more of us they see the more they exercise it. All politicians must practise the art of television and take the opportunity to broadcast their views. My most memorable warning against vanity was conveyed in one television dealer's shop: all 25 sets were flatteringly tuned to a recording of me holding forth eloquently but silently to an empty shop.

I have no doubt that the Conservatives won mainly because of the performance of the economy; but the result was also a verdict on the first phase of the Tory revolution. The electors liked it, and invited us to take it further.

Beneficiaries of Conservatism, the enfranchised council tenants, the popular share-owners, the newly self-employed, the new small businesses, are everywhere. In my own constituency I met the proud owner of a council house which had appreciated by £10,000 in each of the six years since he had bought it. He was no doubt typical of many in the south of England, but there are beneficiaries in all parts of Britain. The election day poll for ITN showed that of owner-occupiers, who are now two-thirds of households, 47 per cent voted for the Tories, and 25 per cent each for Labour and the Alliance. Of those who bought their first shares during the last Parliament – some 18 per cent of voters – 56 per cent voted Tory, 16 per cent Labour. While canvassing in Barrow for Cecil Franks, I saw these chill warnings for the Labour Party, and wondered how it could ever hope to regain this single-industry town, dependent on the building of submarines for Britain's nuclear deterrent, which it held for forty years from 1945 to 1983. I met workers at Vickers who had bought shares in that company now worth £2,600, which Labour proposed to take back for £600.

It was gratifying to see during the election campaign the fruits of the first phase of that revolution. Many of the compartments into which British society was so long divided have been broken down. The council estates are no longer the exclusive preserves of the Labour Party but increasingly house articulate, confident people who have taken the opportunities which eight years of Conservative government have put before them. Indeed, the working class and the owning class have merged. As the new owner-workers of former nationalised industries, they now have material stakes in their communities, helping with visible pride and commitment to manage enterprises which only lately were steered by remote control.

One other conspicuous and greatly encouraging change which I encountered in my travels was the success of black Britons on a scale not seen before. I did not find many blacks in senior posts – far from it – but everywhere I found that, in the four years since the previous election, they had begun to climb the ladders of advancement. This upward movement is not as rapid as one would wish; but it is marked and widespread, and in sharp contrast to some of the negative forecasts recently made. The monuments of which I wrote in Chapter 8 are beginning to emerge. All the same, there is a long way to go, and the distance which black and brown Britons must yet travel helps to make the case for tackling the concentrations of poverty and hardship which the inner cities still display.

This settled determination of the electorate to return the Conservatives is important. The greater the confidence shown, the greater the burden of responsibility.

For the Conservatives returned to Parliament must remember that there are many – we all met them in our campaigning – who believe that the revolution of the 1980s has passed them by. Among these are white-collar workers in the public sector – teachers and civil servants, for example – whose incomes have suffered through wage restraint by comparison with those in the private sector. In absolute terms they are better off, but they believe that they are having more of a struggle to meet their mortgage payments than their neighbours who work for private companies. Nor are such doubts confined to the services in the public sector. I recall the wife of a junior manager in Austin Rover who feared that a Conservative government would close the business down. I could not persuade her that, after having put hundreds of millions of pounds into her husband's company, we were unlikely to abandon it. Perhaps it was as well for us that the incoherence and foolishness of Labour's defence plans and other policies repelled many of the people who would otherwise have been natural recruits for the main opposition party.

But we must recognise that Labour did recruit supporters

in the industrial cities. It is a matter for concern that those living in the cities who are most in need of Tory remedies may at first be the least able to respond to them. Our task is made harder because many of them are alienated from the Conservative Party. The further decline at the general election in our representation in the northern cities shows that we are not even holding our limited ground. This estrangement from Tory values and suspicion of Tory intentions is aggravated in a few areas by hostile local authorities. I do not believe that those very few councils who offer the Government entrenched opposition will be able to block a determined assault on urban squalor; but a sullen witholding of co-operation by local government all across the land could make progress very difficult, and I am troubled by the ill will which the proposed poll tax seems likely to engender. The lawyers are right when they say that hard cases make bad law. There is great mischief in the abuse of the present unreformed rating system by some irresponsible Labour councils, but I have yet to be persuaded that, in order to discipline a limited number of malefactors, the Government is wise to undertake a partial change in local government finance which will extend its consequences to every constituency in England and Wales, with incalculable but not unpredictable effects.

The prospect of a long and costly fight with local government and local interests, both Conservative and anti-Conservative, must make it less likely that urban communities will seize, without active encouragement, the opportunities for self-help which they are now to be given. Labour councillors, trade unions and self-promoting political activities strengthened by combining their opposition to the poll tax, can be expected to offer every possible discouragement. Against the chorus of local advice parents of children in troubled schools and tenants of the more dismal housing estates will be the less willing to vote to take those schools and estates into an uncertain future. All our experience shows that vested political interests have great power to delay social progress and to deny people things which they want. Even some Tory authorities withheld from council tenants the opportunity to buy their own homes until it was conferred by statute. Ministers should therefore have enough confidence in the benefits they are offering to take reserve powers to overcome local obstruction. Legislation should ensure that any freedoms from local bureaucracy which Parliament decides to confer will be available without restriction to those who wish to take them up.

Since the election it has been gratifying to see signs of our revolution advancing as I had hoped, and on the lines for which I have argued in this book, in such vital fields of social policy as housing and education. The common thread is our understanding, confirmed by experience, that the more that people are enabled to take responsibility for arranging their lives the more likely they are to better themselves and their communities. This is the belief behind our pursuit of policies which will allow parents, governors and head teachers to withdraw their schools from local authority control and become self-governing. It is also the basis for the proposed Housing Action Trusts, which will build on the experience gained at Stockbridge Village, and soon at Thamesmead.

There remain great practical questions to be answered. In allowing autonomy to schools, for example, the Government will have to anticipate a consequential problem. Falling rolls in inner city schools are making many of them unviable and liable to closure. What is to happen when, in desperation, parents opt to move out of local authority control? Will the Secretary of State turn away empty-handed the very people whose hopes have been so raised? There will continue to be hard choices and unpopular decisions.

However, to free schools and housing estates from the constraints of bureaucratic control is clearly good. Where bureaucracies retain their responsibilities the aim must be to prod them into greater sensitivity and efficiency in meeting the citizen's needs; and that is the purpose of the admirable proposal, quickly brought before Parliament, to require local councils to put their services to competitive tender. The Bill takes our earlier policy the necessary step further, and is a sign that the Government has understood the dangers of public sector disease, with its twin symptoms of palsy and of proneness to financial haemorrhage, and that it means to find a cure.

One statement in the aftermath of the election stands out. It was the Prime Minister's public promise, made in the small hours of 12 June, as soon as victory was assured, to 'do something about the inner cities'. The manifesto on which the Conservatives fought had already promised that 'the regeneration of the inner cities must be tackled', and linked this prospect with the removal of the barriers with which some Labour councils had blocked private investment and enterprise. Justifiably it made much of the success of the two Urban Development Corporations, the development of the Urban Programme and the steps taken to bring derelict and under-used land back into use. What was new was the sudden post-election elevation of the needs of deprived city dwellers above all the scores of other manifesto pledges. For myself, I welcomed the new priority wholeheartedly and at once. The 1987 public expenditure survey will provide the first real indication that the will matches the words. As I write, we have yet to learn whether there is to be a practical and determined programme to bring the benefits of the Tory revolution to those in the cities whom it has not yet reached.

So what is 'doing something about the inner cities' to mean? Does the Conservative Party really wish and intend the whole nation to enjoy its good government? Has it found the wisdom and courage to do what I have urged in this book and rebuild the physical and social fabric of our old industrial towns and seaports? I am confident that the cost of such extensive rebuilding is manageable; indeed, I am certain that, by the end of this century, any possible increase in the outlay of public funds which may be made, starting early in this new Parliament, will be seen to attract a growing commercial return from the private sector. But it is much more than simply a question of cost. The glittering prize is the restoration of life and hope to derelict communities and the lifting up of broken spirits. This achievement would remain to testify to the social concern of the Tory Party. The prosperous rural constituencies would also add a word of grateful thanks as the pressure of urban sprawl on the countryside eased.

A minimal injection of public funds can be self-defeating. We dare not settle for the smallest scale of expenditure which the Treasury calculates we can get away with. I have written about the liveliest city dwellers who achieve success against the odds in their concrete prisons, but then take the first chance to escape with their precious skills and energies. There is a sound general truth in the story often told in the Western Highlands of the remote crofting village which pleaded for 30 years for the building of a road link with the wider world. On the day the road opened the canny crofters brought in the removal van and moved out. There were too few incentives to persuade them to stay.

The Government must demonstrate that it is in earnest in wishing to bring the ingredients of civilised living back to the cities. We have shown that large-scale projects of urban renewal can work. The decision announced in 1986 to set up five new Urban Development Corporations, which will build on the experience of the pioneer corporations in the London and Merseyside docklands, is proof that this lesson has been well learned. The critical question at the outset was whether the pump-priming with public money would produce an adequate flow of private investment, and the experience of the first UDCs has given an exciting affirmative answer.

Nothing happens quickly in urban renewal, and we must move fast if we are to be able to show results on which the country may pass favourable judgement before the next election.

The visible success of our programme once launched will ensure that the work of reconstruction is not imperilled by any change of Government; but to bring about that success the seriousness of the Government's effort must first convince two categories of sceptical observer. The private investors who will be our indispensable partners must know that the Government's ardour is not going to cool before each autumn's expenditure review; and ordinary city-dwellers, whose goodwill and energy will be equally critical for success in each selected neighbourhood, must be able to see for themselves that the Government's interest is in the welfare of the poorest families and not solely in the fortunes of the entrepreneurs whom we seek to attract.

The most carefully drafted legislation cannot guarantee success. There is also a propaganda battle to be won, and we cannot count on extreme Left-wing local authorities again discrediting themselves with the voters in what Neil Kinnock described as 'the obscenity of playing politics with people's lives'.

All the success stories to which the Government can point were the product of partnership between the public and private sectors. The public sector had to lead, to clear away the legacy of the past and open for the private sector the prospect of profit tomorrow. There is no other way.

The first and second year costs of any programme will be small. The pattern of cash flow from the first UDCs, to which the commitment was made in 1979/80, showed how slow is the build-up. So far the UDCs announced in 1986 have cost virtually nothing. After the initial years, I believe that the Government's programme of asset sales could be adjusted to provide the sums required. I understand the principle that public accounting must be indivisible and that no source of income should be earmarked for specific expenditure, but it would make sound political sense to bring these complementary parts of the Conservative revolution together in the public mind. Those whom it has not yet touched would more readily begin to appreciate it. Those whose imagination has not yet been stirred by what privatisation is achieving might be fired by the spectacle of our towns and cities being restored with its proceeds.

A whole-hearted commitment to building new towns in old cities might bring returns both material and political from beyond our shores. The world would soon notice what we were doing, and if British architects and contractors became pacemakers in urban renewal, they would find that their skills were exportable to foreign cities. We would ourselves gain the chance to catch up with the skills which other countries have already acquired. Flexible and efficient administration of an enlarged urban programme could be linked with the devolved civil service for which I have argued; and the dispersal of civil servants and military establishments from London and the South-East into the provinces, so beneficial to the economy and so stoutly resisted until now, should be delayed no longer. The new office technologies overcome all the difficulties of dispersal – the fax and video machines, the closed-circuit television conference systems – could perforce be adopted and mastered. British industry would gain from these changes.

As for political gains, it is none too soon for our party's good for us to start bringing Tory values back to the cities. We have taught other countries, some of them with Socialist governments, what advances they can make by returning State assets to the citizen body. They will have more to study when we have brought our revolution to maturity and spread the benefits of the enterprise economy to all our people. As a party we must never accept that regaining control of the cities is beyond us. When I first entered Parliament we ran Liverpool, Manchester, Newcastle, Birmingham and many others, but the flight from these areas has included many who, had they stayed, would have led the fight against Socialism and all it stands for. In persuading a new generation to live and invest in the inner city we shall, amongst other things, create the communities from which tomorrow's local leaders of our party will come.

Progress on one front of this Conservative revolution requires simultaneous progress on the others. The most deprived parts of our inner cities will in the end be the chief beneficiaries both of the reform of the public service and of better-run schools and housing. But the urban soil will need more thorough preparation, and the greater independence and responsibility which Conservatives want to spread is unlikely to take root in it quickly. Many inner city stress areas and run-down estates have little experience of the stimulus of self-reliance and little of the energy which it both requires and releases. Running one's own show takes practice. These communities may hesitate to leap from total dependence to full independence, and could need a transitional stage. To help them to find the confidence to take responsibility for their housing estates they should first be involved in detaching those estates from city hall control so that they can be managed within the public sector each as a separate unit. They will quickly realise what we are about when they discover how the breaking up of the bureaucratic leviathans enables school and housing managers to respond faster to their clients' wishes.

Differences between city and suburb, deprived and comfortable districts, in part between north and south, will also oblige the Government to adapt other policies to local conditions. The experience of the election campaign and its outcome did not change my view of the pattern of unemployment or of how it should be tackled. The fall in the headline figure for May 1987 to below 3m, announced in the week after the election, was a heartening sign of improved economic activity, but for most of those millions without work it gave no grounds for hope that there would be early relief of their plight. Over much of the country unemployment was hardly an election issue in that, in spite of our opponents' efforts, there was little disposition among voters to blame it on the Government. However, I found many who shared my concern about whether the management of unemployment was sensible and whether the whole of the £6b annual cost of maintaining 3m people in idleness was necessary.

There is at last a welcome recognition that payment of unemployment benefit for young people should be conditional on their acceptance of training opportunities. This principle should be extended more widely, because people who receive benefit should not assume that they need do nothing for the community in return when there is so much that needs to be done. But in my campaign travels I again encountered the several nations to which I referred in Chapter 11, who differ greatly in the severity of the difficulties which they face in finding work and in their willingness to seek work. So I would repeat that sensitivity is needed in assessing entitlement to benefit. There will be many people in many parts of the country for whom no work can be found, and others who are not capable of work. There are concentrations of poverty, hardship and unemployment where to make any changes to the present pattern of unemployment benefit will be impossible until we have started to rebuild those communities; but in many parts of prosperous Britain there is a broad perception that the unemployment problem, the black economy, the lack of incentive to take available work and the lack of grip in the administration of benefit all require a new and positive approach that sees the unemployed not as a lost generation but as offering a challenge. Such an approach rejects the spending of £6b a year for no return. It recognises that a problem on this scale needs managing by men and women who see their task as one of turning despair into opportunity, rather than putting cheques in the post with few questions asked.

There is one other critical field for Conservative reform still untouched since the election – the Civil Service. There is no sign yet that individualism is to be encouraged. The centralist assumptions of the past century appear all too unquestioned. The application (for which I argued in the opening chapters) of the principle of pushing personal responsibility as far down the chain of command, and as far outward from the centre, as possible should be on the agenda. The evidence grows that the service is ripe for the harvesting of those same benefits, in greater effectiveness and responsiveness, which the delegation of responsibility promises to yield in the management of schools and housing estates.

It is a question of applying ideas which we have already tested and proved. The simplest and clearest solution, with the most obvious economic pay-back, is to privatize many activities and expose them to competition. Where full privatisation – the transfer of assets from public to private sector – may be inappropriate, we know that there will often be scope for the stewardship of those assets to be transferred, under contract, to private sector managers. In recent months the benefits of contracting out on these lines at the Devonport and Rosyth naval dockyards have begun to appear. Some 20,000 employees have moved out of the public sector and into the employ of private sector companies on contract. The threatened disruption failed to emerge. At Devonport a nuclear submarine refit has been completed ahead of time; and men have been dismissed for sunbathing during working hours in yards where, under the recently ended public regime, each worker used to take an average of four weeks' paid but unauthorised extra holiday a year.

Savings are available on a dramatic scale from an efficiently managed Civil Service, restructured to allow the greatest local autonomy. Ministers should advance along this line. The need for reform is too pressing and obvious for it to be neglected any longer. It is impossible to overstate the effect on the enterprise economy if those who manage and work for the public sector behave within a set of disciplines and practices that slows the pace, adds to the cost, refuses to accept responsibility and prevents the transfer of men and women across the frontiers of public and private sector.

Where management remains within the public sector the aim must be to create separate management units able to take decisions, including financial decisions, at local level wherever possible. The Department of Health and Social Security should examine the scope which the health service offers for such improvement. Below the level of regional and district authorities, the local hospital unit, which is the real focus of public interest and pride, could only gain from delegated management. As well as tending to be more sensitive and intelligent in the use of resources, local managers will also be more likely to stimulate and enlist local loyalty.

One student of Whitehall lore, Peter Hennessy, discussed in the *New Statesman* last March the ideas put forward in this book for improving the efficiency of the Whitehall machine. I suggested in Chapter 1 that it would require only four weeks to take the different departmental management systems and mould them into a common form. He suggested that it was up to me to demonstrate what could be done, by putting together a model accounting system with the help of others who knew from experience what was required. I recognise that this challenge deserves a response. It is vital that the Government should not lose its appetite for reforming institutions, so that they will serve the citizen better and charge him less, and I hope that the ideas upon which I am working will contribute to the debate.

The Conservative Party is now presented with a remarkable opportunity. Privatisation is not a dogma maintained in defiance of experience, as our critics have said. On the contrary, we were returned to power in 1979 with little idea of where we might find ourselves if we pursued the instinct which lay behind the sale of council houses. Since then we have stumbled on a philosopher's stone, of which Government and people together have gradually been discovering the potency. This discovery was not made entirely by accident. We were led to it by our belief in the motive power of the individual spirit and our willingness, in accordance with the best of all Tory slogans, to 'trust the people' with the wealth which was theirs and which the State had locked away from them. The social programme which is being placed before this Parliament is based on our determination to trust people not only with their own possessions but with their own lives.

We have some way to travel before all the British people, in the cities, in areas of high unemployment, in the discontented parts of our land, can be counted on to reciprocate that trust. The Conservative Party emerged triumphant from the polls, but a party of the whole nation will not forget that its support fell in the summer of 1987 to less than 30 per cent of votes cast in Wales, and in Scotland to only 24 per cent. Here is ground that must quickly be won back, and happily we have the means of winning it. The world is indeed turning to our ideas, even as Socialism is in retreat in Britain, in the Soviet Union and worldwide.

The next election will take us to the threshold of the twenty-first century. What more inspiring vision for our party than that it should lead our nation into the next millenium, secure again in the allegiance of thriving cities whose present misery and squalor will by then be a vanishing memory?

Index